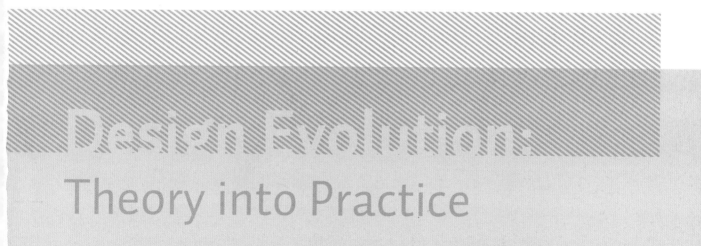

Design Evolution:
Theory into Practice

ROCKPORT

© 2008 by Rockport Publishers, Inc.

First published in the United States of America by
Rockport Publishers, a member of Quayside Publishing Group

100 Cummings Center, Suite 406-L

Beverly, Massachusetts 01915-6101

978.282.9590 *Telephone*

978.283.2742 *Facsimile*

www.rockpub.com

Library of Congress Cataloging-in-Publication Data
Samara, Timothy.
   Design evolution : handbook of basic design principles
applied in contemporary design / Timothy Samara.
        p.   cm.
    ISBN-13: 978-1-59253-387-9
    ISBN-10: 1-59253-387-6
    1. Graphic design (Typography) – Case studies 2.
Commercial art – Case Studies I. Title.

  Z246 .S227
  686.2'2–dc22   2007019661
                                             CIP

While this volume is written to complement *Design Elements: A
Graphic Style Manual*, (ISBN 1-59253-261-6) the contents of *Design
Evolution: Theory into Practice* are relevant on their own merits.

ISBN-13: 978-1-59253-387-9
ISBN-10: 1-59253-387-6

10 9 8 7 6 5 4 3 2 1

Cover and text design
STIM Visual Communication New York

Contributing writer
Laurel Saville

Printed in China

Design Evolution:
Theory into Practice

TIMOTHY SAMARA

KNOW ing DO

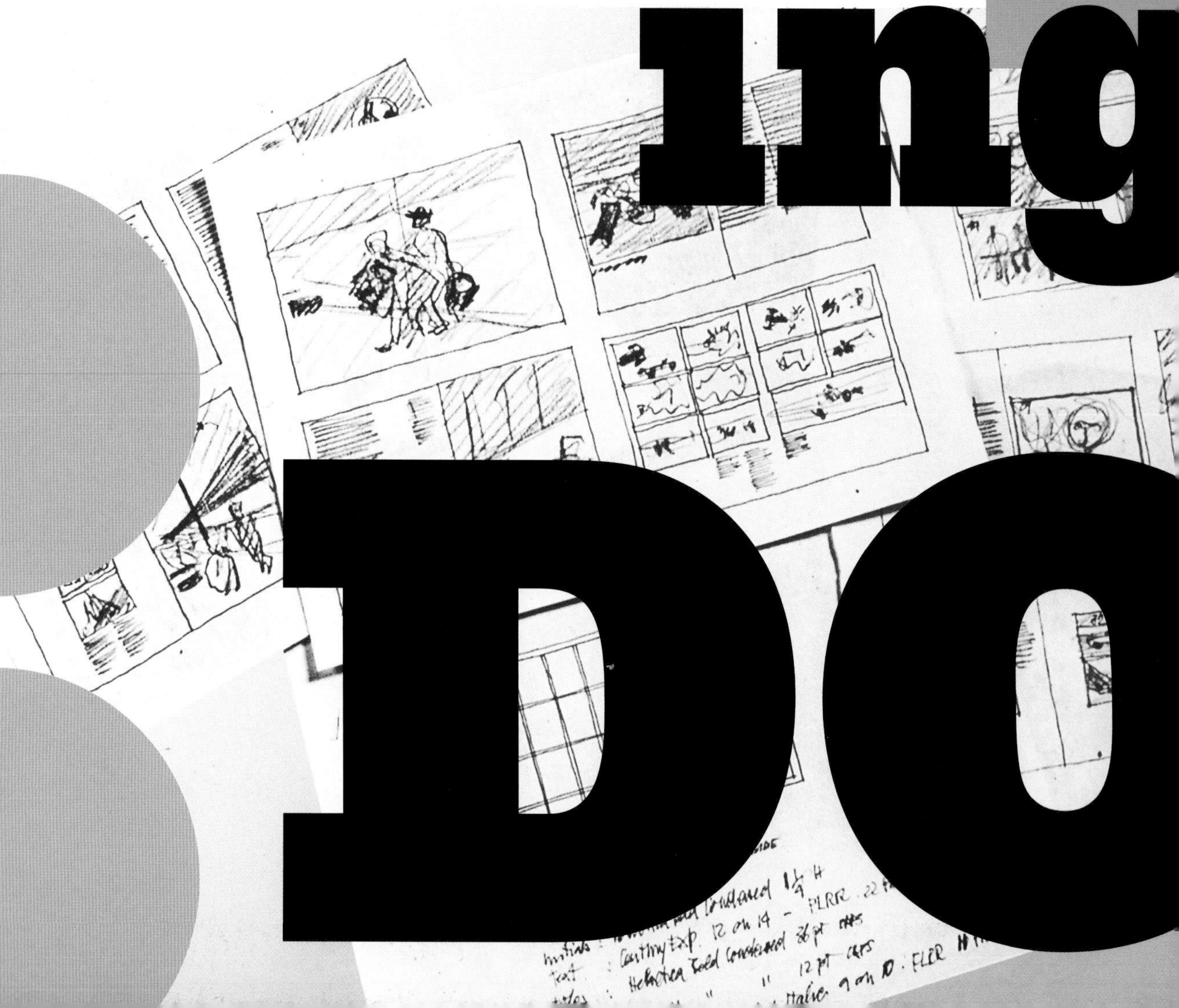

built. *Design Elements: A Graphic Style Manual,* the volume that this one accompanies, focused on these aspects and the fundamental principles needed to understand them. How to apply all this knowledge in a real design project—so that the work comes alive as a beautiful experience and does its job really well—is another issue altogether and that with which *Design Evolution* is concerned. ▌When starting out, designers usually have to think consciously about each design element. As they develop their skill through experience, visual decision making and problem solving become much more intuitive—even unconscious. After a while, most designers aren't even aware of how their

extremely methodical and analytical, looking to understand each step as they go, and even to make decisions intellectually; others work in an intuitive way, relying on feelings supported by their mastery of the basics. ▌Still others jump back and forth between each method, letting analysis and intuition play off each other. These approaches often translate into the way designers structure their fees and business interaction. ▌Many (but not all) define a series of steps for their clients, usually to demystify the process for business people who are easily spooked by creativity—especially when they're paying for it. These steps are generally divided into a beginning, a middle, and

Making the Leap from Study to Real-World Practice

tilled into a document called a creative brief. The designer or design team refers to this brief as a guide while exploring visual ideas to convey concepts. Some designers present one concept; others present three or five. The number of concepts a designer presents may be driven by preference, by budget, or by the complexity of the project. ▍The middle portion, or phase, is usually a period of more focused investigation and refinement, once the client has agreed to pursue one of the concepts developed in the first phase. During this stage, the physical and formal aspects of the project take shape: decisions as to imagery, typography, color, pacing, and production are made. It is

work, such as exhibits or signage, it means the materials are fabricated or built and installed on location. In Web-based projects, the production phase most often focuses on programming and debugging code to ensure functionality. ▍As easy as that sounds, however, the design process is far from linear and methodical, even for the most talented or experienced designers. Creativity is iterative in nature—that is, some backtracking or reinvestigation is needed once a certain point in the process is reached, so that an idea can be tested and altered for clarity. Very often, some aspect of an earlier idea or form becomes relevant later on and must be incorporated. ▍Design development can also

standing of how stimuli—whether abstract or concrete, purely visual or verbal—can be constructed and manipulated to convey richer, more complex ideas and to engage, persuade, and inspire.

The design process can be a long road to travel, even for seasoned professionals. Here, the author tracks the development of his own process for the cover of *Design Elements*. The first round of concepts produced mainly typographic solutions, from which the client selected one idea for further exploration.

The requested revisions focused mostly on color relationships and specific details, such as the placement of certain text

Among the new concepts presented, two offered some similar elements that both designer and client felt could be combined for a richer composition.

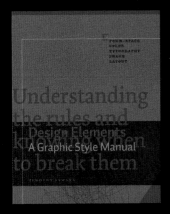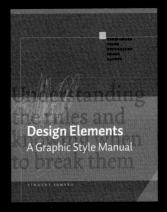

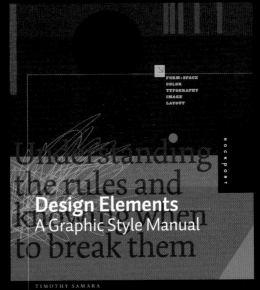

Following another study of color, the final cover layout developed as seen here. Along with a generally cooler color palette, a few abstract elements made an appearance among the layered typography.

CLAUDE FOUCHY-BILLANCOURT

A discussion of the physics of speech and cognition as related to the development of sexual power.

Mr. Fouchy-Billancourt is a professor of linguistic anthropology at the University de la Sorbonne in Paris, France. He is a recognized authority on linguistic ideology.

Language, Sensuality and Power

INCORPORATIONS: THE BODY AS SOURCE

Thursday Oct.12, 8:00pm
The Cooper Union
for the Advancement of
Science and Art
**The Great Hall
One Cooper Square
New York City**

Three lectures fee: $125
Individual lectures: $60

Cooper Union faculty and students attend free, but must register in advance. Please provide your Union faculty or student ID number to waive the registration fee.

The lectures are open to the public. Advance reservations are required. Please call The Cooper Union Office of Public Programs at 212-436-0187 or go online to www.cooper.edu/body to register.

This lecture poster is playing by the rules—all twenty of them, in fact. It's grounded in a strong concept and incorporates only that which is needed to support the concept. A decisive, asymmetrical composition with a great deal of contrast is enhanced by a clear hierarchy and easily accessible typography. The imagery is custom made by the designer, and integrates with type and supporting graphic elements. Variations in compositional states offer density, rhythm, and movement around the format.
Laywan Kwan:
New York, NY; USA

It's such a difficult question to answer in a useful way. "Good," according to who? When people talk about "good" or "bad" design, they're referring to notions of quality that they've picked up from education and experience. Whether aesthetic or functional, they're often grounded in our understanding of how perceptual and cognitive processes work—how we see and what our brains do as a result, on a physiologic level. Understanding these functions and their impact on communication is fundamental to conveying messages—reliably—to large audiences. At the very least, they're guidelines that can help one avoid something unfortunate as a result of ignorance. More likely, they're flexible benchmarks for making a design solution as good as it can be. Here are twenty such items for consideration.

What Makes Good Design?

1

Have a concept.

You need to begin with an idea. It may be very neutral–"It's important to organize this information to be quietly navigable"–or it may be creatively contrived–"These biscuits will seem more delicious if they appear to be made by elves." No idea? No design.

2

Communicate; don't decorate.

Form, it is often said (not often enough, lately) follows function. That means two things. First, every dot, line, texture, shape, color, and image should be related to the concept that must be conveyed (see rule no. 1). Second, each of these forms should add to the concept. If the form is there solely because you think it's cool, you should probably get rid of it.

3

Speak with one visual voice.

All the parts of a project really ought to be recognizably related to each other on a visual level. That is, they must share some similar qualities in order to appear part of the same unified message.

4

Use two typefaces maximum.

OK, maybe three … but seriously, typefaces only get you so far, even stylistically. It's what you DO with the type that really says something. For hardcore, hierarchical concerns, one type family with a range of weights and widths should be enough.

5

Show one thing first.

Speaking of hierarchy… Give visual emphasis to one item to grab the viewer's attention. Then direct them–through a progression of size, weight, and color changes, and so on–down the line of important items or instructions. If they have to figure out what to look at first, they'll get confused and leave.

6

Pick colors on purpose.

As subjective as color perception is, it's not all guesswork. Colors mean things culturally, and colors have optical relationships to each other. Use these "factual" aspects to choose and combine colors in a meaningful way–and in an optically dynamic way.

7

If you can do it with less, do it.

This is another way of saying "Less is more." It's about being economical: Try to show only what's necessary. If "necessary" can be pared down a bit, too, that's a good thing. Think about how many messages, how many resources, how many annoying blobs of information the average viewer has to deal with on a regular basis (never mind the landfill). Now, design accordingly.

8

Negative space is magical: Create it, don't fill it up.

Despite the fact that the space in a format *around* the shapes and pictures and text is apparently empty, it's really a shape unto itself. Consider it as carefully as you would anything that you plop into it. The better integrated the negative space and the more interesting it is, the stronger the composition.

9

Treat type like image.

This is one of the most difficult rules to master. Type *is* an image, even though it looks like something else. It must be considered for its visual qualities, relative to other image material, to integrate it into compositions–even more so when there's a lot of it.

10

Keep type friendly.

If it's illegible, it's not type. If it's illegible, it's not type. And, if it's illegible, it's not type. Consider the audience—their assumed level of education, their schedule, and especially their age—when choosing styles and sizes. Written language exists to transmit information, and your client is paying you to transmit such information on their behalf. If the information can't be read—for any reason—it's no longer useful, and you're potentially out of a job.

11

Be universal; it's not about you.

If you're interested in expressing your fetishes or psychoses, become a painter and work the gallery scene (seriously, it pays better). The purpose of design (regardless of what the MFA people tell you) is populist in nature: you are creating clear messages for other people. The more understandable the images you make, the better.

12

Squish and separate: Create rhythms in density and openness.

The antidote to visual boredom is tension, and there are two easy ways to achieve this antidote: The first is by constantly varying the sizes, weights, and spaces among visual elements so that they appear to be constantly shifting and moving. And …

13

Distribute light and dark like firecrackers and the rising Sun.

Radically vary the lightness and darkness in different areas of a composition, as well as the *quality* of dark and light values: sharp and aggressive, fluid and murky, bold and clean …

14

Be decisive: Do it on purpose, or don't do it at all.

Avoid being wishy-washy in arranging things. Visual elements should be clearly one thing or another, one way or another. Ambiguity can be useful, but even this should be on purpose, not a sloppy by-product of indecision.

15

Measure with your eyes.

A majority of formal relationships play havoc with our eyes—for example, a solid, planar dot and a square will appear to be different sizes if they are mathematically the same measure in height: circles appear to contract in space because of their undefined, endless contour. All visual forms play off each other, so make them behave the way you want them to look like they're behaving. Eyeball it: it usually looks better that way.

16

Make the images you need; don't scavenge.

It's so much easier to find a stock photo and drop some type on top of it. But anyone can do that, and they do. At the very least, alter found images to transform them into the *right* images: customize for your client, customize for your audience.

17

Ignore fashion. Seriously.

What's currently fashionable sells. So does sex. But fashion, like sex, is forgotten quickly. You might make some money, but how will you feel in the morning? And how will your contribution be remembered in 100 years? Keep the word *timeless* in your head, and make decisions based on concept, meaning, and function, not the latest, shallow trend.

18

Move it! Static equals dull.

Two-dimensional images that appear kinetic—in motion—attract greater attention and retain interest longer than those that seem tired, stiff, and lifeless. Arranging visual elements asymmetrically, with differing spatial intervals between them and contrasting directional emphases, creates the appearance of spatial depth and movement. Compose wisely.

19

Look to history, but don't repeat it.

Much successful design borrows from past innovators, as does all human endeavors. That said, applying one's understanding of *how* a famous work achieves its goal and ripping it off are two different things. Show some respect … but don't cross the line between flattery and forgery.

20

Symmetry is the ultimate evil.

Symmetrically organized material creates repetitive, static spatial intervals, violating rule no. 18. Furthermore, symmetry relies on an understood truth about a format—that it has a center—and so it offers nothing new to the viewer. In effect, the format does the designing, not the designer.

The
Tool

A graphic designer assimilates verbal concepts and gives them form, then organizes the resulting form into a tangible, navigable experience. The quality of this experience depends on his or her mastery of very complicated skills and knowledge of the visual effects available for the job. And there are a whole lot of them— a giant toolbox of shapes, colors, perceptual tricks, different kinds of images, and so on—from which a designer can choose.

Design Evolution offers detailed analysis of how designers successfully use these basic ingredients to make powerful visual communications that add up to much more than the sum of their parts. Design is like a tasty stew; sure, the meat, carrots, potatoes, salt, pepper, and gravy are good by themselves, but mixed in just the right proportions, they become something else entirely. A designer is like a good cook. He or she knows how each ingredient tastes and, more importantly, how various ingredients work together.

In this section, we'll review these fundamental visual elements of graphic design.

Visual box

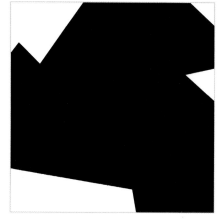

All graphic design—all image making, regardless of medium or intent—centers on manipulating form. "Form" is stuff: shapes, lines, textures, words, and pictures. Our brains use form to identify what is seen; form is a message. Making that form as beautiful as possible is what elevates designing above just plopping stuff in front of an audience and letting them pick through it. ▮ The term "beautiful" has a host of meanings, depending on context; aggressive, ripped, collaged illustrations are beautiful; chunky woodcut type is beautiful; all kinds of rough images can be called beautiful. "Beautiful" as a descriptor might be better replaced by the term "resolved," meaning that the form's parts are all related to each other and no part of it seems unconsidered or alien to any other part, and the term "decisive," meaning that the form feels confident, credible, and on purpose. ▮ Form is considered a positive element or object. Space is considered negative—the "ground" in which form becomes a "figure." The relationship between form and space, or figure and ground, is complementary; it's impossible to alter one and not the other. The confrontation between figure and ground defines the kind of visual activity and sense of dimension perceived by the viewer. ▮ All these qualities are inherently communicative. Resolving the relationships between figure and ground is the first step in creating a simple, overarching message before the viewer registers the identity of an image or the content of any text that is present. Creating a composition by organizing figure and ground, is vitally impor-

tant in design because it affects so many other aspects, from general emotional response to informational hierarchy. ▮ Resolved and refined compositions create clear, accessible visual messages. Resolving and refining a composition means understanding what kind of message is being carried by a given form, what it does in space, and what effect the combination of these things has on the viewer. This, of course, brings up the issue of "clarity," which has to do with whether a composition and the

Form and Space

Form, or "figure," is considered a positive element—the "stuff"—while the space, or "ground," around it is considered its negative, or opposite. Both are mutually dependent—it's impossible to change one without affecting the other. Creating dynamic relationships between positive and negative is the cornerstone of good composition.

Here, simple repositioning and sizing of the form element creates differing degrees of activity within the space. In the last example, positive and negative appear to change places, a state called "figure-ground reversal."

forms within it are readily understandable. Some of this depends on the refinement of the forms, and some of it depends on the resolution of the relationships between form and space and whether these are "decisive." A form or a spatial relationship is decisive if it is clearly one thing and not the other. For example, is one form larger or smaller than the one next to it, or are they both the same size? If the answer to this question is quick and nobody can argue with it—"The thing on the left is larger"—then the formal or spatial relationship is decisive.

Categories of Form There are several kinds of basic form, and each does something different—or, the eye and the brain perceive each kind of form as doing something different, as having its own kind of identity. The most basic types of form are the dot, the line, and the plane. Of these, the line and the plane also can be categorized as geometric or organic; the plane can be either flat, textured, or appear to have three-dimensional volume or mass. ▌The identity of a dot is that of a point of focused attention; the dot simultaneously contracts inward and radiates outward. As seemingly simple a form as it might appear, a dot is a complex object, the fundamental building block of all other forms. Every shape or mass with a recognizable center—a square, a trapezoid, a triangle, or a blob—is a dot, no matter how big it is. ▌A line's essential character is one of connection and unites areas in a composition. This connection may be invisible, defined by the pulling effect on space between two dots, or it may take on visible form as a concrete object, traveling back and forth between a starting point and an ending point. Unlike a dot, the quality of linearity is one of movement and direction; a line is inherently dynamic, rather than static. While dots create points of focus, lines perform other functions. They may separate spaces, join spaces or objects, create protective barriers, enclose or constrain, and intersect. ▌A plane is simply a dot that has become so large within its format that its outer contour has become recognizable and, therefore, attained some importance for the viewer—for instance, that it appears angled or curvilinear. At the point where the plane transcends its dotlike identity, it assumes a kind of weight or mass, even if it appears to be optically flat. Planes are more commonly referred to by another word: "shape." ▌There are two general categories of shape, each with its own formal and communicative characteristics that have an immediate effect on messaging: geometric form and organic form. A shape is considered geometric in nature if its contour is regularized—if

*pose
marré
das
quartier

possemarré
tor bismarckstraße
alt-erkrath

der erlös geht zugunsten
»erkrath initial«
erwachsene 8 euro
ermäßigt 5 euro
vorverkauf
buchhandlung weber
hochdahler markt
fon 021 04.940 20
kreuzstraße 37
fon 02 11.900 39 73

10te
erkrather
kriminacht

3. juno 2005
20:00uhr
hubertus
v. thielmann
»streif«

This poster demonstrates complex interactions among positive elements and between elements and format. Note the wide variety of shapes and sizes of the spaces between forms, as well as the differing relationships between forms and the edges of the format. Hesse Design: Düsseldorf, Germany

its external measurements are mathematically similar in multiple directions—and, very generally, if it appears angular or hard-edged. It is essentially an ancient, ingrained expectation that anything irregular, soft, or textured is akin to things experienced in nature, and therefore organic. ▎The quality of surface activity helps in differentiating forms from each other, just as the identifiable contours of form itself does. There are two basic categories of surface activity: texture and pattern. The term "texture" applies to surfaces having irregular activity without apparent repetition. Because of this inherent randomness, texture generally is perceived as organic or natural. "Pattern," however, has a geometric quality—it is a specific kind of texture in which the components are arranged on a recognizable and repeated structure—for example, a grid of dots. The existence of a planned structure within patterns means they are understood to be something that is not organic: they are something synthetic, mechanical, or mass produced.

Composition: Breaking and Activating Space

Space is defined and given meaning the instant a form appears within it. Each element brought into the space adds complexity and creates new kinds of space, forcing it into distinct shapes that fit around the forms like pieces of a puzzle. The proportions of positive and negative might

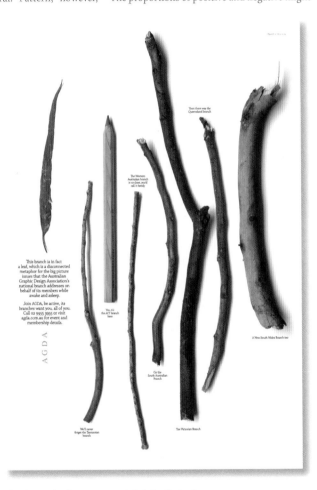

All forms—whether photographic or abstract—can be distilled into four categories: the dot; the line; the plane or mass; and surface activity (pattern or texture). Forms in any of these categories may be described as geometric or organic. Dots are nondirectional; they focus attention and radiate outward. Lines connect, separate, and move. Planes are really large dots whose outer contours have become differentiated. Of surface activity, "pattern" is repetitive and systematic, while "texture" is irregular.

This ad is a study in line rhythm. The various sticks and implements, although recognizable as such, are simply lines as far as composition goes. Some are absolutely vertical, while others are rigid. The designer has taken great care in the placement of each element with regard to their vertical relationships top-to-bottom, as well as in exploiting their individual shapes to lead the eye through them and across the page.
Studio Pip & Company: Melbourne, Australia

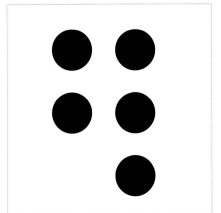

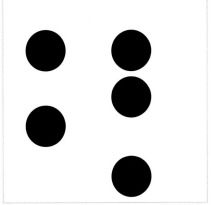

be generally static or generally dynamic. Because the picture plane is already a flat environment where movement and depth must be created as an illusion, fighting the tendency of two-dimensional form to feel static is important. ▌The spaces within a composition will generally appear static—in a state of rest or inertia—when they are optically equal to each other. Altering the intervals between forms, or between elements and format edges creates a dynamic composition. The movement of the eye is enhanced as these intervals exhibit more contrast with each other. ▌Within a compositional format, a designer can apply several basic strategies to organizing forms. Just as the identities of selected forms begin to generate messages for the viewer, their relative positions within the format, the spaces created between them, and their relationships to each other all will contribute additional messages. In addition to side-by-side arrangements at the picture plane, a designer may also organize form in illusory dimensional space—that is, by defining elements as existing in the foreground, in the background, or somewhere in between.

Overlapping and bleeding, as well as the rotation of elements compared to others, may induce a feeling of kinetic movement. Forms perceived to occupy dimensional space are often perceived as moving in one direction or another—receding or advancing. Juxtaposing a static form, such as a horizontal line, with a more active counterpart, such as a diagonal line, invites comparison and, oddly, the assumption that one is standing still while the other is moving. Changing the intervals between elements also invites comparison and, again, the odd conclusion that the changing

spaces mean that the forms are moving in relation to each other. The degree of motion created by such overlapping, bleeding, and rhythmic spatial separation will evoke varying degrees of energy or restfulness; the designer must control these messages as he or she does any other.

Symmetry and Asymmetry The result of making all the proportions between and around forms in a composition different is that the possibility of symmetry is minimized. Symmetry is a compositional state in which the arrangement of forms responds to the central axis of the format (either the horizontal axis or the vertical axis); the forms might also be arranged in relation to each other's central axes. Symmetrical arrangements mean that some set of spaces around the forms—or the contours of the forms around the axis—will be equal, which means that they are also static or restful. ▌Asymmetrical arrangements provoke more rigorous involvement— they require the brain to assess differences in space and stimulate the eye to greater movement. From the standpoint of communication, asymmetrical arrangements might improve the ability to differentiate, catalog, and recall content because the viewer's investigation of spatial difference becomes tied to the ordering, or cognition, of the content itself. Content is always different and always changing, and an asym-

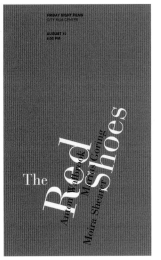

When form enters space, it changes it. The breaking of space has an immediate impact on the overall feeling the composition evokes simply because of the degree of contrast among areas and of optical activity. The first example shows a static arrangement of form and undifferentiated spatial intervals.

The second example shows the effect of altering spatial intervals to create tension and openness. All of the spaces within this composition are involved and, therefore, considered "activated." There are numerous strategies for arranging form in space. Each contributes differently to the degree of spatial activity and organization within a composition and, therefore, its potential meaning.

A comparison of these two images—a promotional card for an Australian wine, and a poster for a dance performance—shows how different are the apparent spatial qualities of symmetry and asymmetry. Parallax Design: Melbourne, Australia

STIM: New York, NY; USA

metrical approach allows a designer to be flexible, to address the spatial needs of the content, and to create visual relationships between different items based on their spatial qualities.

Activating Space During the process of composing form within a given space, portions of space might become disconnected from other portions. A section might be separated physically or blocked off by a larger element that crosses from one edge of the format to the other; or, it might be optically separated because of a set of forms aligning in such a way that the eye is discouraged from traveling past the alignment and entering into the space beyond. Clustering active combinations of form in one part of a format, for focus, may result in spaces that feel empty or isolated from this activity. In all such cases, the space can be called "inert," or "inactive." ▌An inert or inactive space will call attention to itself for this very reason—it doesn't communicate with the other spaces in the composition. To activate these spaces means to cause them to enter back into their dialogue with the other spaces in the composition.

Compositional Contrast Creating areas of differing presence or quality—areas that contrast each other—is inherent in designing a well-resolved, dynamic composition. While the term "contrast" applies to specific relationships (light versus dark, curve versus angle, and dynamic versus static), it also applies to the quality of difference in relationships among forms and spaces interacting within a format together. The confluence of varied states of contrast is sometimes referred to as "tension." ▌A composition with strong contrast between round and sharp angular forms in one area, opposed by another area where all the forms are similarly angular, could exhibit a tension in angularity; a composition that contrasts areas of dense, active line rhythms with areas that

In this composition, various elements work together to activate one another. The paper clip interrupting the black rectangle, the tilting overlay contrasting with the strong diagonal lines of the photo, and the white question mark scribbled on top of it all create an exciting tableau that engages the reader and demonstrates the designer's skill and confidence.
Studio Pip & Company:
Melbourne, Australia

Opposite, top: The line detail in this annual report for a cancer research center is an abstraction of DNA arrays. Its use an a texture communicates that idea very directly—and the movement of these forms is translated into the arrangement of text and image—but the designer also exploits this rhythmic quality to communicate the idea of "energetic pace."
Ideas On Purpose:
New York, NY; USA

one group or part more subtly, while exaggerating the difference between others. Because tiny adjustments in form are easily perceived, the difference between each group can be very precisely controlled. By differentiating elements from others within an overall grouping, a designer creates a focus for consideration, allowing the viewer the chance to identify one set of elements and compare them to another. This comparison elicits several questions: "What is the nature of each grouping? How are they different? What does this difference signify? Does the difference make one grouping clearly more important than the other? ▌ Forms acquire new meanings when they participate in spatial relationships; when they share or oppose each other's mass or textural characteristics; and when they have relationships because of their

rotation, singularity or repetition, alignment, clustering, or separation from each other. Each different state tells the viewer something new about the forms, adding to the meaning that they already might have established for the viewer.

are generally more open and regular might be characterized as creating tension in rhythm. **Seeing Is Believing** What is the result of all this form and space interacting? At this most fundamental level, the result is meaning. Abstract forms carry meaning because they are recognizably different from each other—whether line, dot, or plane (and, specifically, what kind of plane). ▌ There are numerous strategies for creating comparisons between groupings of form or among parts within a group. The degree of difference between elements can be subtle or dramatic, and the designer can imply different degrees of meaning by isolating

In this poster, the symmetrical arrangement focuses attention on the forms and creates a kind of inward contemplation. The circular element, created from overlapping ellipses, is a large dot that hints at a halo or corona. The dot also acts as an eye, whose scale is commanding and dominates the format.

All of these messages communicate the omnipotent qualities associated with the deities of monotheistic religions—those in which there is only one god figure.
Studio di Progettazione Grafica: Cevio, Switzerland

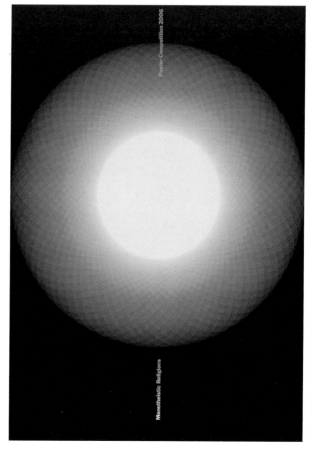

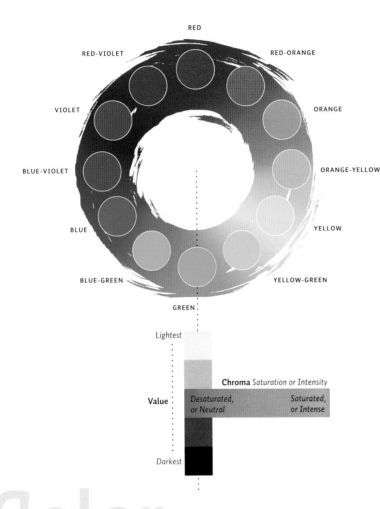

There are few visual stimuli as powerful as color. It is a profoundly useful communication tool. But the meaning transmitted by color—because it results from reflected light waves transmitted through an imperfect organ (the eyes), to an imperfect interpreter (the brain)—is also profoundly subjective. The mechanism of color perception is universal among humans. What we do with it once we see it is another thing altogether, and controlling it for the sake of communication depends on understanding how its optical qualities behave. ▌A single color is defined by four essential qualities related to our perception of its essential nature as waves of light: **Hue** refers to the identity of a color—whether it appears red, violet, orange, or yellow. This identity is the result of how we perceive light being reflected from objects at particular frequencies. Of color's four intrinsic attributes, the perception of hue is the most absolute: we see a color as red or blue, for example. But all color perception is relative, meaning that a color's identity is really knowable only when there's another color adjacent with which it can be compared. A color's **saturation** describes its intensity, or brilliance. A saturated color is very intense or vibrant.

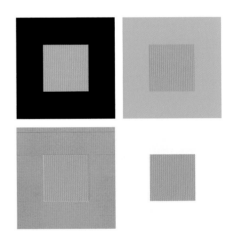

Relationships between colors are defined by their relative position on the Munsell color wheel. The various hues—differences in light wavelengths—exhibit a value (darkness or lightness) and a chroma, also called saturation or brilliance. These attributes are mapped along different axes in the model diagram.

Color is relative—the perception of hue, temperature, value, and saturation of a given color all change depending on the colors adjacent to it. This effect—demonstrated by the changes in apparent color of the central swatch in combination with other colors—is called "simultaneous contrast."

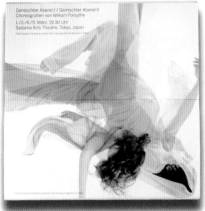

Colors that are dull, but whose hues are still perceivable, are said to be desaturated. Colors in which almost no hue is visible—such as warm gray—are said to be neutral. As with hue, the apparent saturation of a color will change if it can be compared to an adjacent color. A color's **value** is its intrinsic darkness or lightness. Yellow is perceived as being light; violet is perceived as being dark. Again, it's all relative. One color can be considered darker or lighter only compared to another. Yellow, for instance, even appears darker than white,

which has the lightest possible value of any color. An extremely deep blue or violet appears quite luminous against a maximal black, which has the darkest value of any color (black being technically the absence of any reflected light). The **temperature** of a color is a subjective quality that is related to experiences. Colors considered "warm," such as red or orange, reminds us of heat; cool colors, such as green or blue, remind us of cold environments or materials, such as ice.

Color Interaction A color model is a tool that helps describe relationships between colors. One such model, the color wheel, was developed by Albert Munsell, a British painter and scientist. It is a circular representation of hue—the differences in wavelength that distinguish blue from yellow from red—modified along two axes that describe the color's darkness or lightness (its value) and its relative brilliance (its saturation). By using a model such as the color wheel as reference, designers can create purposeful relationships among color combinations to harmonize them or introduce tension as a counterpoint.

Hue Relationships Designers can create interaction between different hues, independent of their saturation or value, according to where they lie on the color wheel. The closer together the colors appear on the wheel, the more similar their optical qualities and, hence, the more harmonious or related. The further apart colors are on the wheel, the more their optical qualities contrast each other.

Value Relationships Regardless of their specific hues, the colors selected for a palette will have relationships of darkness or lightness. By varying the number of jumps from value to value, or by how dramatically the values among the colors change, a designer can create contrast and rhythm among darker and lighter areas even if the number of hues used—or the differences among them—is limited.

Saturation Relationships Saturation relationships may occur independently of hue relationships, but will usually have an effect on value or temperature—as a hue is desaturated, it may appear to become darker adjacent to a different hue of greater saturation, but it may also appear to become cooler if the adjacent hue is a warm color. Grouping analogous hues of similar intensity, but changing the intensity of one, will create a rich, intimately harmonious palette. Grouping complementary hues, or split complements, all with similar values but different saturations, will create a richly diverse color experience.

Temperature Relationships Designers can establish relationships within a color palette based on relative temperature. Grouping colors with similar temperature, together with one or two variations on the same hues that are warmer or cooler—for example, a cool green, blue, and violet with a warmer green—can generate enormous possibilities for combining the colors while maintaining a tightly controlled color environment. ▌One optical response that affects all color relationships—whether hue-, value-, saturation-, or temperature-based—is that of simultaneous contrast: an effect whereby one color appears to be different when shown in close proximity to colors that dramatically alter its apparent identity. For example, a slightly yellowish green may appear to be hotter and even more yellow when it comes in contact with a deep blue-violet, but cooler and more subdued adjacent to an intense yellow-green. Always consider simultaneous contrast—and the potential bonus of more apparent colors—when choosing a palette.

Color: Form and Space Color exhibits a number of spatial properties. Cool colors appear to recede while warm colors appear to advance. Of the primary colors, blue appears to recede and yellow to advance, but red appears to sit

Relative to the skin tones of the dancers in this collateral for a dance company, the color of the clothing creates complementary and analogous relationships. Within the overlap of transparent images, relationships of intensity and value are explored.
Surface: Frankfurt am Mein, Germany

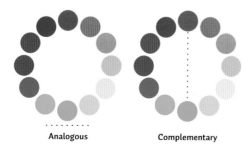

Analogous   **Complementary**

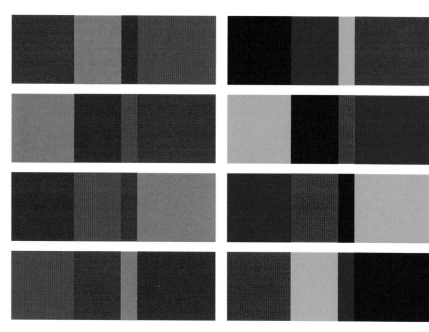

statically at a middle depth within space. Applying color to a composition will have an immediate effect on hierarchy, the relative order of importance of the forms in space. The intrinsic relationships in a black-and-white composition might be exaggerated through the application of chromatic color, or made purposely ambiguous. The application of color to the ground within a composition can further enhance the hierarchy. A form in one color, set on a field of another color, will join closely with it or separate aggressively, depending on their color relationship. If the colors of foreground elements and background are related, the two elements will occupy a similar spatial depth. If they are complementary in nature, the two will occupy very different spatial depths.

Color Stories: Coding with Color Within a complex visual environment, color can help distinguish different kinds of information, as well as create relationships among components or editions of a publication. A designer might develop, for example, a palette for graphic and typographic elements that helps readers distinguish between specific text components (headlines, subheads, and body) or between sections of information. Or, a designer might use a general palette for all elements that is based on the color or thematic content of photographs. Perhaps this palette has a consistent base, like a selection of warm neutrals that remains constant, while accent colors change. The use of colors can be coded—assigning colors to identify sections or components—or not. █ Color coding is one option for using color as a system. To be effective, color coding must be relatively simple and easily identifiable. Using more colors for coding creates confusion, as the viewer is forced to remember which color relates to which information. Color coding within a related set of hues—a deep blue, an aqua blue, and a green—can help distinguish subcategories of information within an overall grouping but ensure that the viewer is able to perceive the differences between the colors. █ Pushing the colors further apart in relation to each other might help. For example, the deep blue might be skewed toward the violet while yellow is added to the green. The components in a system—say, a family of brochures—might change over time, or new components might be added later, so the various parts of the system need to be distinguishable from each other while maintaining a clear family appearance. The color coding not only helps a viewer separate the components from each other quickly but also continues to enhance the unity of the system. The number of colors selected, and how closely they are related, will be determined by evaluating how many components within the system must be delineated.

Limited Color Systems While a great number of projects call for full-color imagery—process, or CMYK—choosing to use specific colored inks instead, called "spot" color, offers exciting possibilities. Spot color does not need to be limited to small-run or low-budget projects; a palette of even two thoughtfully selected colors may communicate just as powerfully

Color has a pronounced effect on the perception of spatial location. Red is perceived as resting at a position equivalent to the surface of an image (the picture plane). Yellow and warmer colors other than red appear to advance in space, while cool colors such as blue and violet appear to recede.

Keeping some variables consistent, while altering only two—or even one—provides a great deal of flexibility in creating palettes that are unified, but rich and complex.
(left) Single-variable system
(right) Two-variable system

spring

shower gel

Gentle Daily Cleansing for All Skin Types

Infused with Pure Flower and Plant Essences

8oz/240ml

as a four-color job and further unify materials. This approach is particularly useful for branding, where the interrelation of inks can be used to differentiate publications in a literature system while reinforcing the identity of the brand.

❚ When a designer is working with only two or three ink colors, choosing colors with dynamic chromatic interaction is integral. Printing a job with two complements as counterparts, for example, is an intuitive first possibility. Their complementary nature need not be exact. For example, skewing blue and orange can create interesting combinations and retain their inherent contrast, such as a blue-violet and orange. Most printing inks are translucent, so a designer has the option not only to print each ink at full strength—or "tint" them to lighten their values—but also to print the inks on top of each other, either at full strength or in combinations of tints. Printing one ink on top of another is called "surprinting," and creates new colors from the overlap.

Color Psychology With color comes a variety of psychological messages that can be used to influence content, both imagery and the verbal meaning of typography. This emotional component of color is deeply connected to human experience at an instinctual and biological level. Colors of varying wavelengths have different effects on the autonomic nervous system. Warmer colors, such as reds and yellows, have long wavelengths, and more energy is needed to process them as they enter the eye and brain. The accompanying rise in energy level and metabolic rate translates as arousal. Conversely, the shorter wavelengths of cooler colors—such as blue, green, and violet—

require far less energy to process, resulting in the slowing of our metabolic rate and a soothing, calming effect. ❚ The psychological properties of color also greatly depend on a viewer's culture and personal experience. Many cultures equate red with feelings of hunger, anger, or energy because red is closely associated with meat, blood, and violence. By contrast, vegetarians might associate the color green with hunger. In Western cultures, which are predominantly Christian, black is associated with death and mourning, but Hindus associate the color white with death. Clearly, selecting a color for specific words in a composition can add meaning by linking its associations to the verbal message. A headline or title set in one color

might take on a different meaning when set in another color. Comparing color options for type simultaneously helps determine which color is most appropriate for the communication.

Limited color palettes are useful not only for saving money, but also for creating coding systems to enhance navigation or distinguish products in a collection, as seen in the bath products here.
Hyosook Kang: School of Visual Arts: New York, NY; USA

The optical qualities of the intense red and the cooler red-violet enhance the dimensionality suggested by the planes in this poster.
Leonardo Sonnoli: Rimini, Italy

Case	Weight	Width	Contrast	Posture	Style

The well of typographic knowledge is vast and the skills needed to master its complexities are many. There are hundreds, if not thousands, of interrelated pieces of information a designer must hold in his or her head while navigating the bigger issues of concept and layout: tiny differences between the shapes of letters, the systematic, rhythmic relationships between letter strokes and the counterspaces between them; the spacing between letters, words, sentences, and paragraphs; conventions for aligning blocks of type and separating others, and so on. Becoming sensitive to these optical details and understanding their effect on spacing, organization, stylistic communication, legibility, and composition is crucial.

Visual Variations The letterforms in all typefaces vary from their archetypes in only six aspects: case, weight, contrast, width, posture, and style. Type designers subtly alter and combine the variables in these six aspects to create individual type styles. Different approaches to the drawing of typefaces have evolved, become popular, or been discarded over time; as a result, the formal aspects of particular typefaces often carry associations with specific periods in history, cultural movements, and geographic location. ▌More important, the drawing of a typeface will often exhibit a particular kind of rhythm, or cadence, as well as provide a distinct physical presence in a design that may connote feelings—fast or slow, aggressive or elegant, cheap or reliable. Consider that not all viewers will perceive the same associations in a given typeface; the designer must carefully evaluate his or her typeface selection in the context of the audience for a particular piece.

Typography

All alphabets differ from each other only through the variation of five aspects: weight, width, posture, contrast, and style. Within these variables exists a limitless array of textural, spatial, and expressive possibilities.

Combining Type Styles The conventional wisdom for mixing typefaces is to select two type families for a given job. As a basic bit of advice, this is a good start; it provides a framework for finding a maximum amount of contrast, and it forces a designer to exercise some restraint. As with all typographic rules, of course, context plays an important role in deciding whether or not to adhere to such a limitation. The complexity of the information being presented is one variable; the overall neutrality, consistency, and expressiveness are others to consider. ▮ Contrast among typefaces that are juxtaposed is critical. The only reason to change a typeface is to gain an effect of contrast, and so the contrast achieved by the combination should be clearly recognizable. Otherwise, why bother? Opposing the extremes of weight (light against bold), of width (regular against condensed or expanded), or style (neutral sans serif against slab serif or script) is a natural starting point. But somewhere in the mix, even among extremes of this nature, some formal relationship must exist between the selected fonts to enrich their visual dialogue. Choosing a sans serif and a serif that are about the same weight or width, for example, creates a tension of similarity and difference that can be quite sophisticated. Selecting two serif faces that are similar in weight, but very different in width or contrast, achieves a similar tension. ▮ Generally, avoid combining two faces of a similar style unless the difference is pronounced enough for the average reader to notice. Mixing Caslon and Baskerville, for example—two transitional serifs with similar axis, weight, width, and terminal shapes—isn't such a great idea. But combining a modern serif of extreme contrast with a slab serif of uniform stroke weight but similar width and axis, might be effective.

Spacing and Text-Setting Issues The drawing of a typeface has an impact on the perception of its size. A sentence set in an old style serif and a similar-weight sans serif at the same point size will appear to be two different sizes. The discrepancy results from the sans serif's larger x-height: its lowercase letters are larger in relation to the cap height than those of the serif. The difference in set size and apparent size can vary as much as two or three points, depending on the face. A sans-serif face such as Univers might be perfectly comfortable to read at a size of 8 points, but an old style such as Garamond Three at that size will appear tiny.

Alignment Logic Type can be set in several different configurations called alignments. It can be set so that every line begins at the same left-hand starting point (flush left) or right-hand starting point (flush right), or with an axis centered on the paragraph width (centered). In this case, there are two options: in centered type, the lines are different lengths and are centered over each other on the width's vertical axis; in justified type, the lines are the same length, aligning on both the left and the right sides. Justified text is the only setting in which the lines are the same length. In text set to align left, right, or centered, the uneven lengths of the lines create a soft shape on the nonaligned side that is called a "rag." ▮ The alignment of text has an effect on the spacing within it. In a paragraph set flush left, ragged right (FLRR), the word spaces are uniform. This is also true in a paragraph set flush right, ragged left (FRRL) and in a centered paragraph. The word space in a justified paragraph, however, varies because the width of the paragraph is mathematically fixed, and the words on any given line must align on both sides—no matter how many words or how long they are. ▮ In justified text, word spacing variation is the single most difficult issue to overcome. The result of poorly justified text in which the word space constantly changes is a preponder-

All ways

The world is an idea you think despite yourself. An idea larger and more real than you, vanishing infinity of all this appearance. Titan Atlas, geographer of wind, bears the world he has dreamt on his own shoulders, all the while crying that gravity is getting him down; little Eros, pudgy cherub, also carries the world, but effortlessly, grinning cheese of love.

ok

Typographic color—the degree of density, value, and contrast within type—is largely determined by spacing and weight. A layout with "good color" is one with variations in tightness and openness, darkness and lightness, linearity and mass, texture and solidity.

This page spread shows a tremendous variety of textures, densities, and perceived spatial play—typographically, it would be considered very "colorful," even though the majority of material is monochromatic. Studio Pip & Company: Melbourne, Australia

FLRR
Lorem ipsum dolori sit amet consecti tur adipscing elitamu duis nonem eratus umma quae coelis at in dolor quamet.

Lorem ipsum dolori sit amet consecti tur adipscing elitamu duis nonem eratus umma quae coelis at in dolor quam

Lorem ipsum dolori sit amet consecti tur adipscing elitamu duis nonem eratus umma quae coelis at in dolor quamet

Lorem ipsum dolori sit amet consectitur adipsc ing elitamu duis nonem eratusumma quae coeli surus atine dolor quam

FRRL

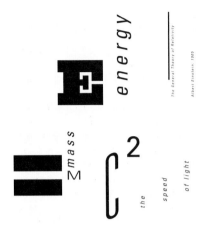

E = energy

M = mass

the speed of light

C²

The General Theory of Relativity
Albert Einstein 1905

ance of rivers—chains of white negative space that visually join each other from line to line. In particularly bad justified setting, the rivers are even more apparent than the interline space, causing the paragraph to become a jumble of strange word clusters. ▌One method of minimizing this problem is to find the optimal flush-left paragraph width for the size of the type before justifying—and then to widen the paragraph slightly or shrink the type size by a half-point or a point.

Exploring the Ragged Edge The rag of a paragraph might range from deep to shallow and active to subtle, but its uniformity and consistency from the top of a paragraph down to the bottom are what make it desirable. The ragged line endings are considered optimal if they create an organic, unforced "ripple" down the edge of the paragraph, without pronounced indents

or bulges—usually, if the rag zone hovers between one-fifth and one-seventh of the paragraph's width. That said, a deep rag is acceptable if it remains consistent throughout the text, and its activity mitigated by introducing more interline space. ▌What is never desirable, however, is a rag that is all over the place as the text progresses. Hyphenated word breaks are a constant source of frustration. Too many hyphens in a row are considered undesirable, and a slight adjustment in text size or paragraph width might correct the problem. The width of a paragraph depends heavily on the size of type being used and therefore how many characters can be fit onto a single line. Regardless of the type size or the reader's maturity, between fifty and eighty characters (including spaces) can be processed before a line return. With words averaging between five and

Deep Funk
Raw Soul
Nu Jazz
Broken Beat

STYLE No. PBA-99

Pretty Baby   *Natural Look*

SHE WILL
LOVE YOU

DJ TILL RUPRECHT & DJ GERALD WILDENAUER

FINE LIKE WINE

Fr 11. Nov - 22.00 Uhr PODIUM, BAYREUTH

ten letters, that means approximately eight to twelve words per line. ▌A desirable paragraph setting is one in which a constellation of variables achieves a harmonic balance. A designer might first make some assumptions about the text typeface, based on his or her sense of its conceptual appropriateness and its visual attributes, and set a text paragraph at an arbitrary width and text size. Judging from this first attempt, a designer might opt to adjust the size of the text, loosen or tighten its overall spacing, open and close up the leading, and change the width in successive studies. ▌By comparing the results of these variations, a designer will be able to determine the most comfortable text setting for extended reading. *At what point is the type size too small—or uncomfortably large? Are the lines relatively even in length or varying a lot? Is excessive hyphenation occurring, meaning that the paragraph is too narrow to allow a useful character count? Is the leading creating too dense a field of text to feel comfortable?* During this study, it might become clear that several options for width and leading are optimal, but a designer will need to choose one as a standard for the publication. The choice that the designer makes has implications for the page size, the number of columns of text that might fit on it, and optimal sizes for other text groupings, such as captions, callouts, and so on.

The Visual and the Informational Design students and novices often make the mistake of ignoring the abstract visual nature of type and, as a result, use type in a heavy-handed way that doesn't correspond with image material—in effect, separating the two things completely. Type is visual; in space, it acts the same way that dots, lines, squares, fields of texture, and patterns do in any composition. In addition to how type is placed within a format, its rhythmic, spatial, and textural qualities are important considerations. The term for these qualities, as

The alignment logic of text creates structure as text elements break space, and the voids in between text elements—as they do between positive shapes—help establish movement and rhythm. It is equally true for type, as it is for other kinds of form, that regularized scale and spatial intervals, along with symmetry, produce restful—potentially monotonous—compositions, whereas irregular relationships, and asymmetry, produce dynamic compositions.

The interaction of alignments and voids in this poster creates a rhythmic and active spatial experience.
Doch Design: Munich, Germany

The fluid movement of image across the format of this concert poster is echoed and extrapolated by the type elements, which respond to the image's changes in scale, density, value, and movement with a counterpoint of changes in scale, density, value, and movement.
Paone Design Associates: Philadelphia, PA; USA

a whole, is "typographic color." Typographic color is similar to chromatic color—like red, blue, or orange—but deals only with changes in lightness and darkness, or value. Moreover, it is different from the qualities of chromatic color in that it describes changes in rhythm and texture. ▌Changing the typographic color of text elements separates them from the surface and introduces the illusion of spatial depth and a sense of changing rhythm. A larger chunk of type, for example, appears closer than a smaller one, while a lighter element appears to recede into the distance. Typographic color, composition, and verbal clarity are inseparable: a change of color automatically alters not only the spatial and textural quality of the type, but its mean-

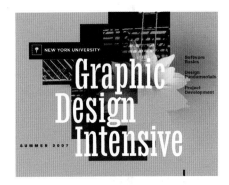

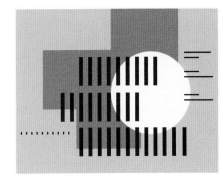

Never forget that type is visual material—just like pictorial or abstract form—and must share some compositional logic with images in order to actively integrate with it in composition. The diagram accompanying this poster demonstrates the visual similarities between image and type—both of which are reduce to their underlying formal identities as dots and lines.

STIM: New York, NY; USA

ing. A typographic color change allows a designer to highlight structure and invigorate a page.

Establishing Hierarchy Information is systematic. Most often, it appears as a collection of parts, each having a different function: for example, callouts, captions, and sidebars in magazine articles; or, primary content, supporting content, and menus on a Web page. These various parts often repeat, appear within the same space, and support each other. ❙ One of the designer's most important tasks is to give information an order that allows the viewer to navigate it. This order, called the information's "hierarchy," is based on the level of importance the designer assigns to each part of the text. "Importance" means "the part that should be read first, second, third . . ." and so on; it also refers to the "distinction of function" among the parts: running text, or the body of a writing, as measured against other elements such as page folios, titles and subheads, captions, and similar items. ❙ Determining a hierarchy is the result of reading the text and asking some simple questions: What are the distinguishable parts of the information to be designed? What should be the main focus of the reader's attention? How do the parts that are not the main

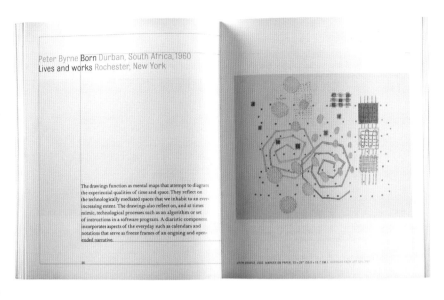

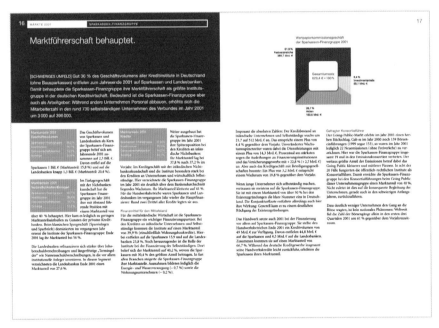

Hierarchy—the order of importance given to text elements—can be achieved through a number of strategies that, in general, focus on the issue of similarity and difference. Text elements that are uniform in appearance diminish in importance in comparison to one that is treated differently. Similarly, viewers consider information treated in the same way to be related; they consider information treated differently unrelated.

The designers of this exhibition catalog used size, color, and position to create a clear hierarchy for text components. Color is used to distinguish different portions of information within contiguous text.
Studio Blue: Chicago, IL; USA

The designers of this page spread spent a great deal of time crafting the text. They paid attention to larger issues, such as rhythmic change in the sizes and spacing of headline, deck, text, callouts, and captions, as well as to the finer points of paragraph indentation, spacing of numbers, avoiding widows and bad line breaks, and so on.
Hesse Design: Düsseldorf, Germany

focus relate to each other? Does the viewer need to see a certain grouping of words before they begin to focus on the main part? ▌All text looks equally important in raw form. If placed on a page as is, the words form a uniform field of texture. By manipulating the spaces around and between text, the designer's first option is to create levels of importance through spatial distinction. The designer might group the majority of elements together, for example, but separate a specific element—maybe a title—and give it more space. ▌The uniformity that is usually desirable to keep the reader moving is thereby purposely broken, creating a fixation point that will be interpreted as deserving attention and, therefore, more important than the other elements. Enhancing such spatial separations by changing the typographic color of separated elements will further distinguish each from the other. Blocks of information that are treated similarly will be assumed to mean similar things, or be closely related in function. ▌At the same time, all the components within a hierarchy must respond to each other's visual qualities. Readers acknowledge minute changes in typographic quality—hence, the focus on achieving a uniform texture in running text to avoid optical fixation—but too much difference among hierarchic levels creates a visual disconnect. The danger of pushing stylistic differences between informational components is that, as a totality, the typography—indeed, the entire project—will appear busy and lack a fundamental cohesion or "visual voice." This is

why designers are admonished to employ only two or three type styles in a project and, as often as possible, to combine styles that share qualities such as proportion, weight, terminal shape, and so on. Limiting the degree of stylistic difference to just what is needed to signal a change in information allows the reader to understand such changes while maintaining visual unity and more clearly creating interrelationships within the content.

The Effect of Color on Type Chromatic color can greatly enhance the textural qualities of type—its boldness, lightness, openness, density, and apparent location in "three-dimensional" space—reinforcing these qualities as they already exist in black and white. The relative value of colors, their darkness or lightness, is an aspect of chromatic color that demands great care in regard to how it affects type, especially legibility. As their values approach each other, the contrast between type and background diminishes, and the type becomes difficult to distinguish from its surrounding field. ▌All the qualities of chromatic color have a pronounced effect on hierarchy because of the way they affect the apparent spatial depth and prominence of the typographic elements to which colors are applied. Color presents the possibility of altering the meaning or psychological effect of words by introducing an added layer of meaning independent of the words themselves.

Dokument 1
1. September 1933
„Die deutsche Kunst als stolzeste Verteidigung des deutschen Volkes" [1]
Rede auf der Kulturtagung des Parteitags der NSDAP in Nürnberg [2]
VB vom 3./4. 9. 1933

Am 30. Januar 1933 wurde die nationalsozialistische Partei mit der politischen Führung des Reiches betraut. [3] Ende März war die nationalsozialistische Revolution äußerlich abgeschlossen. Abgeschlossen, insoweit es die restlose Übernahme der politischen Macht betrifft. [4] Allein, nur der, dem das Wesen dieses gewaltigen Ringens innerlich unverständlich blieb, kann glauben, daß damit der Kampf der Weltanschauungen seine Beendigung gefunden hat. Dies wäre dann der Fall, wenn die nationalsozialistische Bewegung nichts anderes wollte, als die sonstigen landesüblichen Parteien. Diese pflegen allerdings am Tage der Übernahme der politischen Führung den Zenith ihres Wollens und damit auch ihrer Existenz erreicht zu haben. Weltanschauungen aber sehen in der Erreichung der politischen Macht nur die Voraussetzung für den Beginn der Erfüllung ihrer eigentlichen Mission. Schon im Worte „Weltanschauung" liegt die feierliche Proklamation des Entschlusses, allen Handlungen eine bestimmte Ausgangsauffassung und damit sichtbare Tendenz zugrunde zu legen. Eine solche Auffassung kann richtig oder falsch sein: Sie ist der Ausgangspunkt für die Stellungnahme zu allen Erscheinungen und Vorgängen des Lebens und damit ein bindendes und verpflichtendes Gesetz für jedes Wirken. Je mehr sich nun

Readers are acutely aware of tiny changes in treatment, meaning little is needed to accomplish a clear distinction in hierarchy or meaning. The headings in this book, for example, are distinguished only by a change in weight; in all other aspects, they are the same as the running text. Surface: Frankfurt am Mein, Germany

Chromatic color has a pronounced effect on spatial perception, compounding the richness and complexity of hierarchic distinction already possible in black and white. Contrast in value and intensity can enhance an established hierarchy—or purposely contradict it to introduce ambiguity. In this example, the larger type—which would normally appear in front of the smaller text—appears to recede because its hue, value, and intensity offer less contrast against the background field than does its companion.

Image making is perhaps one of the most complex human activities. An image is a powerful experience—a symbolic, emotional space that replaces physical experience. In graphic design, there are myriad image possibilities—symbols and photomontage, drawing and painting, and even type—that perform different functions. Images provide a visual counterpoint to text, helping engage the audience. Images also offer a visceral connection to experiences described by written language. They can help clarify very complex information—especially conceptual, abstract, or process-oriented information—by displaying it concisely, "at a glance." ▌ Every image falls on a continuum between the literal, or representational, and the abstract. Purely abstract images communicate ideas that are grounded in the human experience. Even a photograph that purports to represent something real is an abstraction on some level. Using the intrinsic messaging of abstract form to influence the composition of a photograph will enhance its messaging potential. Similarly, suggesting concrete, literal experience within an abstract composition will help ground the message in reality for a viewer,

making it more accessible without sacrificing the abstraction's simplicity and visceral evocative power. ▌ The form of an image's representation is called its "mode," and this includes not only its degree of simplicity and abstraction but also its medium. A designer must consider a number of things in choosing the right image mode. Among these are the evocative, emotional qualities of the project's content; the number of different modes needed to differentiate specific messages; the expectations of the viewing audience for certain image experiences over others, because of their demographic makeup or the social and historical context of the project's content; and production issues, such as budget, lead time, and fabrication concerns. ▌ How far from its "natural" state the image gets (how much the "pure" depiction of the subject gets altered by the designer) is described as how "mediated" it is. The level of an image's mediation can be evaluated in a couple of ways. First, it can be considered in terms of its physical expression, or how it's made—for example, a realistic drawing shows a greater level of mediation than a photograph of the same subject. Second, an image's level of mediation can be considered in how complex the messaging in the image is—a somewhat literal drawing of an image is less mediated than a highly contrived photograph or collage.

Stylization An icon is a visual sign that shares a structural similarity with the object it signifies. Usually, icons are devoid of detail and are literal representations of their signified object. An indexical sign is an image that points to its signified object indirectly, or "indexes" it—for example, a nest indexes a bird. Symbols are highly mediated forms of image, drawing on common understanding and cultural contexts that elevate them beyond mere representation. A supersign superimposes more than one

Image

The presentation of images falls on a spectrum defined at one end by representation and at the other by abstraction. Images that lie closer to the representational end of the continuum are more literal; images that approach abstraction are more interpretive.

 **Der Deutsche Schulpreis**

This symbol combines iconic representations of a bird and a school desk. The combination of these elements creates a simple supersign that takes on symbolic qualities because of the audience's agreement association of certain meanings with the idea of "wings." Hesse Design: Düsseldorf, Germany

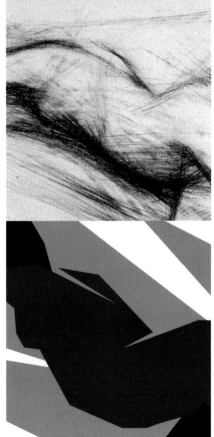

sign (and often more than one type of sign) in a single, gestalt combination in which all the signs included are accessible immediately—a logo is an example of a supersign.

Illustration and Photography The choice of illustration over photography opens up tremendous possibility for transmitting information. The designer is not only unencumbered by the limitations of real-world objects and environment but also given the potential to introduce conceptual overlay, increased selectivity of detail, and the personal, interpretive aspect of the designer's visualization—through choice of medium, composition, and gestural qualities. An illustration might be a concrete depiction that calls upon the traditions of classical drawing and painting—its goal being to reproduce the empirical world in a way that responds to actual conditions of light, form, and perspective. Alternatively, an illustration might be a graphic-

ally stylized image that approaches abstraction, referring to the real world as a grounding point but favoring the expressive qualities of gesture, ambiguous space, and the process of making the image. Between these two extremes lie the possibilities of mixing elements of each state. ▌A line is a line is a line … or not. Every drawing and painting tool makes characteristic marks and affords a designer a specific kind of visual language. The language of the tool has a powerful effect on an illustration's communicative value, not just on its visual qualities relative to other elements in a design solution. Above and beyond the fundamental selection of subject matter, composition, and degree of stylization, the medium a designer chooses with which to create the illustration carries meaning—in terms of feeling (softness, hardness, fluidity, and stiffness) and, sometimes, conceptually (for example, using a drawing

All these images depict the same subject, a figure, but using different modes. The modes range between literal and stylized, and each mode intrinsically mediates the image to varying degrees. The "pure" photograph is the least mediated in this study. The two drawn images are inherently more mediated than the

photographic image—the designer has invented his or her own depiction of the subject—but, between the two, the naturalistic drawing is less mediated than the other.

The montage in this collateral combines illustrative and photographic elements—as well as icon and literal modes of representation. The alteration of the cello image, along with the mixture of modes itself, creates not only a more complex symbol, but a highly mediated image—the designer has interfered to a tremendous degree in order to manipulate meaning. Studio Pip & Company: Melbourne, Australia

tool native to a certain region or historical period for a project related to that region or period). ▌ Choosing illustration for image presentation, however, means potentially sacrificing a kind of credibility or real-world connection for the viewer. Despite the fact that most audiences realize that a photograph might just as easily be manipulated and therefore made misleading, the audiences will still instinctively respond to a photograph as though it were "reality." This provides the designer with an upper hand in persuasion, on behalf of a client, because the work of convincing a viewer that he or she can believe or trust the image is already well on its way to being achieved: "I saw it with my own eyes." ▌ As with any other imagery, photographic content must be decisively composed. The photographer has two opportunities to control the image's composition, however: first, within the frame of the camera's viewfinder; and second, during the printing process in the darkroom (or in cropping a digital photograph using software). In photography, tonal range—the number and depth of gray values—is of particular concern. Traditionally, a "good-quality" photograph includes a clean, bright white; deep black; detail present within

shadow areas; and a fluid range of grays in between. Pushing the tonal range toward generally brighter values decreases the contrast in the image and, to some degree, flattens it out; pushing the tonal range toward the shadow end also tends to flatten the image but increases contrast and causes highlight areas to become more pronounced.

Type as Image When a letter or word takes on pictorial qualities beyond those that define their form, they become images in their own right, and their semantic potential is enormous. Words that are also pictures fuse several kinds of understanding together: they are

supersigns. As their meaning is assimilated through each perceptual filter—visual, emotional, intellectual—they assume the evocative stature of a symbol. Understanding on each level is immediate, and a viewer's capacity to recall images makes such word-pictures highly effective in recalling the verbal content associated with them.

Mixing Image Styles As with all compositional strategies, creating contrast among visual elements is key to surprising, refreshing, and enlivening layouts—and this is no less true for imagery. Aside from the big-picture contrasts afforded by changing sizes, shapes, color, and spatial arrangement, combining different modes of image offers an important and highly effective method for introducing contrast. Very textural, linear illustration, for instance, will contrast richly with photography—which tends to be continuous in tone—as well as with flat, solid graphic elements. ▌ It's important that, while the different styles being combined contrast each other decisively, they also share some visual qualities. The designer must combine image styles selectively to support a given purpose, using the qualities of each to appropriately convey intended messages and interact with each other in a unified visual language that assimilates their differences as part of their logic.

Image and Narrative Putting photographs together increases their semantic power and creates narrative, or storytelling; the instant two images can be compared, whether juxtaposed or arranged in sequence, a viewer will try to establish meaningful connections between them. Every photograph will influence any others around it, changing their

Type may be transformed into an image using a number of strategies. The substitution of the clock icon for the O in the word *not* transforms not only the word into an image, but also creates a supersign.
Studio di Progettazione Grafica: Cevio, Switzerland

The form alteration in this logotype creates the perception of three-dimensional perspective as well as back-and-forth motion.
Surface: Frankfurt am Mein, Germany

Removing the vowels from the word is a syntactic deconstruction that alludes to the meaning of the client's name.
Parallax Design:
Melbourne, Australia

Altering the form of the type creates a three-dimensional image.
GollingsPidgeon:
Adelaide, Australia

The form of the lowercase G is altered and pictorialized to suggest a physical object.
Parallax Design:
Melbourne, Australia

Always evaluate similarities, as well as disparities, in visual form to determine what mix supports the project's visual language and concept the best. In this example, each composition combines the same subjects—one in iconic form, the other as concrete photograph.

individual meanings and contributing to a progression in narrative as a result. ▎As more images are juxtaposed or added in sequence, their narrative reinforces itself based on the increasingly compounded assumptions initially made by viewers. By the time viewers have seen three or four images in a sequence, their capacity to avoid assumptions decreases, and they begin to look for meaning that completes the narrative they have constructed. This "narrative momentum" increases exponentially to the point that the semantic content of any image that appears later in the sequence must be related to that delivered earlier. ▎Every image is susceptible to change when words appear next to it—so much so that a designer can easily alter the meaning of the same image over and over again by replacing the words that accompany it. In a sequential arrangement in which the same image is repeated in subsequent page spreads but is accompanied each time by a new word or phrase, new experience and knowledge about the image are introduced to the viewer. Not

surprisingly, the ability of images to change the meanings of words is equally profound. The mutual brainwashing effected by words and images depends a great deal on the simultaneity of their presentation—that is, whether the two are shown together, at once, or in succession. ▎If seen simultaneously, word and image will create a single message in which each reciprocally advances the message and neither is truly changed in the viewer's mind—the message is a gestalt. However, if one is seen first and the other second, the viewer has a chance to construct meaning before being influenced.

Ever Metaphor? In writing and speech, a metaphor is an expression—a word or phrase—that refers to an unrelated idea, creating additional meaning. Images can be used in much the same way: a designer may present an image that means something else entirely, refers to a much broader concept, or combines concepts to evoke a third concept that is not explicit in either of the combinants. ▎One option for creating a visual metaphor is to use an object to define the form of something else—for example, laying out an invitation to a travel-themed fund-raising event to look like an airline ticket, using the type styles, colors, and other visual details of such tickets as a source. Another option is to depict one thing behaving, pictorially, like another—presenting products in an urban cosmetics brochure, for instance, configured as a city skyline. ▎There are as many ways to create metaphors as there are ideas and images—in short, an endless array limited only by imagination. While the literal content of images provides a baseline communication, a thoughtful designer can use images to evoke higher-level concepts above and beyond what they merely show. The result is a richer, more inventive, and more memorable and meaningful experience for the audience.

Words and images each profoundly affect the meaning of the other. In these pairs, compare the effect of image on image; word on image; and word on word.

The designers of this desk calendar use words to qualify the meaning of the photographic image. In these two-page spreads, similar environments are changed in their meaning because of the headings with which they are paired. Strichpunkt: Stüttgart, Germany

JUKE JOINT

The Bottleneck Blues Bar isn't the only place to hear live entertainment at Ameristar St. Charis, but its got to be the most visually exciting one. There's so much going on here that it's hard to know where to look. Giant crystal chandeliers sparkle against the black ceiling. A blow-lit saxophone hangs from a wall. A sign tells you that, "If you ain't been blue, you ain't really been."

Everything here comes at a surprise, from the bar stools and tables veneered with bottle caps, to the multihued glass teardrops lit from below, dangling colorfully from the bar. The Bottleneck's stained "junk wall" contains just that: it's a three-dimensional collage of bottle jukes, an old bugle, doughnut dials, street signs, all manner of bottle-bottle-case, and more.

"We just wanted it to look like it was a juke joint from the Mississippi Delta," designer Tom Hutch said. "We wanted to make the building look like an old Victorian theatre, but one from a worldly area." As if the proprietor of the blues bar came along and added his layers of cultural funk."

Well, somebody did. And the experience is by no means just a visual one. Free music is a regular feature here, as an ticketed concerts by such names as Merle Haggard and David Mac. The 8-element punch also exists at our Vicksburg location features jazz and rock 'n' roll, too. And on the guitar and LP-shaped menu indicate, the Bottleneck also serves lunch and dinner — inventively, of course. Why not try wild in dishes as Popcorn Lobster and Crispy Gator with cajun ranch dressing? There each choices, there's no excuse for singing the blues.

Layout

In this spread, the type and image work together to convey the emotional pull of the content, with no one element outstripping, conflicting, or competing with the other. The image is vibrant, the cropping draws attention to the expressions of the people, the type is classic, while the difference in the size of the two words in the headline makes the statement bold and contemporary. Kuhlmann Leavitt, Inc.: Mineapolis, MN; USA

Design solutions really come together when all the components are clearly interrelated. First off, a format's proportions should begin to evoke appropriate feelings in the viewer—intimate, expansive, or confrontational—right from the moment they come in contact with the work. Content organization should respond to the format, as well as the requirements of the information presented; the selection of images and type styles should support each other stylistically, reciprocally reinforcing mood and concept. The arrangement of type and images should respond to each other visually, and their composition within the format space should again augment the emotions or associations that are more literally apparent in the content of both images and writing. ▌ Furthermore, the pacing and sequencing of the content should respond to emphases within the content and create visual highs and lows—alternations of sequences that are dramatic and sedate—to continually refresh the viewer. Thoughtful consideration of typographic and abstract details should be apparent in the way they refer to large-scale compositional elements or spatial interaction. Last, the physical, experiential quality of the work should be considered in the context of its production medium, whether electronic or printed and bound. When a designer sees the project through in all these aspects, the result is a powerful totality of experience: one that is evocative, emotional, useful, enjoyable, and memorable.

Organizational Strategies: Structure and Intuition Figuring out what goes where, in what order, and how it should be arranged from a compositional standpoint demands a lot from a designer. A client might supply some content in a particular order, but the designer really has to understand the content and, potentially, reorder it when necessary to improve its clarity or enhance its conceptual aspects. Strategies for organizing content involve sorting the material into manageable parts that are related to each other: by part to whole; by kind; by frequency; by complexity; chronologically; and by relevance. Some strategies are often applied to particular kinds of publications because of convention—usually driven by the expectations of the audience. Newspapers, for example, exhibit an organizational strategy of part to whole based on local relevance; packaging divides information among its sides based on complexity.

The Grid System Pictures, fields of text, headlines, and tabular data: all these pieces must come together to communicate. Using a structure called a grid is simply one approach to achieving this goal. A grid consists of a distinct set of alignment-based relationships that serves as guides for distributing elements across a format. Every grid contains the same basic parts, no matter how complex the grid becomes. These parts can be combined as needed or omitted from the overall structure at the designer's discretion, and the proportions of the parts is similarly dependent on the designer's needs. ▌ Grids can be loose and organic, or they can be rigorous and mechanical. The benefits of working with a grid are simple: clarity, efficiency, economy, and continuity. Before anything else, a grid introduces systematic order to a layout, helps distinguish between various types of

Pacing and sequencing material helps the audience understand and assimilate it; in addition, it provides opportunities to create rhythm and surprise from part to part or from page to page. Here are several ways to organize content:

by kind, which emphasizes differences in meaning; by specificity, moving from the general to the specific; by complexity, moving from the least to the most complex; or by relevance, according to the importance of each item.

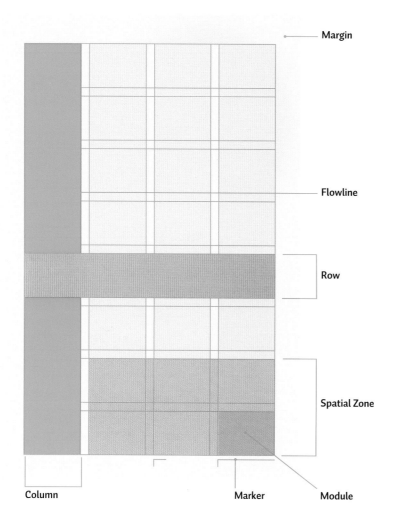

Margin

Flowline

Row

Spatial Zone

Column

Marker

Module

information, and eases a user's navigation through them. Among other things, a grid can help solve complex communication problems. ▌Building an appropriate grid for a publication involves assessing the shape and volume of the content, rather than trying to assign grid spaces arbitrarily. The shape of the content, whether text or image, is particularly important—its proportions become the source for defining the grid spaces. When considering text as the essential building block, the designer must look at variations in the text setting. The

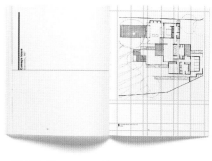

All grids are made up of columns, which contain content, surrounded by margins, an open area that separates the columns from the edges of the format. A grid may have any number of columns appropriate to the complexity of

the content it must organize. A column grid that is also divided by a number of regular horizontal rows is called a "modular grid."

The benefits of working with a grid are simple: clarity, efficiency, economy, and continuity. Shown here are diagrams of two publications' grids, superimposed on their respective spreads to demonstrate how the grids provide consistency and flexibility as well as help integrating text and imagery.
GollingsPidgeon: Adelaide, Australia
Hesse Design: Düsseldorf, Germany

sheer amount of text that the publication must accommodate is an important consideration. Achieving an optimal setting for text at a given size and in a given face will indicate a width for columns, and, from there, the designer can explore how many columns will fit side by side on a single page. Adjusting the size of the text, its internal spacing, and the gutters between columns will allow the designer to create a pre-liminary structure that ensures optimal text setting throughout. ▌Considering image as a source for the grid spaces is another option. If the publication is driven by its image content, this might be a more appropriate direction. The proportions of the images, if they are known, can be used to determine the proportions of columns and modules. Beginning with a universal height or depth for the images, and a consistent alignment among them, will allow the designer to assess how varied they are in format—squares, verticals, and horizontals. The designer must then decide how the images are to be displayed in terms of their size relationship to each other: will the images be shown in sizes that are relative to each other, or will they be allowed to appear at any size? If all the images hang from a particular flowline, their depth varying, the designer will need to address the images with both the shortest and deepest depths to determine what is possible for text or other elements below these variations. From these major divisions in space and the logic that the designer uses to govern them, a series of intervals might be structured for the images and for text areas surrounding them. ▌The way in which columns of text interact with negative space is an important aspect of how a grid is articulated. The spaces above and below columns play an active part in giving the columns a rhythm as they relate to each other across pages and spreads. The options available to a designer are endless but can be described as fitting into three basic categories: columns that

justify top and bottom; columns that align vertically at top or bottom and rag at the other end; and columns that rag top and bottom. ▌A grid is truly successful only if the designer rises above the uniformity of its structure; the greatest danger is to succumb to its regularity. Remember that the grid is an invisible guide existing on the bottommost level of the layout; the content happens on the surface. Grids do not make dull layouts—designers do. Violating the grid is a necessity of designing, sometimes because circumstance dictates it—content that must occupy a specific spread won't quite fit—or because it is visually necessary to call attention to some feature of the content, or to create some surprise for the reader. A simple trick to achieving layout variation is to arbitrarily clus-ter images toward the top of one spread and then toward the bottom on the following spread. Sometimes forcing a small, medium, and large image onto a spread—and then using the same sizes but placed in different locations on the next spread—will quickly create move-ment across the grid.

Intuitive Strategies Sometimes content has its own internal structure that a grid won't necessarily clarify; sometimes the content needs to ignore structure altogether to create specific kinds of emotional reactions in the intended audience; and sometimes a designer simply envisions a more complex intellectual involvement on the part of the audience as part of their experience of the piece. The first option is splitting apart a conventional grid, even a very simple one. A designer might "cut apart" major zones and shift them horizontally or ver-tically, perhaps aligning informational compo-nents in a way that creates a new verbal connec-tion. A conventional grid structure repeated in different orientations could be used to explore a more dynamic architectural space by creating different axes of alignment. ▌Another interest-ing way of creating compositions is to derive a visual idea from the content and impose it on the page format as a kind of arbitrary structure. The structure can be an illusory representation of a subject, like waves or the surface of water, or can be based on a concept, like a childhood memory, a historical event, or a diagram.

A grid can be successfully vio-lated as long as the page maintains a structure that ori-ents the reader and maintains a connection between images and text. In this example, the images are beautifully bal-anced across the spread, while the text flows harmoniously around them, a fitting tribute to the content itself.
Ah-Reum Han: School of Visual Arts, New York, NY; USA

Whatever the source of the idea, the designer can organize material to refer to it. For example, text and images might sink underwater or float around like objects caught in a flood.

Visual Relationships between Words and Pictures Getting type to interact with imagery poses a serious problem for many designers. The results of poorly integrated type and image fall into two categories. The first category includes type that has nothing in common with the images around it or is completely separated from the image areas. The second category includes typography that has been so aggressively integrated with image that it becomes an illegible mass of shape and texture. ▌Images are composed of lights and darks, linear motion and volume, contours, and open or closed spaces, arranged in a particular order. Type shares these same attributes. It is composed of lights and darks, linear and volumetric forms, and contours and rhythms of open and closed spaces, also arranged in a particular order. ▌Similarities between type elements and pictorial elements make a strong connection between the two. Every image portrays clear relationships between figure and ground, light and dark, and has movement within it. When typographic configurations display similar attributes to an adjacent image or expand on those attributes, the type and the image are said to be formally congruent. ▌Although seemingly counterintuitive, relating typographic elements to images by contrasting their visual characteristics—creating formal opposition—can help clarify their individual characteristics. By their very difference, two opposing visual elements become more clearly identified and understood. The caveat is that some congruence between the elements must also exist so that the opposing

In this composition the type responds to the photograph's visual language—its structure, rhythmic movement, and tonal values—so that both type and photograph are mutually dependent and equally vital components.

A rough composition study for a poster series yields a multitude of possibilities for a consistent, yet flexible, visual language. In each set of examples, one aspect of the visual language has been called out for variation without disturbing the other aspects. In the first, scale change is the variation that is exploited for flexibility; in the second study, the shape of the organic forms changes, but their essential identities remain recognizable; in the third, position of elements is the only variation. STIM: New York, NY; USA

characteristics are brought clearly into focus. In the same way that a hierarchy is destroyed if all the elements are completely different, so too is the strength of the contrast in opposing forms weakened if all their characteristics are different. Consider, too, the location of the type relative to the image and the attributes of the image's outer shape in relation to the format. An image cropped into a rectangle presents three options: the type might be enclosed within the image; the type might be outside, or adjacent to the image; or the type might cross the image and connect the space around it to its interior.

Design as a System The vast majority of designed works—printed, interactive, and environmental—are systematic in nature. Publications or websites with multiple pages, office signage, ad campaigns, families of brochures, and so on all involve part-to-whole, puzzle like relationships that must function together. Because of this, a designer's understanding of the visual language he or she is creating for such work is terribly important. It not only ensures the user's unity of experience from one part to another—directing them through changing levels of information—it provides flexibility in visual presentation appropriate to whatever such changes may be. Being able to control variations within the system also prevents the experience from becoming monotonous for the audience.

Consistency and Flexibility Establishing tension between repeated, recognizable visual qualities and the lively, unexpected, or clever manipulation—even violation—of those qualities in a system-oriented work is a difficult task. At one extreme, designers risk disintegrating the visual coherence that makes for a unified and memorable experience by constantly altering the project's visual language in his or her effort to continually refresh the viewer. At the other extreme, treating material too consistently will kill the project's energy. In some instances, it might also do the material a disservice by constraining all elements into a strangled mold that decreases the clarity of either the concept or informational relationships by not allowing these to flex as they must. ▌There are two fundamental variables in any project that a designer can investigate while looking for strategies to keep the work visually consistent as well as flexible. The first variable has to do with the way material is presented, what its actual form and color are. Within a given project, there may already be a range of possibilities that the designer has established—the options within a selected color palette present one possibility of changing the presentation of material; the kinds of images the designer chooses to use might also offer a range of options. The second variable is pacing—altering the frequency

of different page components in some kind of pattern so that the kinds of images or shapes, the number of images, and the amount of specific colors from within the palette are constantly changing. ▌Pacing can be understood as a kind of visual rhythm, a cadence or "timing" the reader will apprehend from part to part— whether from home page to subpage within a website, or between page spreads in a magazine, or between brochures in a literature system—almost like a film. By varying this rhythm from slow to fast, or from quiet to dynamic, for example, the designer can accomplish several goals. One result achieved is strictly visual: each turn of a page engages the reader in a new way by varying the presentation. Another result might be that the reader is cued to a significant content change; the informational function is clarified by the pacing. Magazines, for example, are often divided into sections: a series of "department" pages that recur in the same order every issue and a sequence of feature stories that changes every issue. Within each section, too, the designer must establish visual variation so that the reader, while recognizing a consistent structure, doesn't become bored.

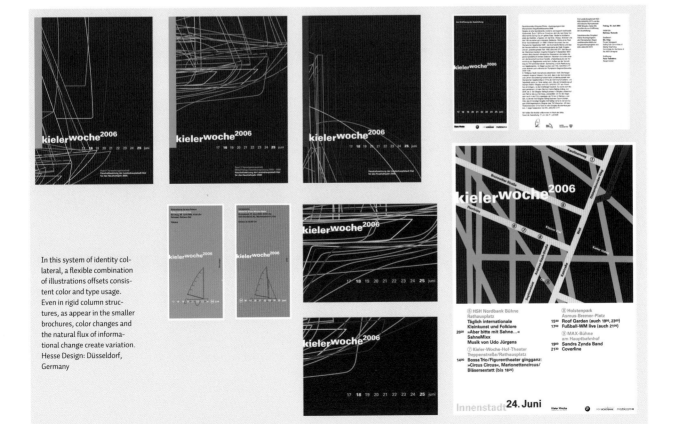

In this system of identity collateral, a flexible combination of illustrations offsets consistent color and type usage. Even in rigid column structures, as appear in the smaller brochures, color changes and the natural flux of informational change create variation. Hesse Design: Düsseldorf, Germany

THEOR

PRAC

Project

Y INTO

TICE

Case Studies

How to Use This Book

Every project presented in this section has an individual design process—whatever it may be—from beginning to end. We follow the progression of forty different projects on the following pages, including a description of the process, images of design concepts from napkin sketches to final artwork, along with insightful quotes and informative captions that illuminate how the design team worked together and how specific qualities of each design phase support the overall communication goals. Each case study concludes by showing the project as it was ultimately produced.

01

Lunar Productions Identity
Tactical Magic, LLC | Memphis, Tennesee, USA

The television production field is a crowded one and, as a result, getting the attention of advertising agencies can be tricky. Lunar Productions, based in Memphis, Tennessee, needed a bold identity to get them noticed, and one that would emphasize their creative potential in providing a valuable commercial service—providing smart and client-friendly business video. They turned to the strategic branding partnership of Tactical Magic to develop a logo that would set them apart from competitors. Equal doses of simplicity, humor, and conceptual thinking yielded a mark that demonstrates the power of visual story-telling. "The challenge was to make Lunar Productions big-time business feel as creative, smart, and friendly as their process and work actually is," says Ben Johnson, a partner in Tactical Magic, the firm that spearheaded the development of the Lunar logo.

Straight to the Moon

All of the designers' concepts—good and bad—are displayed together on the wall of a "war room." Comparing concepts simultaneously allows stronger ones to differentiate themselves more quickly. Concepts that appeal to both client and designers are tagged with sticky notes.

> We create a war room and cover the walls with our strategy, audiences, competition, benchmarks, reference material, and most of all—concepts, concepts, concepts. Our clients are involved early in the process. They see the war room in process. They see our strategy become concepts—good and bad—and collaborate with us to contribute ideas and narrow the field.
>
> Ben Johnson, Partner

"Ad agencies want to see creativity, a sense of humor, and excellent craftsmanship," he adds. For he and his partners, this process begins with a sound strategy that outlines the client's goals and proceeds directly into visual exploration–sketching. The designers sketch together, filling walls in a "war room"–devoted to that sole project–with potential candidates. ▌While many designers edit the first presentation of concepts to a small number of more refined options, Tactical Magic brings the client in during this early phase. "They see the war room in process. They see our strategy become con-cepts–good and bad–and collaborate with us to contribute ideas," says Johnson. Over a several-day period, clients and designers visit and revisit the concept wall, using sticky notes to tag concepts they like and dislike. The designers help guide the client's evaluations based on their sense of what makes a strong logo, from both a conceptual as well as formal vantage point. "Logos need to be so simple that they can work a third generation fax," Johnson says, "so photography is rarely an option." ▌The first round of concepts produced a wide range of approaches–from the strictly typographic to

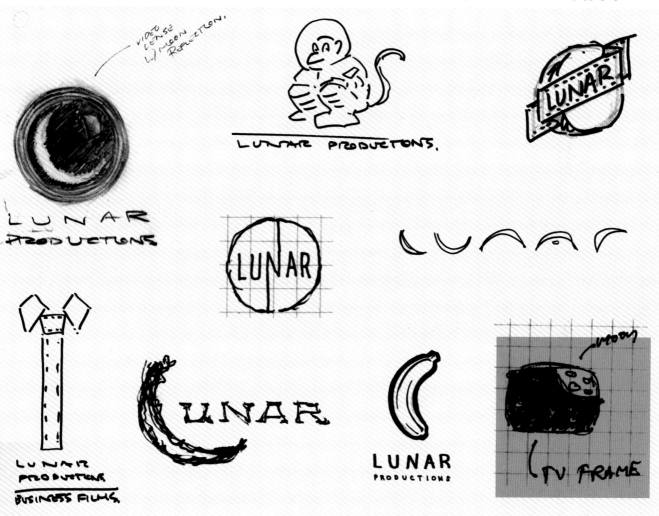

The first round of sketches produced concepts that were strictly typographic, as well as those incorporating symbols and illustrations. Combining symbolic references–for example, the filmstrip with the tie and collar–provides an opportunity to communicate complex ideas quickly and with a minimum of information.

Type can easily be trans-formed into an image by manipulating its structure. Here, the basic strokes of the letters–all angle forms–are replaced with crescent-like shapes that evoke the shape of the moon.

Replacing the initial letter L with a crescent could have created a strong image, but in this execution, its scale relative to the rest of the word–as well as its curvilinear shape–disconnects it from the remaining letters and impairs legibility.

the illustrative—but concentrated on evoking associations with the client's memorable name. Client and designers were drawn to ideas that were direct, but communicated bigger concepts. Illustrations involving a crescent moon, for example, were direct and formally strong, but lacked the depth or humor the client was after. ▌Conversely, more complex, narrative concepts—such as one depicting a monkey cosmonaut, referring to early space missions—seemed overly frivolous, or required too much knowledge on the part of the audience to understand. "Decisions are made with the gut—

because that's how consumers react to the work. But choosing one means saying 'no' to dozens of other ideas," Johnson explains. "That's a tough job." ▌In the end, the candidates were narrowed to three, including the winning logo that combined the images of a lunar landing module and a television set. The chosen direction captured the nature of the client's business, and it told a story about pop culture and history. The lunar module and the television set, both iconic symbols and sharing similar forms, could be fused into a memorable image.

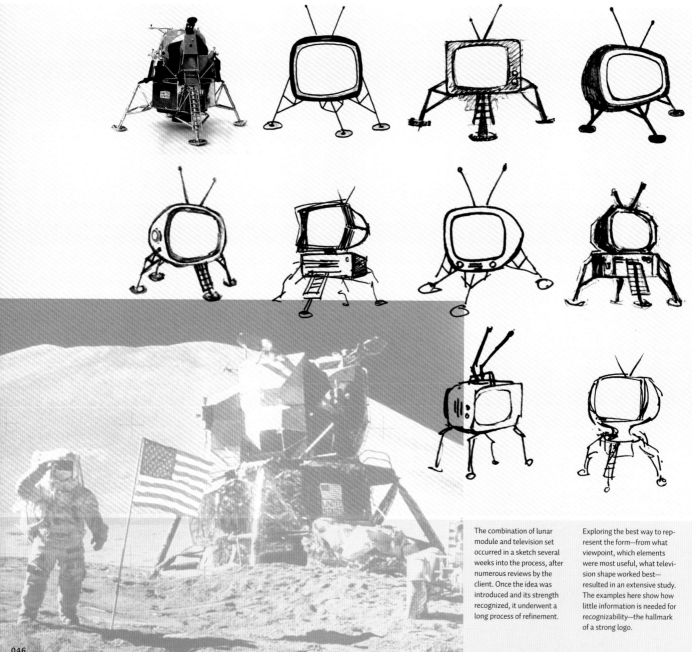

The combination of lunar module and television set occurred in a sketch several weeks into the process, after numerous reviews by the client. Once the idea was introduced and its strength recognized, it underwent a long process of refinement.

Exploring the best way to represent the form—from what viewpoint, which elements were most useful, what television shape worked best—resulted in an extensive study. The examples here show how little information is needed for recognizability—the hallmark of a strong logo.

"When we finally decided on this direction we explored the world of retro TVs and old LEM (lunar excursion module) schematics. We looked at old *Jetsons* cartoons to give the LEM/TV mutation a personality," Johnson notes. Along the way, the designers noticed that the TV form was recognizable over the image of the LEM. ▌After experimenting with more complicated LEM details, they decided to add a simple rocket booster underneath. Various positions and degrees of three-dimensionality were explored. A three-quarter view gave the hybrid image a confident presentation,

> We do our best to let the priorities of our client's situation and our resulting strategy guide the creative tactics.

Ben Johnson, Partner

Curving the back of the TV set alludes to an earlier, "retro" version that evokes an association with pop culture in the 1950s and '60s, as does the inclusion of antennae—now an obsolete technological detail. The designers felt that the landing module wasn't conveyed quickly enough. Rather than complicate the form with technological detail, however, they opted for a silhouetted rocket booster under the television. The simplified hand-drawn symbol was scanned and traced using Illustrator, where the designers made changes to proportions and contours.

LUNAR
PRODUCTIONS

LUNAR PRODUCTIONS

LUNAR PRODUCTIONS

STANLEY L. WENDER
SENIOR CONSULTANT

C01 722-8571 | 901 276-2407 F
SWENDER@LUNARPRODUCTIONS.COM

1575 MADISON AVENUE
MEMPHIS, TN 38104

LUNAR
PRODUCTIONS

MARK O. WENDER
PRESIDENT

1575 MADISON AVENUE
MEMPHIS, TN 38104
901-722-8571
901 276-2407 F
LUNARPRODUCTIONS.COM

The supporting logotype is an altered form of sans serifs that were popular in the 1920s and '30s. Its condensed proportions contrast the mass of the logo symbol, and its historical association with Hollywood star-power adds a sense of prestige and glamour.

The stationery focuses attention on the mark. Decisive margins in the letterhead set off the area for the letter body and activate space around the page. All the stationery applications respond to the logo's shape with rounded, diecut corners—a simple detail that helps reinforce the identity.

and the fourth leg was edited out to simplify the form. ▮ Upon refining the mark itself, the team's attention turned to supporting elements, such as color and type. "In this case," Johnson remembers, "the client was particularly concerned with balancing the logo's humor with more conservative typography." Johnson and his team explored classic typefaces with ties to the 1920s and '30s, Hollywood's Golden Age. "We modified an existing modern typeface to feel more Art Deco and produced several variations to work with the mark," he continues. Color was kept to a minimum, with the logo in black for boldness and a supporting blue to give depth, as well as hint at the notion of space. The logo was given maximum exposure. ▮ "The design became all about the logo as the hero. All other elements played a supporting role–to the point that the company name appears on the back of the business cards to give more drama to the "bug" on the front."

The designers had fun with the restroom signs in the clients' offices. A clever alteration of the familiar iconography extends the concept initiated by the logo itself.

"It has a big personality. It delivers a big smile. It's a bold logo in a competitive marketplace, and it works hard for the client.

Trace Hallowell, Partner

DESIGN EVOLUTION

02

Vorarlberg Regional Transit Communications Program
Sägenvier | Dornbirn, Austria

The network of public transportation in Vorarlberg, the Western-most region of Austria, is covered by a variety of municipal agencies and by Verkehrsverbund Vorarlberg (VVV), which coordinates between various administrative units. The complexity of this management system, with its many bureaucratic levels—along with the constant need for public communications, often with extremely short production timelines and small budgets—drove the bus, so to speak, for designers Sigi Ramoser and Hermann Brändle. Their approach addressed these needs—communicating quickly and simply—from a very intuitive standpoint. Spirited, dynamic arrangements of type and vividly colored illustrations convey the fun and benefit of riding the buses and trains while drawing the community together.

Easy Does It: Leave the Car at Home

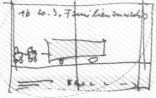

Rapid sketching in pencil and digitally, with type, begins the process of creating advertising posters and other collateral. A number of possibilities are explored very quickly, but without being overly analytical. Relying on intuition helps assure the images are fresh and loose, as well as easily understood.

Helvetica, a robust sans serif typeface with uniform stroke weights and a very neutral presentation, was a given—it was part of the client's corporate identity guidelines, already in place. Its neutrality, however, provides a universal appeal and its lack of stylistic details ensures clear legibility—an ease of use that can be interpreted as friendly.

"After winning the pitch, we gathered a lot of examples from transit advertising," says Ramoser. "We noticed that they concentrated more on technology and rates, rather than on the benefits of using the public transport or the experience of it." ∎ Having also encountered what he describes as a "hard-nosed, must-have" sentiment among the client's communications department—a budget- and time-conscious practicality without much regard for what the communications looked or felt like—Ramoser and Brändle decided to work for the opposite. While the client felt that good design was "nice to have," but not a necessity, it became their goal to make sure that "nice to have" is a must!" Ramoser opines. ∎ Sagenvier fought to rewrite the communications to be sharp and witty, but relaxed. "We followed a hidden agenda," Ramoser says, "to avoid bare information and highlight emotions instead." At the same time, they concentrated on finding a way of illustrating ideas that would set the advertising apart and unify the plurality of styles across the ads produced by the various agencies involved. "We were looking for simple visual signs that would communicate to all the target

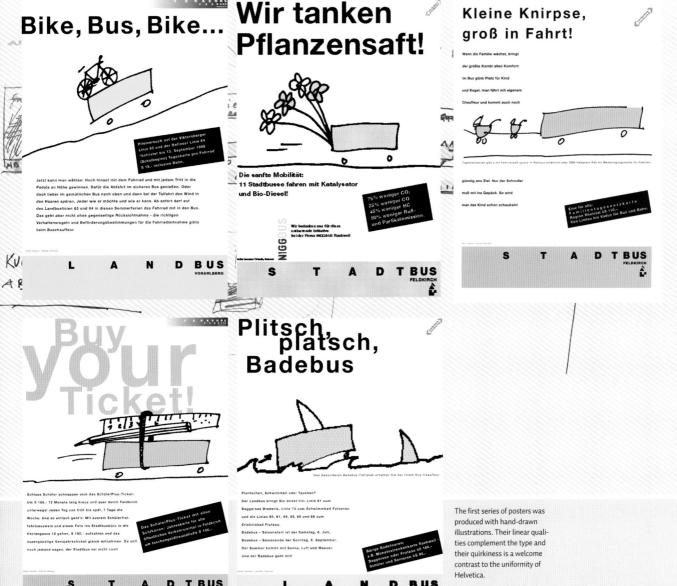

The first series of posters was produced with hand-drawn illustrations. Their linear qualities complement the type and their quirkiness is a welcome contrast to the uniformity of Helvetica.

groups," Ramoser says. The result was what Ramoser calls a "speaking illustration," a kind of image that tells a story. In the first series of posters for the client, these illustrations were drawn by hand very quickly and combined with strong, direct typography—mostly Helvetica, the ubiquitous sans serif face designed by Max Miedinger and Edouard Hoffmann at the Haas Type Foundry in the 1950s. ▍The typeface choice came from the VVV's limited corporate style manual. It suited the directness of the ads, as well as contrasted the quirky illustrations, which also came to include rough cut-paper shapes and high-contrast photocopied images. ▍The visual language—simple images, witty writing, and vivid color—were well received and made a strong impact in the community. Their graphic boldness was recognizable and memorable against other advertising, and their friendliness resonated with the public, helping to counteract the slick media superiority of auto industry advertising. Still searching for ways to communicate more universally, Ramoser and Brändle rediscovered the world of pictograms, popularized in the 1970s by airport signage, corporate identities, and Olympic events. "These little signs are able to simplify difficult messages and supplement the written words," Ramoser says. The pictograms could be used much as they were, and they could be altered and combined to create new ones very fast, which suits the rapid design schedules. ▍The process for each project is quick: "Briefing, brainstorming, concept, sketches, presentation, refinement," according to Ramoser. The refinement phase accounts for about 30 percent of the total time period, from a day or so up to a couple of weeks, depending on the scope of the project.

In a subsequent round of posters, the image style expanded to include iconic silhouettes and high-contrast photocopied elements. Even with added textural detail, as in the fish tail, the outer form retains its strength as a dynamic, simple shape.

The concept of using pictograms—icon-based forms reduced to pure geometry to enhance recognition across cultures—came about during the concepting for the next set of ads. The simple construction of the images gives them greater mass than linear, drawn illustration; it also means they can be produced or altered quickly. Because of their semiabstract nature, the designer need not conform to empirical reality in order to communicate—ideas can be very specific, somewhat symbolic, and even surreal, as needed.

**V E R K E H R S
V E R B U N D**
VORARLBERG

Mobil mit Bus, Bus, Bahn.

Der Bus ist los!

Am 27.2. ist großer Faschingsumzug in Feldkirch. Damit alle „Mäschgerle"
gut hin-, an- und zurückkommen, schicken wir mehr Busse ins närrische Treiben.
Vom Vorderland und vom Walgau sind an diesem Tag zusätzliche
Verstärkerbusse nach Feldkirch und retour unterwegs (Linie 60 und Linie 73).
Einfach einsteigen, gute Laune mitnehmen und ab geht die Post!

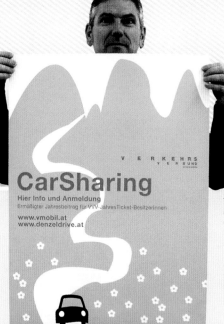

„Als was gehst du?", fragte der Stadtbus. „Als gelbe Kutsche!", lachte der Landbus.

L A N D B U S
VORARLBERG

In evolving the program visually and emo-
tionally, Sagenvier has expanded the role of
typography, integrating decorative styles for
holidays and so on, and the role of the studio—
producing radio spots, novelty giveaways,
"Happy Bus Day" events for the public, story-
brochures placed in the regional trains, and
short animations shown on the website and on
screens in the buses themselves. "We shot a
short movie about a train journey across
Vorarlberg to show in local cinemas," Ramoser
laughs, clearly enjoying the work and the
process. "It's close to everyday life."

**V E R K E H R S
V E R B U N D**

Mobil mit Bus, Bus, Bahn.

**Alles schläft.
Nur das Geschenketicket
nicht!**

S T A D T B U S
FELDKIRCH

Benzinpreise, noch normal?

Bus und Bahn, echt super.

Ein halbes Kilo
Bus und Bahn, bitte.

CarSharing
Hier Info und Anmeldung
Ermäßigter Jahresbeitrag für VVV-JahresTicket-BesitzerInnen

www.vmobil.at
www.denzeldrive.at

The choice of bright primary
and secondary colors helps
distinguish ads and images in
busy environments. The colors
all share a similar value, approximately 60 percent the value
of black, which helps soften
the stark quality of black icon
forms and typography.

Usually, only one color is used
with black in a single ad or
poster, for simplicity as well as
to be economical.

With successive posters, the
manipulation of iconic subjects
became more complex. Along
with adding details, the
designers often distort the
forms and integrate photographic effects such as blurring
or gradations.

The arrangements of images and type are not bound by any grid or regular structure. The designers compose the material on the fly, looking for dynamic tension between positive and negative, line and mass, light and dark.

Near-complementary color relationships, such as the combination of green-blue with yellow, are often jarring. By bringing the values of the two colors closer together and desaturing the complements, the designer maintains strong color contrast while adding depth to the mixture. Note the effect of temperature on spa-

tial perception: The cool blue-green appears to recede, creating the appearance of deep space, while the warm yellow advances into the poster's foreground. Variation in value and temperature contrast the flatness of the icons.

Scale change, a rhythmic back-and-forth arrangement, and contrast of soft, clustered forms with linear movement all contribute to communicating the humanity and benefits of the various forms of public transportation.

Extending the iconic language to the website was a natural progression; the vector-based images load quickly and reproduce well on screen. The simplicity of the images corresponds to the strong grid structure evident in the developing page layouts; unlike the print materials, the Web environment demands rigid structure. Early page layouts separated the image area from the navigation; an evolutionary stage incorporated the main navigational links into the image frame. As a result, the image could be larger and the two areas visually unified. The site uses a hierarchic grid, breaking content areas into different proportions to help the user more easily distinguish their respective functions. Primary content resides in the wider, left-hand column, while secondary fucntionality is found in the narrow right-hand column.

The saturation of the yellow branded callout provides focus within the overall neutral page. Situating it as a header over the right-hand column enhances the page structure. Value is used to establish a hierarchy in the content, with brighter elements commanding more attention than darker ones.

03

Marc Montplaisir Photo Website
Orangetango | Montréal, Canada

Marc Montplaisir is a photographer who is well known in the Montréal area for his work in corporate, advertising, fashion, and portrait projects, as well as his personal artistic endeavors. He enlisted OrangeTango to create a portfolio site to spotlight his work and talent—but to also reflect a professional who is serious about his work without ever taking himself too seriously. The site's potential visitors were easy to identify from the start—creative heads from different agencies and others who would potentially require his services. This particular clientele is artistically attuned, familiar with the Internet and what it has to offer, and—for lack of a better expression—has seen it all before. These individuals are also professionals who do not want to spend hours pointlessly browsing the Internet.

Well-Developed Navigation

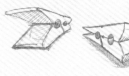

The client's company moniker, "M2," developed rapidly from a simple, clean typographic solution to a photographic concept, once the designers noticed the similarity of the shape to a Scrabble letter. The photographic presentation is a direct link to the nature of the client's business, but the game piece is more conceptual.

Quick sketches—while listening to specially created music—served to distill ideas about environments that could organize the client's photographs. Some of these sketches played with the gaming idea as the "logo" was being developed, but seemed to distract from the environment concept.

The environments contain objects related to the various areas of Montplaisir's practice.

Although the client would sell his services mainly by spotlighting his work, the site's feel "needed to play a key role in helping visitors learn more about Marc's personality," says Mario Mercier, the project's creative director. ▌He established early on that the site, in contrast to the overdesigned, high-tech style currently in vogue, should use very neutral color and understated imagery, acting as a backdrop to Montplaisir's sophisticated photographs. Additionally, the site should be clearly organized. Creating an interesting environment and navigation to express the client's personality—without competing with it—became the challenge. ▌Oddly enough, music was the source of inspiration for the site's designers. The songs that resonated in their minds were that of an era gone by—tunes that were both joyful and nostalgic. Mercier's colleague and brother, Jean-Marc, created songs especially for the project as a starting point. The songs are somewhat like elevator music, and yet vaguely exotic. As the music took shape, with Montplaisir's enthusiastic encouragement, the designers began to sketch visual environments that corresponded, in their

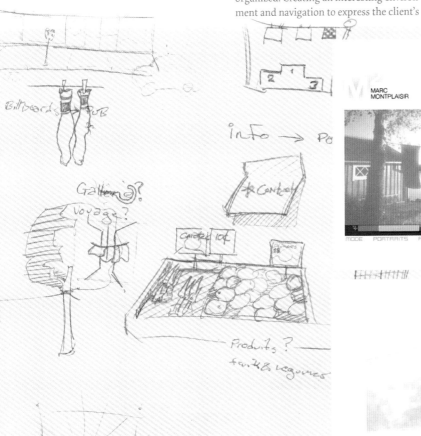

Early digital studies used soft-focus photographs as backdrops to help communicate the dreamy quality of the music. The full-color images hanging on the clothesline are navigational buttons that lead the user to individual galleries.

Because both background and navigation buttons are photographic, they seemed to blend together a little too closely.

In another iteration, the designers first tried removing the color from the background image—desaturating—so that, while not quite black and white, the color feeling is almost completely neutral. Still, the separation seemed inadequate, and the environments are either too literal or not closely enough related to the given subject area.

minds, to the songs—and to the various subject areas, such as fashion, editorial, or portraiture. The first series of sketches approached these environments photographically, but in muted colors and with details blurred slightly to make them more dreamlike. ▌Montplaisir's photograph's, in thumbnail form, would be part of these environments, and act as navigation to the gallery areas. For the fashion section, photos are hung from hangers near a mannequin. Travel photos are presented on a clothesline that seems to hang over an alleyway somewhere in the Mediterranean. The advertising photos

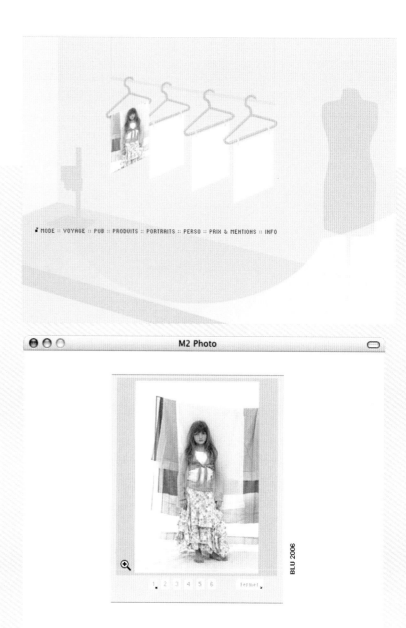

The site launches with a short animation sequence in which the latent image of an exposed sheet of paper is developed in a darkroom tray.

Within the individual galleries, the user can select from a number of photographs listed in numerical form below the image area. A simple "close" button returns the user to the previous level.

are shown on what appears to be Times Square-like billboards. Portraits, for their part, are strewn on a string next to what looks like a Rodin and a Giacometti. ▌ Upon reviewing the initial studies of screens, however, it seemed that while the idea was appropriate, the visual competition between the environmental backgrounds and the client's photography was too great. Since both were photographic, their relative textural detail and tonality was still too similar for clear separation. As a solution, Mercier's team experimented with desaturating

the color of the backgrounds, but eventually opted for flattening the scenes into vector-drawn areas of warm, neutral beiges and grays, following the input of designer and illustrator Martin Fontaine. ▌ "These images are so light and subtle," Mercier explains, "that they serve only as a fuzzy background to the most important element of the site: the active windows leading to the artist's photos, which, by contrast, literally pop against the background." This simple solution left the supporting typographic navigation to be handled in an equally

simple way. Although more classical typefaces were explored, a bitmap face—all caps—was chosen for onscreen clarity and its modern, but quiet, personality.

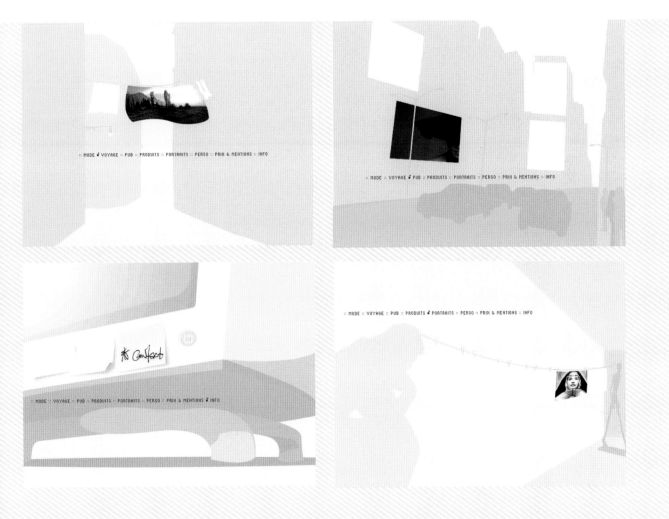

These screens, from the implemented site, show the clarity of separation between navigation image and background, as well as the three-dimensionality achieved in the flat, vector-drawn illustrations. Careful attention to spacing, scale, and rhythmic change creates a surrealistic space in what are very flat images.

A bitmap typeface, in a muted blue tone, lists the primary navigational areas in a single horizontal strand of text across the screen; a red highlight indicates mouse-over and selection. The bitmap typeface is far more legible than the screen-resolution version of a classically drawn typeface, and complements the vector-based illustrations.

04

Formica Corporation 2005 Trade Stand
Kuhlmann Leavitt, Inc. | St. Louis, Missouri, USA

In creating three-dimensional applications, all the visual aspects of composition are extrapolated into real space, and hierarchy and flow are of paramount importance. This is especially true of a trade show presence—where crowds of people, exhibitors, products, and colors all compete for attention—such as the one here, created for Formica Corporation's hospitality design trade stand. The design challenge was to design a space that would attract exhibit goers from near and far in a busy exhibit hall, while communicating Formica's vast offering of commercial and residential surfacing products. Adding to this challenge? "Members of the hospitality design industry expect to see highly designed spaces," says design studio principal Deanna Kuhlmann-Leavitt.

Building Block as a Centerpiece

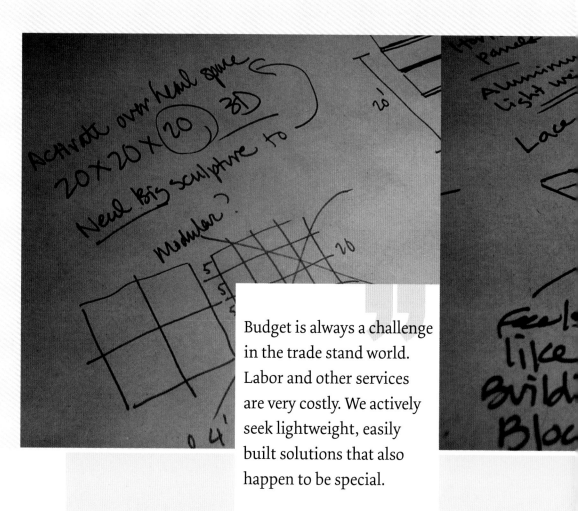

> Budget is always a challenge in the trade stand world. Labor and other services are very costly. We actively seek lightweight, easily built solutions that also happen to be special.

Deanna Kuhlmann-Leavitt, Principal

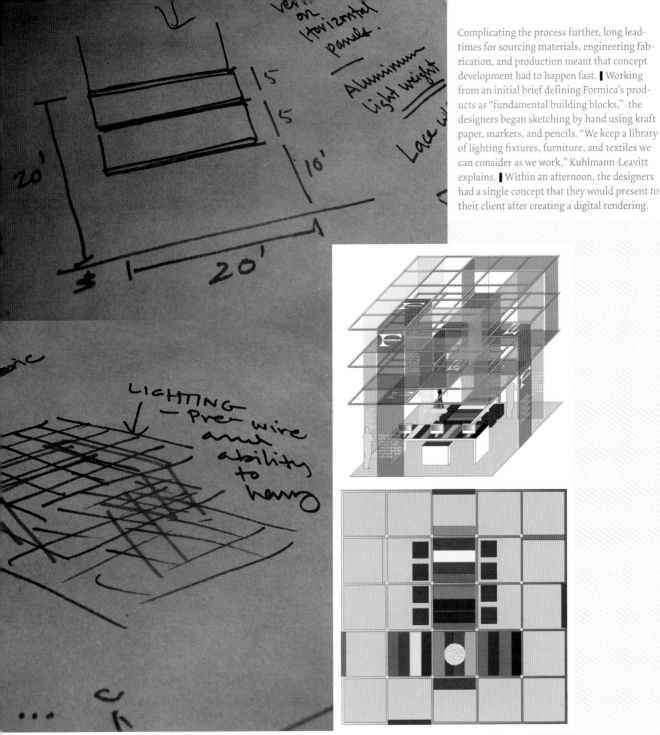

Complicating the process further, long lead-times for sourcing materials, engineering fabrication, and production meant that concept development had to happen fast. ❚ Working from an initial brief defining Formica's products as "fundamental building blocks," the designers began sketching by hand using kraft paper, markers, and pencils. "We keep a library of lighting fixtures, furniture, and textiles we can consider as we work," Kuhlmann-Leavitt explains. ❚ Within an afternoon, the designers had a single concept that they would present to their client after creating a digital rendering.

Two designers—armed with kraft paper, markers, and a stack of furniture reference—churned out sketches for a strong visual concept in about four hours.

Notes and measurements annotate the basic idea in these drawings: a giant open-work cube. The cube concept derives from a premise that the client wished to convey: that their products are the building blocks for interior designers.

Upon defining the basic idea, the designers transformed the sketch into a digital rendering, using drawing software. Including silhouetted human figures in the space shows scale. In this first presentation, the cube form is constructed from a lightweight armature from which colored banners wrapped and hung. Both the client's branding, as well as marketing text, are shown printed on the banners. The first floor plan shows the single long table intended to display the client's products, along with sales literature and monitors to access the Internet or sales data.

Neutral carpeting keeps focus on the brightly-colored product displays, while complementary color combinations among the banners brings that visual activity upward into the space.

According to Kuhlmann-Leavitt, cost is a primary factor in developing solutions for exhibits of this nature. "Budget is always a challenge in the trade stand world. Labor and other services are very costly. We actively seek lightweight, easily built solutions that also happen to be special." ▌ For this project, the solution was bold and simple, focusing on a large display table situated under a lightweight hanging structure that creates an extraordinary centerpiece. Built from aluminum tubing and wrapped with preprinted fabric banners, the structure forms a three-dimensional, transpar- ent cube that ascends over the floor space, demanding attention from across a crowded exhibition hall. The cube allows for flexibility in various spaces and abstractly reinforces the premise of "building blocks." ▌ "In trade stand design, we 'build' the 3D perspective from the floor covering up," says principal Deanna Kuhlmann-Leavitt in describing her presentation strategy. "In other words, we layer the main components sequentially so the client can understand the space. It's an 'additive' style presentation."

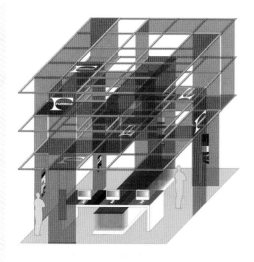

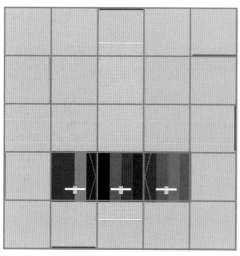

A revised floor plan shows the banner coloration simplified to one red throughout. While simpler than the first iteration, the space also seems less dimensional because of the loss of hue contrast.

Subtle patterning of the client's logo adds depth and dimensional ambiguity to the sheer banners. The hint of surface activity conflicts with the fabric's translucence. Similar value and intensity between background and pattern prevent the effect from being too jarring.

With the concept approved, the designers had to integrate a few requests from the client, develop specifications to fabricate the structure, and coordinate production and materials. First, the client asked that the banners include photography, along with the vibrant colors and typography. "There is a brief (somewhat tested) that Formica specifiers prefer to see real product in real settings," Kuhlmann-Leavitt says.

▌The studio picked up photography that the client had shot for various uses, including trade shows, and had it printed on the banners. Because the banners are constructed from mesh fabric, the images became transparent at different angles, overlapping the solid-colored bands and the aluminum structure in a way that dramatically enhanced its dimensionality.

▌The client also suggested the single table be split into three separate units to delineate product offerings. Alternative floor plans were presented, including one in which the table remained a single unit but with one section raised to bar height. This simplified traffic flow within the exhibit area and retained the presence of a large, single display surface. "We showed changes to the client three times,

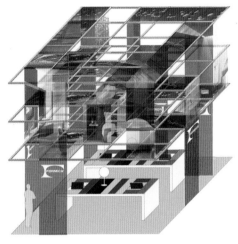

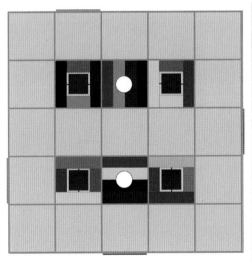

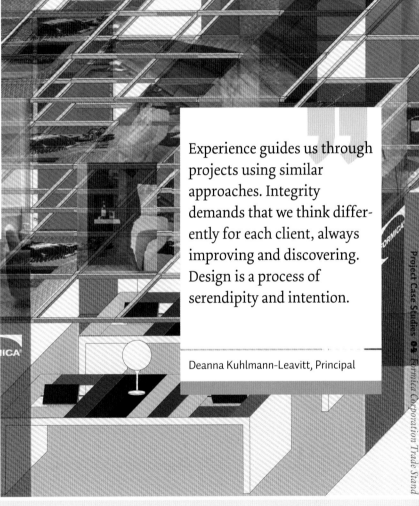

Experience guides us through projects using similar approaches. Integrity demands that we think differently for each client, always improving and discovering. Design is a process of serendipity and intention.

Deanna Kuhlmann-Leavitt, Principal

The second revision separates the tables into two groupings and introduces photography into the hanging banners. The images create an even more dimensional experience than did just the type and color; their softness contrasts the geometry of the structure and the flat color of the displays.

which is about right," says Kuhlmann-Leavitt. Although the period of concept exploration was especially short, Kuhlmann Leavitt spent nearly two months refining the structure and revising specifications for materials and layout of components. Mostly because on-site setup must happen very quickly, the designers spent a great deal of time building small hanging-grid models made of balsa wood to determine the exact placement of banners. Installation, therefore, turned out to be seamless.

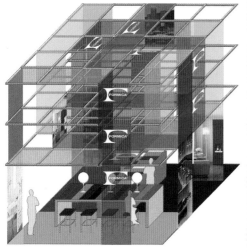

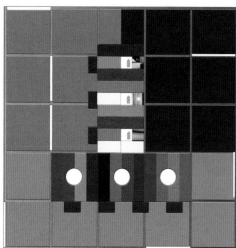

In the final floor plan, the designers returned to the single-table configuration but raised one of the surfaces up to bar height while the other remained low, at conventional table-height. The floor's carpeting is divided into three areas, separated through color in an analogous scheme that helps unify the space, as well as creating a complementary relationship with the warm red tones of the banners above. Additional colors were returned to the banners.

> We had the notion to incorporate vibrant colors. Carpet was decided first, and then banner colors were printed to match. Many of the new colors shown on the tables were vibrant, which we offset with white and wood laminate on the table bases.

Deanna Kuhlmann-Leavitt, Principal

From outside the space, the cubic form of the tables and hanging armature, wrapped in bands of mesh fabric, create a coherent structure visible from a distance. The overlap of near and far transparent panels helps create dynamic three-dimensional space.

Surfaces in the display are covered in neutral colors to contrast the products, which are brighter and more varied in hue and texture. Bulbous white lamps exude a soft, warm light that brings curvilinear form into the mostly linear form into the mostly

angle-based space; the curvilinear quality is restated in the tulip-shaped seating at the table display.

05

Podravka 2006 Annual Report
Bruketa & Žinic | Zagreb, Croatia

Podravka is a food company located in Koprivnica, Croatia, about 60 miles northeast of Zagreb. It's similar to companies in the U.S. such as Kraft or General Foods, and produces prepared and packaged foods for a variety of outlets. Still, it's a relatively close-knit company that approaches business with integrity: "It's a company with heart," says Davor Bruketa, one of the principals of the Croatian firm responsible for designing Podravka's annual report. And that drives the design approach for Bruketa and his partner, Nicola Zinic, who turn the report into something other than the potentially dry collection of figures it could be. "The values of the brand are communicated on more levels than is usually found in annual reports," they say.

The Bottom Line: You've Got to Have Heart

> We work on one file, making little changes, taking something out, moving it. Yes ... it is like sculpture. You tear away layer by layer of stone until you get what you want.

Davor Bruketa, Principal

The team of four designers—Bruketa, Zinic, and two associate designers—often begin sketching by hand in an informal way, as well as cutting and pasting found material together and looking at typography and images on the computer. Because this is the seventh annual report they've designed for Podravka, the designers are familiar with the brand and conveying the company's basic business messages to the report's audience—stockholders, clients, business partners—so they spend time having fun with the material. ▌This time, the team spent about a month developing concepts that would tell the story of a company with heart in different ways than they had previously, and they presented one concept to the client in near-finished form. "Often clients wish to see a few different directions in which the project could develop, but not this time. And we always know that only one concept is the best one," Zinic explains. ▌The design evolved over the thirty-odd days, as some material was altered or discarded in favor of other material, spiraling toward a resolved, finished compilation that grew out of discussion, refinement, and collaboration among the designers. ▌"There are many ideas

Looking for ways to express the client's personality led the designers in many directions. One of the first ideas under consideration was to incorporate personal artifacts related to cooking such as the old recipes and grocery lists seen here. The unstudied, non-precious, and undesigned qualities of such items—rips, stains, and all—provide all sorts of messages: humanity, honesty, accessibility, nostalgia, and warmth. In addition, their texture and color could potentially contrast more refined images or layouts.

Along with collecting, the designers actively sketched by hand. Purposefully drawn layout thumbnails mix with exquisitely refined doodles that hints at the designers' fluid conceptual process. Many of the offhand doodles made their way into the finished annual report—another "personal" element. On this particular page, ornamental letterforms, images of pie tins, heart icons, and floral abstractions weave into and out of each other.

that we don't use; the best ones survive the time test," Bruketa says. This is a common way for the designers to work, although they're quick to point out they don't approach any project in the same way. "I think it is wrong and impossible to solve each problem in the same way," continues Bruketa.

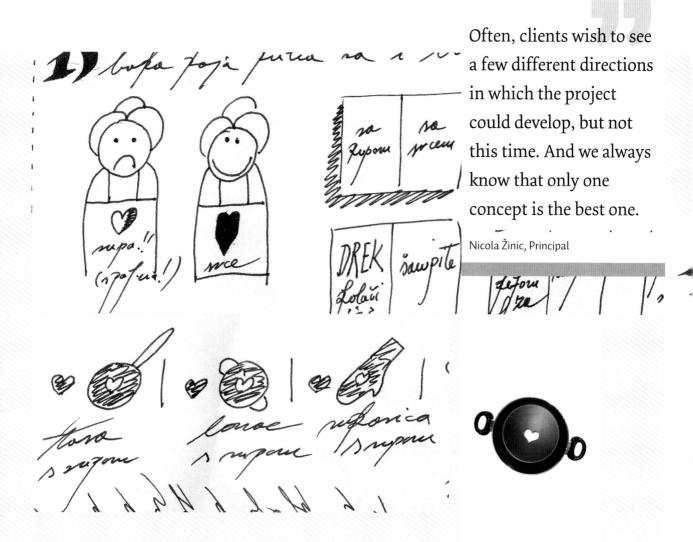

Sketches for a photographic section propose a simple narrative: comparison between a sad cook and a happy cook, ostensibly one who works in the kitchens at Podravka. Conceptually, such directness is appropriate to the overall concept and adds a bit of humor. In the drawing itself, the idea is very clearly represented in the cook's facial

expressions, but even more so in the manipulations of the heart icons on her apron—one colorless and divided, the other full and colored in with red ink.

In sketches for another image sequence, cooking implements such as pots and pans and an oven mitt have the heart cut out of them. The fact that this action renders the item useless in the kitchen suddenly becomes apparent when the designer tests this idea with a photographic rendering.

This book is a collection of reasons that show why it is important to do everything with heart. The various reasons are grouped into five parts, all reinforcing the same message in different ways. Paper, binding, and printing techniques are often an important aspect of communicating within each part. ▌Žinic explains: "In the first part there are people who doubt the importance of the heart; we showed their stories in black and white on a thinner paper. In another part, a heavier-weight paper supports photography that shows that the heart does matter after all. The fourth part is

Thumbnail sketches for yet another photographic sequence envision portraits of questionable characters one would rather not have cooking for them—a woman who seems a little unsavory, an intimidating doctor, and a punk rocker, complete with anarchy symbol. Using stock photographs to flesh out the concept for rough layouts,

the designers' selection of details and color helps bring the characters to life and enrich their unspoken narratives. The choice of an older woman in leopard print, smoking, speaks volumes. Color plays a role, both visually, for contrast, and psychologically; the cool blue-green behind the surgeon is impersonal and almost sickly.

Rough sketches for a section with text shows an interesting detail—a dotlike element that contrasts the central editorial structure, destabilizing the layout's symmetry and activating the space in the margin.

DESIGN EVOLUTION

a financial report from an independent auditor, printed on a traditional "endless" dot-matrix paper to visually separate the part of the book that doesn't come from Podravka, but from the auditor. ▌Along with the mix of paper stocks, the designers varied the kinds of photography used—black-and-white, color scenes, and silhouetted objects—as well as different typographic textures. There are stark whites pages with exquisitely justified text, handwritten notes and scribbles, bright stickers with recipes using some of the client's products, and a narrative section, written by hand, as a letter describing a heartwarming tale about cooking. The mixture of media, icon and narrative, image and text—all produced at a high level of craftsmanship—helps weave the different parts of the annual into a coherent whole, and lends it a highly personal character … just what the designers were after. "We worked with heart."

> In this cynical world, we decided to prove that it is important to do everything with heart.

Davor Bruketa, Principal

Stitched, glued, casebound, and tied, the annual is a book fetishist's dream come true. The cover is robustly embossed and printed with only black ink. Such attention to finishing techniques sends two messages loud and clear: the company is doing well, and it cares about what it produces.

A mix of idiosyncratic details reinforces the personal aspect of the report's messaging: hand-drawn ornamental type treatments, script, and elaborate doodles. The organic qualities of these elements contrasts the open space, sharp typography, and bold geometric stickers.

The photographs exhibit a quiet tonality—not washed out, but intentionally a little more soft, and with a little less contrast in their tonal range. This is highly unusual for annual reports, which tend to reproduce sharp images with saturated color. The tonal softness seems friendly, approachable, and honest.

The final sequence of sad cook/happy cook image pairs is humorous. The seeming simplicity of this concept is countered by the relentless control of every detail within the photographs, from the selection of props to the extremely subtle change in color saturation from left to right page. The desaturated color of the left-hand page is barely perceptible, but adds to the depressing quality of the subject.

The justified text shows an optimal character count—between fifty-five and seventy-five characters per line—resulting in an overall consistent rag and minimal hyphenation. Callouts set in red flush right against the left alignment of the main column, providing detail and an easy way of navigating the content.

Text and tabular data are set in a sharp, transitional serif family, making use of bold, regular, and italic faces to distinguish informational components. Careful attention to spacing, punctuation, rule weights, and alignment provides both legibility and conceptual reinforcement for the report.

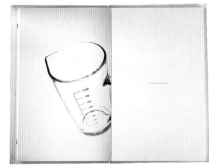

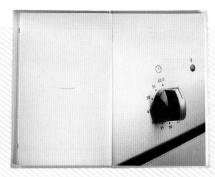

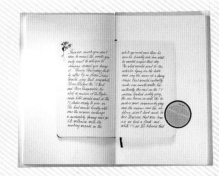

The majority of the images are photographs, which lends instant credibility to concepts because the average viewer will readily trust the content of a photograph over an illustration. In the first photographic section, the images form narrative pairs. In the second, shown here, the images are illustrative icons. Note the care with which the single images are arranged across the spreads, activating negative space and creating areas of tension and openness.

A final, narrative section presents a photographed journal page-by-page across the report's gutter, creating the effect of turning the journal's actual pages. The dimensionality of the images and the personality of the handwriting convey honesty and accessibility.

The saturated recipe stickers are a welcome interruption from the cool whiteness of the pages. Each sticker uses primarily two colors, usually sets of near complements. With the text set in a friendly sans serif that contrasts the serif face used elsewhere, they pop excitedly off the page.

06 The Forsythe Company 2006/2007
Season Collateral
Surface | Frankfurt am Mein, Germany

Twist, Turn, Push, Pull

Sometimes the subject of a design project speaks for itself. Dance is one such subject—it is its own concept and, most often, does a good job of communicating. That is, after all, its purpose. Enter the designer, tackling the problem of representing such a medium in the static world of print. Two possibilities present themselves: Turn on the design pyrotechnics, or keep the design serene and let the medium present itself. Faced with these two options, Markus Weisbeck and Katrin Tüffers of Surface chose the latter. Within the austere, photographic layouts of the 2006/07 season campaign for the Forsythe Company, a contemporary ballet, taut arrangements of figural form and text speak volumes about the nature of dance … all without overstating the case.

Very rough digital studies, such as those shown here, were presented to the client before proceeding with a photo shoot. The images were picked up from those used in a previous season's campaign

to establish the basic premise for shooting and cropping, but no storyboards or art direction took place before the day of the shoot.

The designers and client took advantage of the digital photo shoot by viewing the images on a laptop and making decisions on the spot without interfering in the shoot. Shots were altered and reshot on the fly and then edited for final selection at the photo shoot.

William Forsythe, client and founder of the company, has radically influenced thinking in the field of dance, investigating the malleability inherent in the language of classical ballet. His work is known for exploring alternative encounters with the audience and intense collaboration among musician, choreographer, and dancers. This intuitive and flexible approach, governed by the rigor of classical training, is a strong match with Surface's aesthetic. ▌Surface partners Markus Weisbeck and Katrin Tüffers have collaborated with Forsythe on the development of previous sea-

sons' campaigns, each time finding flexibility in a visually economical approach that is documentary and photographic. ▌Looking for another way to interpret the nature of dance and the forms created by the body, Weisbeck and Tüffers spent about two weeks investigating possibilities. Their rigorous sensibility, and Forsythe's history and work, directed them toward photography again, but the method and style of the photography was yet to be developed. "We had a notion this time to convey the idea of dancer as sculpture," Weisbeck says. "We imagined a neutral background and

the dancer, isolated, but nothing more." After a few quick studies using some captured images from previous campaigns, layered in a Photoshop file, Weisbeck and Tüffers conferred with Forsythe, who approved the rough concept and set up a photo shoot. ▌In true collaborative spirit and following Forsythe's malleable approach, there was no plan for the shoot itself. The specific method was developed on the spot, in conversation between Forsythe, Weisbeck, and photographer Armin Linke during the shoot.

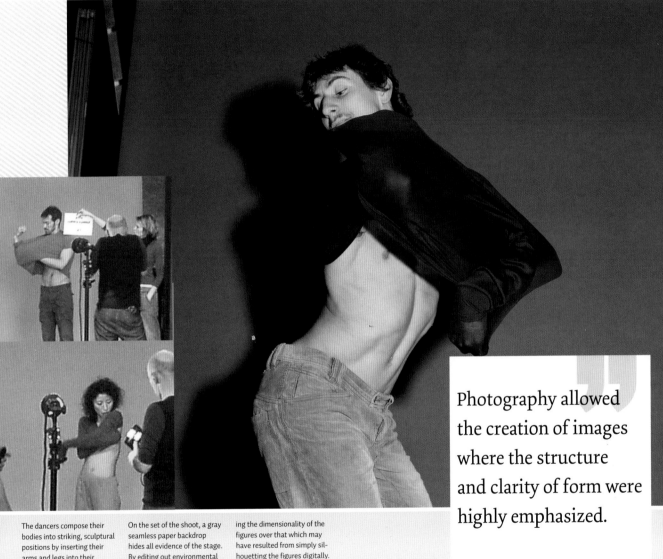

The dancers compose their bodies into striking, sculptural positions by inserting their arms and legs into their clothes. The unusual shapes create an otherworldly, almost claylike character to the mass of the bodies.

On the set of the shoot, a gray seamless paper backdrop hides all evidence of the stage. By editing out environmental activity, the designer and photographer force attention onto the figure as the sole object of focus. The harsh spotlight, however, throws shadow against the backdrop, increas-

ing the dimensionality of the figures over that which may have resulted from simply silhouetting the figures digitally.

Photography allowed the creation of images where the structure and clarity of form were highly emphasized.

Katrin Tüffers, Partner

The day of the shoot, the photographer, dancers, and designers appeared on a set devoid of props or scenery. The designers and photographer determined that a strong flash positioned forward on an individual dancer close to a backdrop, would deliver a high-contrast image and precise, blur-free detail. The flash would capture a dancer in a frozen moment. ▍Unlike images they had photographed before, where a dancer was caught spinning or in mid-leap, the dancer would be photographed in a contorted position to create an amorphous mass. The dancers would exaggerate these positions by stretching their elasticized dance uniforms. The shoot proceeded over several hours, with Weisbeck, Forsythe, and Linke evaluating the shots on a laptop as they were taken and editing down to those they felt best captured the dancers' form. ▍From there, Weisbeck and Tüffers downloaded the images from the laptop and composed them in the various formats—brochures, flyers, ads, posters—to maximize the twisted contours of the dancers' bodies and create space for the accompanying text. A neutral, austere sans serif was selected and necessary information was structured

The designers selected colors for type from within the images by taking samples with Photoshop's eyedropper tool. These base colors were supplemented by two colors that provided contrast, either in temperature, value, or hue. In this case, two blues of slightly different temperature and — value are used to contrast the orange-based warm colors sampled from the image. This color strategy for the type creates a strong visual link between type and image without resorting to more theatrical typographic arrangement.

Composing the images within the frames of the various print formats took the most time. Dynamic cropping creates movement into and out of the format, and helps exaggerate the contour of the pose against the background. Situating a figure with more space around it—and more evenly proportioned space— creates a relaxed, static presentation. Closer cropping, in which the shapes of the spaces between the figure and the format edges are more varied and irregular, enhances the viewer's sense of the figure's sculptural form.

in a simple system of one and two columns, usually of the same width. Colors for text were selected by sampling pixel areas in the photographs with Photoshop's eyedropper tool, and then choosing additional colors to contrast the sampled ones in temperature and hue.

The designers chose the typeface Grotesk for its formal purity to echo that of the images. Grotesk's stark, light, uniform strokes and sharp joints offer a pleasant linear contrast to the massed forms but also respond to the tonal contrast they exhibit.

By cropping the images horizontally in the brochure—within frames of different depth—a kind of short animation is produced for the viewer as he or she flips from page to page. The interval of white text area changes in proportion and the figures almost appear to dance, despite their frozen sculptural presence.

07

Book Design: *100 Years of Magazine Covers*
Research Studios | London, United Kingdom

Magazines—no matter how frivolous or specialized the content—offer a unique window on cultural history, being eminently timely when published and providing a nearly seamlessly sequential record of fashion, food, politics, aesthetics, science, and morality, among other human endeavors. Their covers, in particular, are snapshots of a culture's pulse at any given moment. Such was the thinking for the publishers of this book, tracing the history of these historical snapshots over the last century. Research Studios, a seven-designer concern headed by Neville Brody—a British design maverick with extensive editorial background himself—was perhaps uniquely positioned to undertake the book's visual development. Brody drew on his magazine expertise, deftly mixing bold editorial layout with the restraint of an art-house publication design sensibility to unify a vast collection of powerful images.

History in Multiple Editions

100 YEARS OF MAGAZINE COVERS

> We set out to design a book which would last for some time—not being specific in its style to now. As it is a historical document, we aimed for it to be something kept rather than discarded in a few years.

Neville Brody, Creative Director

The cover study began closely focused on one overarching concept—big type for the title and an intensely colored field. This early layout explodes the title at enormous scale across the width of the format, relying on the active alternation of stroke and counter, as well as changes in proportion, for its power. The idea of incorporating samples of magazine covers shown in the book, however, was of greater interest to the client.

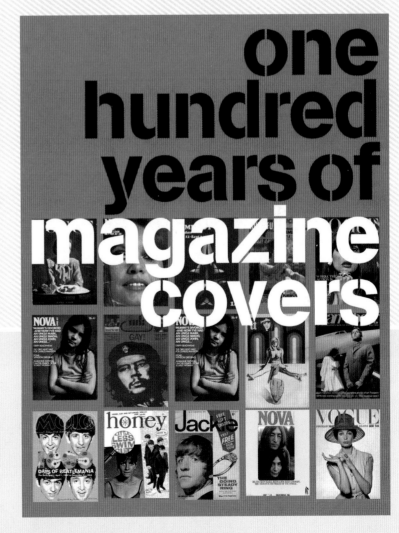

Studying variations allowed the designers to compare subtle differences in relationships: between the values of the type and the background; between the size of the type, its location, and alignment; between the typography and the number or size of images; and so on.

Using a single image was deemed limiting in terms of conveying the breadth of the book's subject; if the covers became too small, however, they lost their visual appeal.

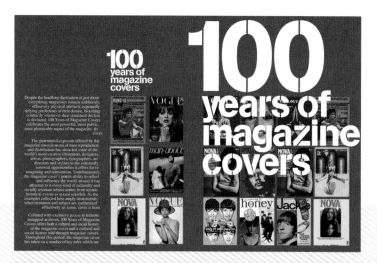

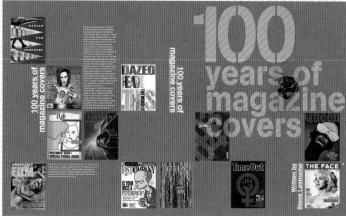

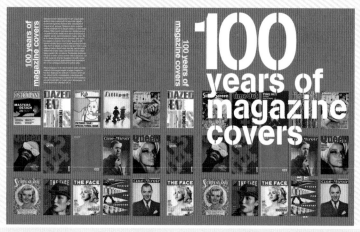

The development process began roughly one year before publication, with Brody and associate designers—Marcus Piper and Nick Hard—working through a series of cover concepts. Their vision for the book, in general, was to be relatively neutral, to showcase the hundreds of sample magazine covers that would appear inside without intruding on them. ▌This strategy guided their thinking about the cover. "There was one main vision from start to finish which evolved into the finished product," Brody explains. The close-in cover studies focused on a large, bold treatment of the title and varia-

The selected cover concept underwent additional exploration. The designers looked at a color variation—a deep, saturated blue, instead of orange—and experimented with other typefaces. While the coolness of the blue deadened the color of the images, the orange seemed to help

them pop. The final decision to use a stenciled face maintained the cover's desired stylistic neutrality, but gave it a kind of identity that then migrated inside the book's pages. A pattern of diagonal lines lifts the type off the surface and introduces sharp detail in contrast to the large shapes.

tions in color. Some of the layouts included selected magazine covers, toward which the publishers gravitated immediately. ▌ "There was a slight evolution of the cover once selected," Brody recalls, "but in principal it was approved as is, and its style informed the design of the internal pages. From there, the majority of the book's evolution happened internally." That said, however, Brody notes that he and his team showed the client evolutionary steps at various points, especially as the editorial content and selection of specific covers needed to merge seamlessly with the book's graphic pacing.

The essentially ephemeral nature of magazines, in general, makes them ideal as both reflectors and arbiters of 'Society'.

23/24

The essentially ephemeral nature of magazines, In general, makes them ideal as both reflectors and arbiters of 'Society'.

25/26

Early layouts for the chapter openings quickly identified the editorial conceit that remained in effect for the duration—bold openers and more text-heavy "content" spreads following. Once the cover treatment was final, the pattern of diagonal lines appeared in the openers, in the giant numerals.

The first layouts for text spreads established a clear hierarchy of sizes for heads, callouts, text, and captions. The column structure drops the text from a low hangline. All of the text components are set in the same sans serif face. Enormous folios are an unexpected element.

Design and Experimentation

As is common to many processes of creative evolution, the dynamic of magazine cover design over the last 100 years follows the shape of an hourglass.

> "The visual form of the project aimed to complement the disparate visual content of the covers while unifying them with one underlying language.

Neville Brody, Creative Director

21/26

26/26

One study of a more transparent, three-dimensional treatment for the chapter opening type was discarded in favor of a simpler line pattern and color gradation.

As the chapter openers evolved, material was separated to enhance impact. A middle-round shows the chapter number and introductory text on the same spread. In the next iteration, the chapter number occupies a spread alone at a much larger size, while the introductory text shifts to the following spread.

The replacement of the neutral, sans serif text face with a typewriter-derived font enhances the textural difference between running text and captions; it also lends a journalistic quality to the text.

"This process was very different from normal in that it was very much a fluid process—back and forth—rather than giving formal presentations. The major changes were to the image content, with the client asking for specific covers to be included. ▌The interior of the book developed stylistically based on the cover, taking cues from magazine layout as a reference to the subject matter without being overt. Brody and his associates created a visual navigation through the book, using bold colors that lead the reader from the contents page through the chapters. Bold opening spreads identify each chapter, segueing from vivid colored fields to light editorial pages, and then into an alternating sequence of black-and-white spreads depending on the images being displayed—each chapter works visually like the feature story of a magazine, and the sequence repeats with the beginning of each chapter. ▌The editorial quality was enhanced with callouts and a soft, typewriteresque font, as well as a diagonal linear hatching motif that occurred during the continued revision of the cover. The hatching was initially used in the chapter opening spreads, but quickly migrated throughout the text

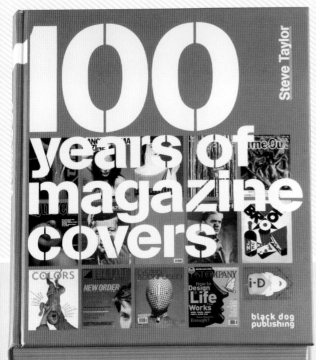

A strong type treatment is carried from the cover, through table of contents, and onto the chapter openers. This diagonal linear pattern becomes connective tissue between images and text, and activates spaces that might otherwise end up static.

spreads in the form of vertical strips housing the side runners, underscoring in the callouts, and in a free-form use behind and between images to help activate space. All, of course, articulated on a tight grid of eight columns that Brody used to arrange content in alternately vertically or horizontally emphasized configurations, instead of enforcing one or the other. Brody elaborates: "As we could not crop covers, the grid was used loosely." ▌ Along with Brody, Hard, and Piper, two additional designers spent the last month of the year's development time laying out and pacing the spreads and coordinating the proofing and file preparation for reproduction. "The collection of so many different magazine covers all presented in one cohesive book makes this a unique publication," Brody says.

The repeating sequential structure of the chapters is evident in comparing the openers and subsequent spreads. This pacing strategy, decidedly editorial in nature, acts as a clear navigational system for the reader. Color plays a navigational role, identifying each chapter individually and coding them in the table of contents. The designers defined an overall palette of intense orange, gray, and black for the book as a unifying identity.

The line pattern also appears as a detail within callouts and as a narrow strip at the left foredge, housing the running side and color-coding a given spread relative to the chapter in which it appears.

Loose interpretation of a relatively tight grid structure allowed the designers to size and position magazine covers without cropping them, one of the publisher's requirements. The movement and scale changes among the covers is carefully considered, creating "bounce" as images alternate between smaller and larger sizes, high and low positions, restate and then refute specific flowlines, and appear singly or in groups.

Vogue gradually phased out the illustrated cover which had been conceived as a total piece of art that incorporated the magazine's logo. The first photographic cover appeared in July 1932 and by the end of the 1940s the drawn cover had become a rarity.

204/20

VOGUE

Under the art direction of Mehemed Fehmy Agha (Dr Agha) from 1929 to 1943, Vogue gradually phased out the illustrated cover which had been conceived as a total piece of art that incorporated the magazine's logo. The first photographic cover appeared in July 1932 and by the end of the 1940s the drawn cover had become a rarity. This one, by leading Mexican artist, anthropologist and writer Miguel Covarrubias, makes clear what the photographers were up against. Covarrubias was a key figure in the cultural exchange between Mexico and the US, rapidly establishing his reputation in publishing shortly after arriving in New York in 1923 with a series of stylish and perceptive caricatures of public figures for Vanity Fair's 'Impossible Interview' feature. This cover, which epitomises the art director's mission in that period to produce a singular piece of commercial art, won the award for 'Best Cover of the Year'. It still puts most contemporary magazine covers to shame for sheer beauty.

Vogue, 1 July 1937

The counter-cultural magazine cover hasn't completely disappeared—it still lurks on the fringes of media in the form of *Modern Toss* and its scabrous satire, for example.

186/1

110/111

This British *Elle* could have been assembled according to the rules devised for magazine cover formatting by post-war psychologists—the framing of the shot, the angle of the head, the orientation of the eyes.

The contrastingly unwelcome status of dissenting covers in the age of globalisation were starkly illustrated by the 2006 launch of the 40-something-year-old music magazine *Rolling Stone* in China, which featured an image of Cui Jian, known as the 'Bruce Springsteen of Chinese music' on the front.

Unfortunately for Jann Wenner, the magazine's legendary American publisher, Cui's most notorious song, "Nothing is My Name", is an anthem to the student demonstrators in the 1989 Tiananmen Square demonstrations, an event that the Beijing government arranged to be excised from both the nation's collective memory and Google's database.

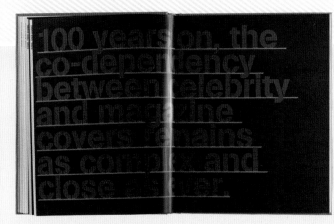

100 years on, the co-dependency between celebrity and magazine covers remains as complex and close as ever.

08

Forgotten Africa Poster Campign
Armando Milani Design | Milan, Italy

Designers struggle against apathy on a regular basis, hoping to garner a meager snippet of the message-weary public's shifting attention. Getting an audience to feel and act is an entirely different matter. This project highlights design's potential to focus public awareness on serious issues and as an outlet for compassion. Produced for Italian humanitarian entity CESPI, the poster delivers a brutally direct reminder of ongoing horror in a visual language that makes the most of what typography has to offer. Its simplicity belies profound complexity.

Denouncing Indifference

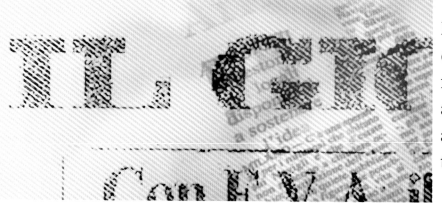

> I hope this project encourages people to not only reflect but also to act on finding a solution to this tragic human problem.
>
> Armando Milani, Principal

A concerned activist at heart, the designer often initiates public awareness projects in collaboration with longtime client CESPI, a humanitarian organization.

Armando Milani is a designer who focuses on communications for humanitarian agencies and cultural institutions. Very often, Milani himself is the creator of such projects and, having longstanding working relationships with agency directors, is able to facilitate their production when the need arises. The impetus for this poster was a newspaper article detailing the slaughter of 800,000 or more people in Darfur—and the apparent lack of concern in the rest of the world. ▌"I was determined to design a poster to denounce the tragedy of these events, but I kept postponing it," Milani relates. Shortly after, he saw another article, this time recounting the deaths of four million African children from famine, war, and AIDS, that galvanized him to produce the poster. "I was shocked by what I saw as total indifference of the entire world," he says, "and I felt an ethical need to do something about it." ▌That "something" began with a rough pencil sketch of a concept based on simple imagery and an appeal to one's sense of shame—Africa: The Forgotten Continent. Initially representing the continent in black—the map made invisible—with the type reversed white, Milani's intent

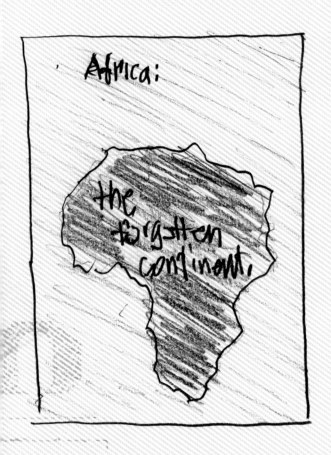

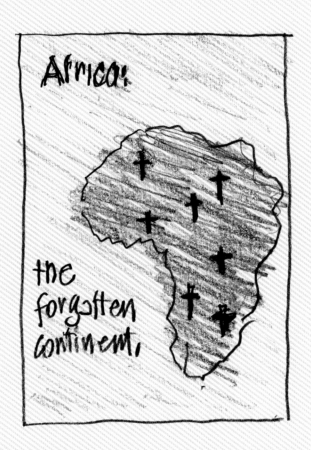

The impact of scale within the format, along with the directness of the verbal message, confronts the viewer with an unavoidable issue. Sensitivity to the continent's shape and size, relative to the space around it, counteracts the potential for its symmetrical placement to be static.

Choosing an iconic representation of the continent's form facilitates quick recognition and adds messages: the field of black color hides detail and, hence, any sense of location or certainty—and Western audiences associate the color black with death and fear.

Shifting the text from inside the continent's contour to the spaces surrounding it provides a place for a new element—a grouping of crosses—which symbolizes burial. In the context of the Africa icon, they help generate new information for the viewer and add size contrast to the composition. Furthermore, the new position of the type creates negative spaces that are more varied in interval—some looser, some tighter—which enhances the overall contrast within the poster's layout.

was to rely on the stark power of the forms for their ability to communicate quickly. Not finding enough message there, however, Milani moved the type outside the landmass's shape to engage the surrounding space and provide space for a secondary image: a field of crosses. ▌It was the next step in the process that took the poster to a new level. "I just start sketching with pencil and then I go digital quickly," Milani notes. In a preliminary exploration of typefaces in which to set the poster's text, he found inspiration in the shape of the lowercase *t*. Set in Futura, the *t* is nearly a per-

fect cross. True to his reductive aesthetic, Milani realized he could better represent the forgotten continent by not showing it at all and instead, letting the intrinsic form of the letters do the talking for him. A quick sketch to position the type, this time incorporating color, created an image of bloody crosses among the text. ▌Feeling that this solution still lacked a certain simplicity, Milani removed the color from the letters—retaining the red only in the three dots of the punctuation— and setting all the type except the lowercase *t*'s in dark gray.

The effect of deep, foreboding space contrasts the stark white of the crosses, which now appeared scattered across a blackened field. By shifting the crosses upward and off their usual baselines, Milani imparts a surreal, floating quality that evokes uncertainty, anxiety, and death. "Creating the image this way is very direct," Milani says in summary, "awakening the emotions and the consciousness of the viewer."

The decision to focus solely on the type occurred after the designer was inspired by a certain lowercase *t*. Comparing the previous version with this new one reveals that the visual impact of the text increased tremendously because it can be set in a much larger size. The spaces around the type also become more decisively irregular.

The lowercase *t* in most typefaces has a curved lower terminal. Futura does not. Recognizing this essential difference was a source for the idea that became the final poster. Still, a slight change was needed to transform the letter into a cross—the left cross stroke is naturally short and needed to be lengthened.

Design: Armando Milani

The fewer the elements, the more important it is to pay attention to their relationships to create a dynamic, rather than dull or empty, composition. The positioning and spacing of the type within the format shows strong geometric relationships; the position of the "crosses" can be considered a study of dot relationships, creating a random floating effect.

Visual elements that are aligned horizontally across a format will appear to not be aligned. It's an optical illusion that's hardwired into our perceptual system. To create a decisive alignment between the bottom edge of one and the cross stroke of another t, the designer "cheats" by moving the lower one up a little.

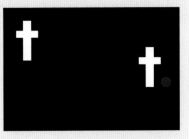

09

Southpaw Vineyard Brand and Bottling
Parallax Design | Adelaide, Australia

The winemaking style of Southpaw Vineyards is unconventional, and its customers are experienced wine aficionados who are looking for something different. The vineyard is biodynamic, and noninterventional—neither chemical pesticides nor insecticides are used, and the vintners take no trouble to ensure a consistent flavor profile. Instead, each year's vintage is directly influenced by the climate and the site, and will change with the seasons. Graphic designer Matthew Remphrey, of Parallax Design in Adelaide, South Australia, took these aspects of his client's winery in designing bottle labels—working only with what happened to be on hand. "The brand," Remphrey states, "had to be consistent with the site and the winemaking philosophy."

Some Varietals Are without Pretension

> I work mostly in the commercial sphere, for commercial clients with products to sell. If I want a brand to communicate something, then I want the audience to understand it. The consumer doesn't have time to decode a designer's musings. This doesn't necessarily mean literal, but I'd say our approach is for a more direct relationship.

Matthew Remphrey, Principal

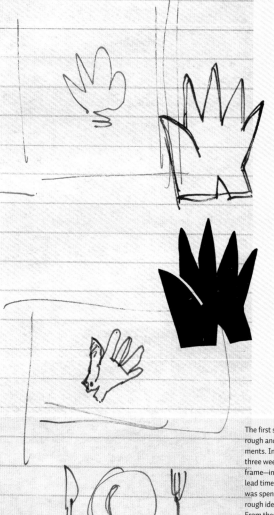

The first stage of sketching is rough and produces fragments. In this project, about three weeks of the total time-frame—including eight weeks lead time for production—was spent developing these rough ideas to show the client. From these roughs, two concepts were singled out to show the client—one pictorial, one typographic.

The pictorial concept focused on a glove as a symbol; stylized translation was discarded for the directness of photography.

The vineyard is located in MacLaren Vale, also in South Australia, and is owned by the designer's friend, Henry Rymill, who Remphrey describes as being very "hands-on" with the vineyard, spending several days a week tending to it. Rymill named the vineyard Southpaw, a baseball term for left-handed pitchers, because both he and his wife are left-handed. ▌This hands-on approach resonates with Remphrey, who began developing label concepts sketching by hand and cutting and pasting things together. "I use a photocopier a lot," Remphrey says. "I find it easier to get a sense of scale and bal-ance, particularly with typography, by working with elements physically … rather than looking at them on a screen. ▌"Initially, we presented the client with a lot of sketched ideas, fragments, thoughts, concepts, and beginnings; not final concepts, but explorations. Mostly, when we have got this right, the solutions present themselves. This was then honed to a presentation of two concepts. Sometimes, we may only hone our thoughts down to one direction," muses Remphrey. "It depends on feedback at the early stage and the solutions we develop. I rarely present three concepts,

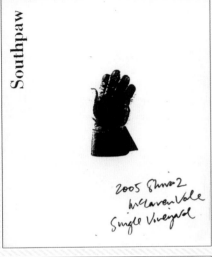

…89, working for a few clients …Iacintosh to use making …ook advantage of the new …control of their typefaces …dentity. As processing …ewspapers followed, and …igital composition raced …ry. Before we knew it, …retail fonts' to corpor- …designers. Eager to reach …hoices, each used type to …r. The number of seekers …hy skyrocketed, and we …ched for you directly, through …endors of operating systems, …velopers. This latest book …expanding *Retail Library* …e also includes the *Studio* …:ion of typefaces commis- …:lients for publication and

The choice of glove, rather than hand, as a possible symbol identifies the winemaker and suggests honest labor. Its iconic quality is rendered more a graphic translation in that its rough, photocopied texture stands in for the rugged quality of the glove itself and as a symbolic reference to hard work in the earth.

The second all-type concept is clear enough in its basic idea—type on the left side of the label. Its texture and position are all that matters to the designer in relating the idea.

and never more. Part of a designer's job is to edit, so I don't believe we should expect the client to do this for us." ▌ The two directions chosen for further refinement were equally restrained—one image-based idea, represented by a gritty, left-handed gardening glove; and the other strictly typographic, a narrow column of type set toward the left side of the label. Both made the journey from rough, pasted photocopy to a more refined state, but at the second meeting with the client, the typographic version won out. ▌ A short exploration of alternate typefaces resulted in the choice of Clarendon, an earthy slab serif, as a principal font. "It is a typeface with no pretensions," Remphrey opines. It is used in a simple way, set flush-left on the left side of the bottle's label, to subtly refer to the left-handed nature of the owner and his wife. Important information—brand name, appellation, and varietal—is called out from the muted, neutral text in a deep, red-brown. ▌ This text is reproduced in hot foil stamping and high build screenprinting (a process by which thickened ink is layered in successive impressions, raising the surface of the printed area) to contrast with the textured

The **Southpaw Vineyard** veniam, quis nostrud exerci tation **McLaren Vale** lobortis nisl ut aliquip ex ea com modo consequat. Duis **2005 Shiraz** in hendrerit in esse molestie conse quat, vel illum dolore eu **single vineyard** facilisis at vero eros et accumsan et iusto odio dignissim blandit.

750ml

I spent a lot of effort refining. Because the label is purely typographic, a lot of time was spent on kerning, adjusting spacing, and so on.

Matthew Remphrey, Principal

The Southpaw Vineyard is a special patch of dirt in McLaren Vale, growing only **Shiraz** grapes. Our winemaking philosophy is simple—let the vineyard speak for itself. This approach can produce variation from vintage to vintage. In fact that is the point of it. But the resulting wine is a true reflection of what this **single vineyard**, together with the rain and the sun, produced.

750ml

Remphrey evaluated a number of typeface candidates in looking for a bold serif with some personality. Among those contenders were Century Bold, Caslon 224 Black, and Bodoni Poster, as well as a few stencil fonts. Unlike these, however, which come with a certain degree of historical baggage, the Clarendon Remphrey ultimately selected had an unpretentious character more in keeping with the client's communication goals. One of the primary differences between Clarendon and the other faces is that it exhibits less contrast and, therefore, smoother transitions (or ductus) between the thicks and thins. Its serifs are also more robust, and the terminals lack stylistic, decorative qualities. The result of these minute details in the drawing of Clarendon is a relaxed, less obviously stylized, presentation that feels more accessible.

uncoated stock. Because of the type treatment, the front label could not be changed every year to update the vintage, so this information was placed on a neck label. The logo, which occupies a place on the neck, is in fact a dingbat, again stressing the nature of the wine by only using what is available and not introducing extras. Cartons continue the story and graphics at a scale to work in a crowded retail environment. ❙ "This label is unique among its competitors," Remphrey emphasizes. "No crests. No script type or flourishes. No scenes of vineyards. No animals or critters. Just an

honest representation of the wine and how it came to be—but still loaded with personality."

We base our early responses on research and getting to know the client, product, and audience. But along the way, design decisions do become instinctive—things feel right. I think experience as a designer allows you to know when something is right. The label simply tells the story of the vineyard and wine.

Matthew Remphrey, Principal

The neutral beige and warmer red-brown were chosen to convey the organic quality of the wines—earthy, muted, nothing artificial.

The hand-pointer logo is a dingbat—selected as a ready-made to underscore the noninterventional approach to the vineyard's winemaking. Its familiar presence as an easily recognizable, existing decorative element communicates the idea that nothing

extra or artificial has been introduced into the wine, no refinement—only what's there from climate and site.

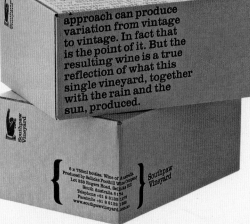

approach can produce variation from vintage to vintage. In fact that is the point of it. But the resulting wine is a true reflection of what this single vineyard, together with the rain and the sun, produced.

10

Nice Lines
for a Nice Line

Identity work is a process of extreme distillation. The need for quick recognition, ease of reproduction, and symbolic richness—all in a small footprint that's memorable and easily differentiated from other identities—means that an astounding volume of exploration is often required for a lean, minimal result. This notion is especially relevant for designers such as Gregory Paone, whose strategy in approaching the design of a logo is always the same, regardless of the client. "I don't preconceive," Paone states, "which means in order to find an original solution that has meaning and strong visual form, I have to sketch every possible option." For Nelson Line, a producer of fine stationery goods, that's exactly what happened.

Paone sketches in a variety of pads, some lined with graph paper and some blank. Word lists appear scrawled in margins for reference as he works.

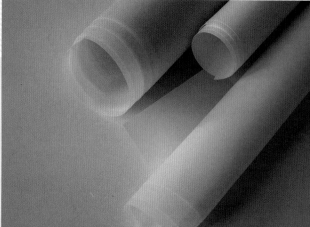

Paone's process begins with developing word lists related to a brief or discussion with his client, which he writes in the margins around the sheets of his pad where he sketches. Always returning to these word lists, which may include adjectives and conceptual phrases relevant to the subject, Paone works through as many possible approaches as he can, such as letterform studies based on the client's initials; wordmarks; alterations of letter into symbol; combination of letter with abstract and/or representational elements related to the subject matter; creation of letterforms from recogniza-ble or symbolic forms, such as icons; purely abstract forms; abstract forms based on tangible, recognizable images; icons and symbols; and nonlogo-based concepts such as typographic or pattern systems applied using recognizable rules. ▌As he sketches, each sheet is dated and sequenced to track recurring ideas that hold his interest or present possibilities for combination with others that occur on different sheets or even different days. ▌The pencil sketches for the Nelson Line identity were extensive. Many of the ideas, however, circulated around the idea of paper sheets or

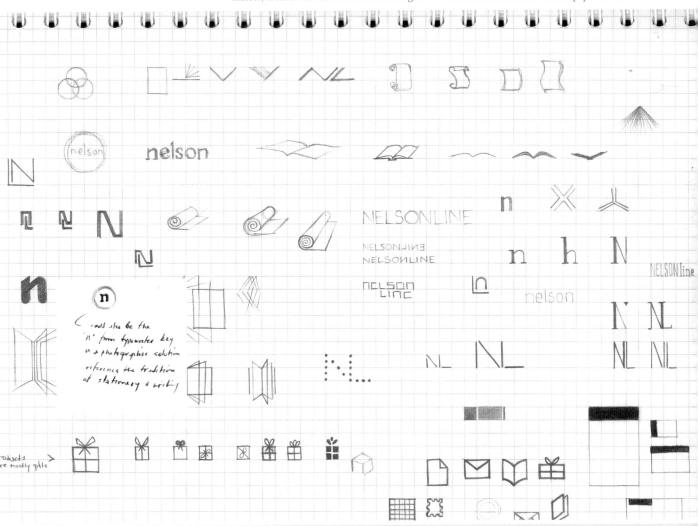

As a starting point for this identity, the designer took digital photographs of paper to get a sense of their form in an easily accessed record. In these two selected images, aspects of transparency, the overlap of sheets, and rolling of sheaves are evident as sources for logo ideas.

Scanning excerpts from Paone's sketchbooks, arranged in chronological order, the ebb and flow of related ideas and new, spin-off concepts creates an organic network of concepts that can intermingle or be pursued individually. Being able to see and compare a variety of images helps create deeper connections and affords an opportunity to consider the reasons for certain forms resurfacing.

books as planes that housed letters, created clusters, or interacted with type forms to produce geometric configurations. ▌Some of these were eventually explored in a photographic way, with images of paper sheets fanned through the contour of a letter *N*. Other concepts included signets made of typewriter keys, configurations of the *N* and *L* initials into a kind of linear monogram, script lockups in circular forms, an icon of a quill pen, and gift packages. In the latter, Paone saw something. ▌"I don't spend a lot of time hammering out an idea if I see it's going somewhere early on," he

says. "I let it sit and keep working out other ideas." This part of the process continues in pencil until he reaches a kind of jumping off point: the changeover to digital work. For Paone, this happens once he has seen all he can see in his drawings, and it becomes important to trade the roughness of the pencil for precision. The jumping off point usually happens two or three weeks into the concept phase; with Nelson Line, it was thirteen days. ▌The precision afforded by drawing software isn't a vehicle for finalization, however; it's another tool for understanding more clearly what, exactly,

his intentions are. Each of the concepts that appears to have some merit is put through a series of alterations, comparing changes in various aspects of its elements—line weights, scale relationships, positioning, interplay of positive and negative space, width to height, and so on. ▌Each concept—and there may be five or ten—will undergo similar testing and play until it becomes a clear idea, viable for presentation to the client, or it plays itself out, discarded because of potential reproduction problems, inappropriate messages, or a sense of cliché.

> I don't preconceive, which means in order to find an original solution that has meaning and strong visual form, I have to sketch every possible option.

Gregory Paone, Principal

Nearly every semiotic variation of sign making is considered in this thorough process: typographic, indexical, iconic, symbolic, supersigns, and combinations thereof.

Initial letterforms offer a powerful medium for communication, especially when they are transformed into image. Such combinations as those seen above, in which planar representations of paper become letters, create supersigns rich in intellectual depth.

Relatively early in the process, Paone discovered the idea for the concept that would eventually become the identity. In its nascent form, it's unresolved—How big? How many? Lines or solids? Leaving it for later allowed Paone to let it percolate while he continued to explore other—potentially more viable—options.

The change from pencil to digital sketching serves to clarify the designer's intentions. In this particular set, the sharpness of the vector line permit an evaluation of weight, as well as rapid variation in proportions, that would otherwise be too time consuming or impossible to achieve accurately with hand drawing.

Digital sketching also provides a quick way of combining multiple ideas. Here, the type lockup with the shared *l* can be seen in tandem with a book icon, as part of the book icon, and inside a circular housing—both with and without a book icon.

Issues of transparency—and, therefore, the hierarchy and sequential cognition of the two initial letters *n* and *l*—can be accurately explored during the digital phase. The potential for legibility and sequence problems (for example, reading the *l* before the *n*) led the designer to discard this otherwise visually interesting candidate.

Eli Nelson, *President*
eli@nelsonline.com

102 Commerce Drive
Number Six
Moorestown, New Jersey 08057

T 800 350 5463
F 856 778 4725
www.nelsonline.com

NELSON LINE

Eli Nelson
President
eli@nelsonline.com

102 Commerce Drive
Number Six
Moorestown, New Jersey 08057
T 800 350 5463
F 856 778 4725
www.nelsonline.com

 nelson line

Elizabeth Judge, Vice President
elizabeth@nelsonline.com

102 Commerce Drive	T 800 350 5463
Number Six	F 856 778 4725
Moorestown, New Jersey 08057	www.nelsonline.com

From this exhaustive search, Paone narrowed his focus to three primary ideas that he investigated more thoroughly. ▌First, a distillation of many concepts involving planes of paper evolved into a single letterform *n*, created by three transparent planes. Merging the abstract representation of pages and the concrete, linear *n* created an elegant supersign that conveyed the client's business in an understated way and reinforced the name through the focus on the initial. Second, a wordmark in which the words *Nelson* and *Line* share a common *l* that became the spine of a book. Last, Paone developed a

nelson line

nelson line

nelson line

nelson line

NELSON LINE

NELSON LINE

nelson line

These three concepts were eventually presented to the client, roughly four weeks following the kickoff meeting. Each logo, or mark, is presented in the context of a business card to test its reproduction at a small size, and to demonstrate how it could interact with supporting elements, such as line rules, dots, informational type, and color.

The approved concept underwent a number of refinements. First off, the line weights of the icons were increased to counter a perceived brittleness in the original version. The original typeface was replaced with a neoclassical, modern serif whose contrast is not as extreme as that of some other such faces, but still introduces a bit of richness into the line language. The height of the type relative to the icons was decisively resolved. The sequence of the icons remained the same, alternating rhythmically in height to create movement that contrasts their baseline arrangement with the type.

series of small icons from one of the earlier sketches of a wrapped package, each showing a kind of stationery item. The icons could be configured in various ways, as solid forms or as outlines, and it was this last iteration that appealed most. Paone presented these three concepts to the client; in discussion, the icon concept was approved, and refinement began. ▎For Paone, the issue now was color and typography, relative to the stationery—the first applications. "Presenting the first time is all about the idea and the feeling," he explains. "The typeface, at that stage, is a detail that I'm

going to deal with later." Several iterations of the type lockup resulted in choosing an old cut of Bodoni over the original sans serif, mostly for the contrast it introduced among the system of lines in the icons and the letters. In terms of color, it was a simplification from the full-color presentation—which caused concern for printing costs—to a limited two-color palette using an analogous green and muted green-blue of similar value and intensity. ▎In the stationery—which also underwent an extensive study over several days—Paone explored variations on layouts he had developed for the first presenta-

tion. "I always show a logo in use, usually on a business card and letter, so we can see how it behaves. The business card is a serious acid test, because it's a limited space with a lot of other information. It helps solve a lot of problems up front." Gill Sans became the secondary typeface for informational text on the stationery applications and a light system of rule lines helps structure the information without distracting from the identity.

Full-color application was reduced to a limited palette of green and blue. The blue is a warmer blue (having some green in it); the green is a bit desaturated, creating a slight yellowing and graying effect; and the two colors are of similar value. This ensures that elements set in either color will still be perceived as spatially unified (neither advancing nor receding).

As a last stage in development, Paone fleshed out the remaining elements of the stationery system based on the rough business card from the first presentation. By sketching in black and white, he is able to focus solely on the composition of each application without distraction.

DESIGN EVOLUTION

The letter content:

March 03, 2006
Mr. Gregory Paone
President
Paone Design Associates, Ltd.
242 South Twentieth Street
Philadelphia, Pennsylvania
19103. 5602

Dear Mr. Paone

Lorem ipsum dolor sit amet, consectetuer adipiscing elit, sed diam nonummy nibh euismod tincidunt ut laoreet dolore magna aliquam erat volutpat. Ut wisi enim ad minim veniam, quis nostrud exerci tation ullamcorper suscipit lobortis nisl ut aliquip ex ea commodo consequat. Duis autem vel eum iriure dolor in hendrerit in vulputate velit esse molestie consequat, vel illum dolore eu feugiat nulla facilisis at vero eros et accumsan et iusto odio dignissim qui blandit praesent luptatum zzril delenit augue duis dolore te feugait nulla facilisi. Lorem ipsum dolor sit amet, consectetuer adipiscing elit, sed diam nonummy nibh euismod tincidunt laoreet dolore magna aliquam erat volutpat. Ut wisi enim ad minim veniam, quis nostrud exerci tation ullamcorper suscipit lobortis nisl ut aliquip ex ea commodo consequat.

Duis autem vel eum iriure dolor in hendrerit in vulputate velit esse molestie consequat, vel illum dolore eu feugiat nulla facilisis at vero eroset accumsan etiusto odio dignissim qui blandit praesent luptatum zzril delenit augue duis dolore te feugait nulla facilisi. Nam liber tempor cum soluta nobis eleifend option congue nihil imperdiet doming id quod mazim placerat facer possim assum.

Sincerely,
Eli Nelson

102 Commerce Drive, Number Six
Moorestown, New Jersey • 08057.4262

T 800 350 LINE
F 856 778 4725
www.nelsonline.com

nelson line

102 Commerce Drive, Number Six
Moorestown, New Jersey • 08057.4262

T 800 350 LINE

sales@nelsonline.com

102 Commerce Drive, Number Six
Moorestown, New Jersey • 08057.4262
www.nelsonline.com

nelson line

Elizabeth Judge
Artistic Director
elizabeth@nelsonline.com

102 Commerce Drive, Number Six
Moorestown, New Jersey • 08057.4262

T 800 350 LINE
F 856 778 4725
www.nelsonline.com

nelson line

102 Commerce Drive, Number Six
Moorestown, New Jersey • 08057.4262

T 800 350 LINE
F 856 778 4725
www.nelsonline.com

sales@nelsonline.com

nelson line

The stationery arranges the logotype and icon lockup in both vertical and horizontal orientation. Sharp, light line rules delineate spaces for different functions and articulate a geometric structure within the formats of the various elements. A playful coaster makes use of the logo in reverse and presents an opportunity for large areas of color.

Paone provided the client with a series of word processing templates for letter- and invoice-writing, as well as production information and measurements for proper usage in ads or creating new forms, business cards, or labels.

one nline nelsonline

nelsonline   nelsonline   nelsonline   nelson line

nelson line   nelson line   nelson line   nelson line

 nelson line   nelson line   nelson line

In this sequence of frames from a flash animation, the designer shows the logo's potential for movement and flexibility in a Web environment. An unexpected color change creates a new meaning in the type as the sequence progresses.

DESIGN EVOLUTION

11

Audio CD Package: *Fear & Desire*
doch design | Munich, Germany

There Are Two Sides to a Story

It's the dream job of many graphic designers: laying out the CD artwork for a band whose music they appreciate. Unfortunately, though, representing the abstract qualities of music so that they resonate with the intended audience is extremely difficult, and can be quite frustrating. Never one to avoid frustration, Maurice Redmond of doch design in Germany undertook just such a project—designing the cover for the band Mr. North's latest CD, *Fear & Desire*. Oddly, frustration would become a key ingredient in the visual language of the cover, whose subtle use of imagery masterfully captures the conceptual and emotional depths of the music. ❙ "Working with a band can be tricky," Redmond says, "as there are usually four completely conflicting opinions. I figured that presenting one idea at a time might be more productive. As a rule, I never present more than two or three variations for a project," he states. "As I see it, my job is to make the selection process easier for the client. Too much choice at the start usually indicates a lack of focus on the part of the designer."

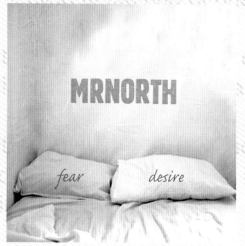

The designer begins his process by writing down ideas he feels describe the image he envisions. This writing forms the first page of the PDF presentation he made to the client.

The album's music explores the darker side of romance. The first proposals focus on the idea of the participants, evoking them through the image of an empty bed and two pillows. Monochromatic color—nearly black and white, but hinting of cold violet—creates a sense of coldness and anxiety that exaggerates the feeling of loss created by the couple's absence—there is no comfort here. The lighting also presents a mystery, being indefinable as to the time of day.

Redmond began this project writing about how the concept should look, a method he uses when working with image-focused projects. "With logos I start with a pencil on paper, with artwork I sit down and write out the idea in longhand and see what visual ideas come to me," he muses. The writing took place after a conversation with the band, during which they discussed the content and theme of the album. "The album is about the underbelly of love…" the notes begin. "It's about the tragically ironic crappy things that we do, that are done unto us, in what should be the enlightening and noble pursuit of love." Redmond listened to the music as he worked. He presented the band with the first concept a day later, a photographic idea revolving around an empty bed, two rumpled pillows standing in for persons unknown and, perhaps the double meaning in the title.

▌The band was appreciative and offered some thoughts on color and the type, which Redmond addressed. He began to think the album was much darker than the current cover was communicating, so he presented a second concept—a black cover with simple, centered title—during the second meeting. "There was a

> All the jobs I do are the result of research, method, gut instinct, self-criticism, and pure accident.

Maurice Redmond, Principal

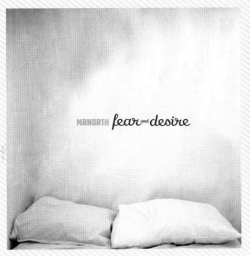

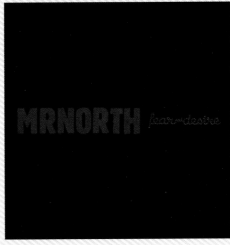

Different crops of the photograph all break the format asymmetrically, but each result in varying effects. When the position of the optical horizon created by the pillows divides the frame in half, the result is a comfortable feeling at odds with the cover's intended message; when the image is shifted upwards to reveal rumpled bedclothes, it suggests a recently inhabited feeling, as if the couple has just left the scene; when the pillows are positioned low in the frame, the stark emptiness of the wall is exaggerated dramatically.

The band's existing logo—a bold, condensed woodcut sans serif—was used for the presentation, along with alternate typeface choices for the album's title. The light, handwritten script is more immediate and less studied. When the words are printed over the pillows, each personifies an emotion related to the invisible couple, and the position suggests the band as narrator. A sweet, refined, and decorative interpretation of the script typeface adds the irony of romance to the scene, while the pink type suggests the feminine aspect of things like lipstick, passion, a handwritten diary. The worn texture of the logo gives an impression of weariness.

Alongside the album concepts, the designer presented a promotional logo to be used for T-shirts and similar merchandise. The symbol plays on the naivete of young love by alluding to the sweets exchanged on Valentine's Day.

week or so of variations and discussions where we realized that a common set of ideas had developed that didn't fit with the initial concept, despite it being liked. I wrote a new concept within an hour and hit the mark." ▌In this new concept, decorative, floral wallpaper would appear almost completely covered in black paint. An important aspect of the concept was that the cover be predominantly black; the subdued colors of the background pattern would provide contrast, and the texture of the wallpaper would affect the surface—a nearly imperceptible texture. Redmond describes his

goal in creating the artwork. "The image needed to look like a painting, like the result of the action of applying paint to a surface." This covering up of the floral wallpaper, not especially the color, conveys the primary symbolism—the loss or destruction of a kind of romantic ideal. ▌Redmond and the band explored a short list of typographic solutions for the cover, settling finally on a sharply serifed setting, all uppercase, with the band's name underneath, smaller, in a light sans serif. "I wanted the simplicity of the typography upon the image to convey that the album is a study of a complicated emotional subject."

FEAR & DESIRE

MRNORTH

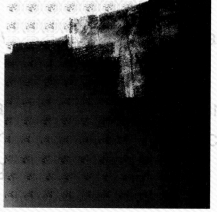

The band's reaction to the first concepts was generally good, but they suggested the image was dry and two dimensional, perhaps needing a window or city view. They also decided to discard the existing logo, as it was related to a previous album. Their sense of the typography was that it should

feel luxurious, as though for a box of chocolates. While still pondering the first concepts, the designer presented a new option with an all-black cover and sharp, serif type set all uppercase. The forlorn absence of image offers irony to the type's elegance. Variations on both the initial

concepts were considered improvements, but the band still felt these directions were not what they wanted to communicate.

A new written concept led directly to the final image— a photograph of decorative wallpaper, almost completely covered over with black paint. It was intended that the paper's pattern or structure could be seen through the paint, creating an almost imperceptible texture.

Redmond experimented with the paint on a chosen wallpaper to achieve the desired transparency so as to highlight the act of brushing it over the paper.

FEAR & DESIRE
MRNORTH

> This isn't just a picture to decorate the album for them; it is the image that people will associate with this collection of their songs … . They have a good visual knowledge of artwork and really care about it. This also makes the disagreements a lot more entertaining.

Maurice Redmond, Principal

The wallpaper acts as a symbol of the idea of an idealized "nest." Its presentation as a photograph grounds the image in physical experience—the "real." The blotting out of this symbol performs a kind of desecration of that ideal.

A transitional serif typeface lends crisp contrast without the contrived classicism of the previous type choice. Setting the title in sans serif, smaller and under a separator rule, creates a signature for the band and focuses attention on the concept.

Harmonie Sempach Anniversary
Concert Poster
Mixer | Lucerne, Switzerland

Making Music for the Eyes

The optical effects of form perception are powerful. Different shapes produce different physical sensations; size changes and arrangement create perceptions of rhythm or loudness. As the underpinning aspect of most graphic design, the abstract formal qualities of composition play a huge role in evoking the designer's intended emotional effect—especially when intentionally exploited within arrangements of recognizable forms. Erich Brechbühl of Mixer, in Lucerne, Switzerland, employs this knowledge to rich effect in this poster for a brass band. Fanfares of exploding dots and lines reveal themselves to be something else on closer inspection. ▌Brechbühl's poster promotes the 125th anniversary of the Harmonie Sempach band in Sempach, a small, lakeside city about 50 miles from Bern, in the north of Switzerland. It draws on a tradition of highly abstract, yet representational posters, popularized by Swiss designers in the early- to mid-twentieth century, and a guiding Swiss aesthetic—economy of means, the idea known commonly as "less is more."

I wanted to capture the rhythmic and sonic qualities of the music.

Erich Brechbühl, Principal

While Brechbühl's work stretches the boundaries of this aesthetic when the need demands it, his working method is classically Swiss: starting with research to find ideas, distilling the idea into a simple form, editing out what seems unnecessary, and creating clearly defined, decisive relationships among the form elements—whether they are abstract, representational, or typographic. ▌"My research always begins anew with every project," Brechbühl says, preferring not to keep an image library as some designers do. He began his research for the poster by collecting images of brass bands playing, but quickly noticed something about the instruments in the pictures—the buttons and valves of clarinets, saxophones, tubas, trumpets, and so on were decidedly geometric, a group of dots and lines. ▌Recognizing this formal quality, Brechbühl radically edited his research to images and diagrams of such mechanical parts. A quick pencil sketch showed him what he needed to know: that configuring dots and lines in various ways would create a rhythmic movement across the page that could very quickly convey a sense of musicality. He roughed out a tighter sketch

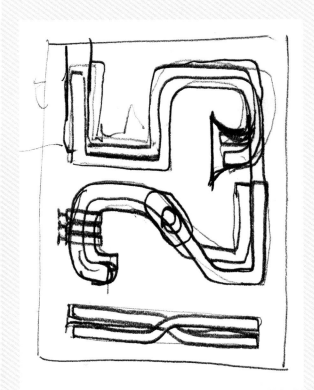

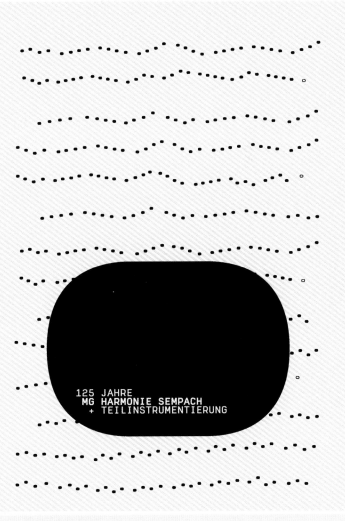

125 JAHRE
MG HARMONIE SEMPACH
+ TEILINSTRUMENTIERUNG

One of the first pencil sketches shows an early fascination with the mechanics of the instruments. The number signifies the client's anniversary, transformed into image through form alteration.

An early digital sketch focuses on the idea of rhythm. The dots abstractly allude to musical notation and provide a kind of rhythmic movement across the format.

for his clients in the brass band, and they approved. "For me it's normal to present one ideal concept. If the client isn't satisfied," he winces, "I'll work on another one and present it another time." ▌Confident in his approach, Brechbühl scanned instrument diagrams and set about tracing them with drawing software, building an extensive library of parts with which he would be able to compose. Following a week's time spent researching and developing the initial concept, he spent a few days preparing the drawings and then arranging them in various iterations to determine the most rhyth-

mic compositions, positioning of light and dark areas, and how these interacted with the resulting negative spaces. The minimal typographic elements, set in regular and bold weights of a neutral sans serif, integrated easily with the linear rhythms and enhanced the visual punctuation of the dot forms.

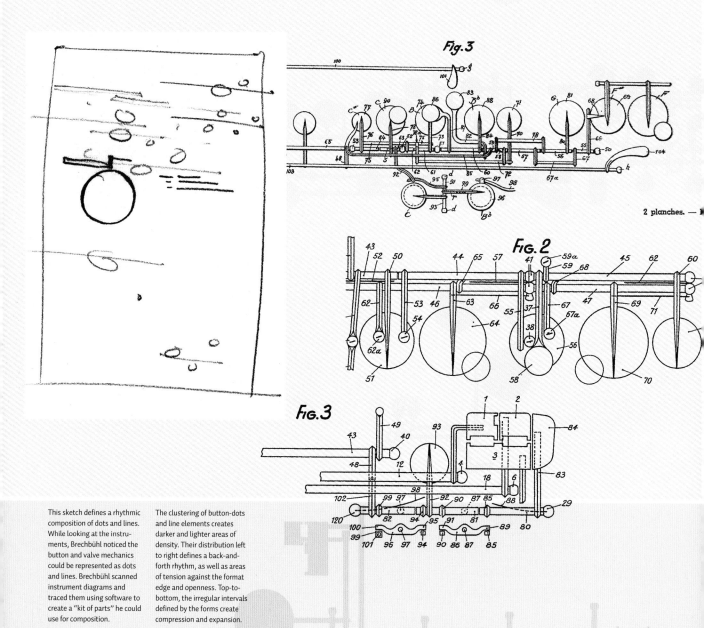

This sketch defines a rhythmic composition of dots and lines. While looking at the instruments, Brechbühl noticed the button and valve mechanics could be represented as dots and lines. Brechbühl scanned instrument diagrams and traced them using software to create a "kit of parts" he could use for composition.

The clustering of button-dots and line elements creates darker and lighter areas of density. Their distribution left to right defines a back-and-forth rhythm, as well as areas of tension against the format edge and openness. Top-to-bottom, the irregular intervals defined by the forms create compression and expansion.

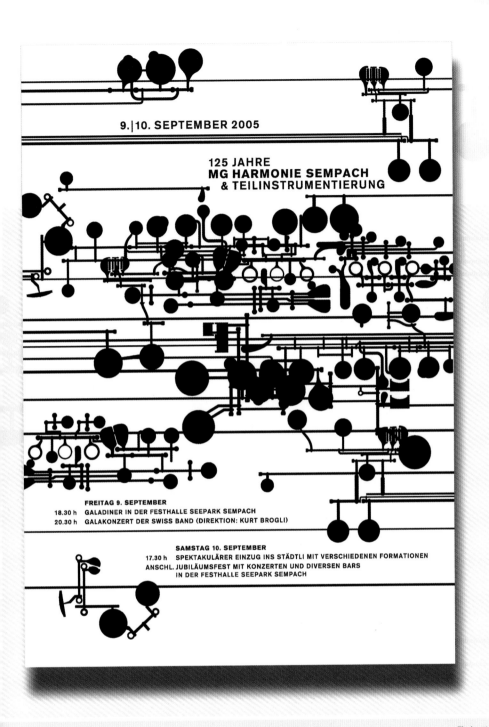

9.|10. SEPTEMBER 2005

125 JAHRE
MG HARMONIE SEMPACH
& TEILINSTRUMENTIERUNG

FREITAG 9. SEPTEMBER
18.30 h   GALADINER IN DER FESTHALLE SEEPARK SEMPACH
20.30 h   GALAKONZERT DER SWISS BAND (DIREKTION: KURT BROGLI)

SAMSTAG 10. SEPTEMBER
17.30 h   SPEKTAKULÄRER EINZUG INS STÄDTLI MIT VERSCHIEDENEN FORMATIONEN
ANSCHL. JUBILÄUMSFEST MIT KONZERTEN UND DIVERSEN BARS
IN DER FESTHALLE SEEPARK SEMPACH

As horizontal configurations of lines and dots, the image also suggests musical notation, a secondary and more abstract allusion that adds to the poster's conceptual depth.

A neutral sans serif typeface echoes the linear quality of the image; bold and regular weights respond to the image's density changes. Setting the text all uppercase reinforces its horizontality by avoiding the up-and-down internal rhythm that lower-case letters would have intro-duced.

The locations of the type's alignments adds a correspon-ding vertical counterpoint to the horizontal rhythm of the image and text itself; this introduces a secondary, subor-dinate structure that helps unify the various areas of the composition.

13

Bizer HVAC Identity and Website
2FRESH | Istanbul, Turkey

By its nature, the HVAC (Heating, Ventilation, and Air-Conditioning) business is a field where high-tech engineering, business, and human talent come together. The benefits of well-integrated systems are low operating costs and increased productivity resulting from improved worker health. In addition, the HVAC business relies on high-level engineering talent; system parts are produced in the high-tech industry sector and most systems are digitally managed. CanBurak Bizer and his team at 2FRESH undertook the redesign of such a company's identity primarily to update it with regard to changing perceptions of the industry, but with a mind to establish a corporate Web presence for the client. Embarking on this process for Bizer HVAC Engineering, Ltd., meant addressing elements from the existing identity before moving into exploration of new concepts, but the results—a clever, energetic wordmark situated within a refreshing, high-tech Web environment—explicitly show the benefits of a thoughtful redesign and brand extension into new promotional media.

Now That's Cool

Rough pencil sketches show the designers' interest in air and movement, spinning, and rotation, as well as with the mechanics of HVAC systems. Experiments with propellers and fans, derived directly from image research, yielded interesting possibilities, including a three-dimensional pinwheel.

This image was too complex and delicate for use a logo, but provided inspiration later.

While developing a custom typeface as an alternate direction, the drawing of both the B and the R caught the designers' attention. Using these type forms to attempt to create fan blades resulted in this idea integrating directly with the word to form a more specific logotype. The rendering of

the blades is a repetition of the lowercase R. By dropping the stem of the lowercase R below the baseline, the letter is made part of the rotating blade forms in the propeller image.

"We focused mainly on air and movement," Bizer says, and looked to the machinery of HVAC equipment—fans, propellers, oscillators, windmills—for inspiration. Image research produced a vast collection of reference for the kinds of forms; hand-drawn sketches led quickly into digital drawings of propellers and windmills. ▌ At the same time, Bizer and his team were developing an alternate wordmark concept, retaining the qualities of a sans serif but creating something more ownable. The initial B, both uppercase and lowercase, suggest-ed some of the blade forms they were seeing in propellers, but it was the lowercase r that struck a chord. "It somehow got our attention," recalls Bizer. This insight led to a harmonic integration of the abstracted propeller form and the type, joined by the r acting as one of the propeller's blades. ▌ Next order of business: the website. Bizer and his team developed a site map to organize the various areas, playing up the list of project references as the most important. There were a tremendous number of projects in the company's history, so they were edited and categorized according to application. Other primary navigational areas, or A-levels, included corporate information, a list of services, and contact. With the site map complete, the designers began to investigate the experience itself. "Instead of making an information-oriented site," Bizer says, "we sought to create an appealing corporate image site. The information would all still be there, but in a secondary position." ▌ The first con-cept was a 3D model of a HVAC system, using its parts as navigation. The central unit signified the home page; and ductwork, the A-levels. The site was to launch with an animated

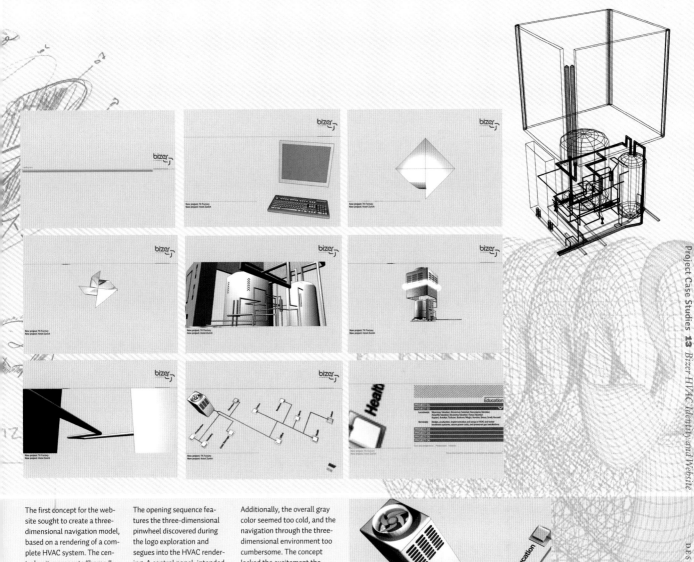

The first concept for the web-site sought to create a three-dimensional navigation model, based on a rendering of a complete HVAC system. The central unit represents "home," while secondary units repre-sent case studies organized by industry.

The opening sequence fea-tures the three-dimensional pinwheel discovered during the logo exploration and segues into the HVAC render-ing. A control panel, intended to provide secondary naviga-tion to corporate information, proved inefficient and techno-logically inaccurate.

Additionally, the overall gray color seemed too cold, and the navigation through the three-dimensional environment too cumbersome. The concept lacked the excitement the client and designers were after.

propeller becoming the central unit's fan; a computerized control unit acted as an alternate navigation device. ▌Bizer stopped the process, however, based on a number of team objections: the information focused too narrowly on the technical aspects, failing to target investors and developers as well as engineers; the renderings of the system seemed dry and not particularly impressive, even though it communicated well; the light colors were cold but not technical enough. In short, "We were in need of something more uncommon and sophisticated," Bizer says. ▌The team developed screen-shot roughs of three new concepts, looking for visual impact and not simply to represent the business. All three directions incorporated "techno" abstractions in 3D space, a kind of distorted reality. One of these centered on an animated, futuristic version of a propeller, and this concept seemed the most appropriate, given the direction the identity had taken.

> What's important is not each unique element but the whole, which is formed by these elements. So, refinement, for us, is about making the whole, and as long as the universe we create works coherently, we are quite happy with it.
>
> CanBurak Bizer, Creative Director

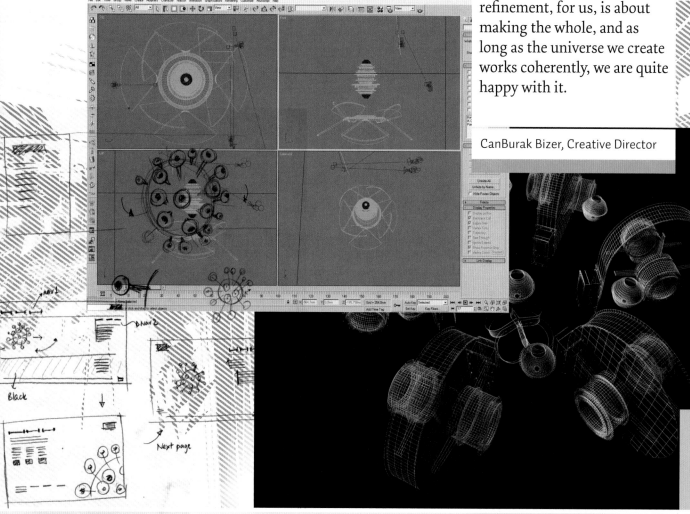

The designers explored more dynamic three-dimensional environments that were completely abstract. The three dimensionality of the site was considered desirable to convey the client's technological sophistication. Especially important was to create a richer color experience; their research focused on cool colors.

New sketches, also derived from subject research, focused on HVAC parts, such as rotors, fans, and propellers. The designers decided to create models of fantasy machines to enhance the futuristic quality of the site; explorations of rendering style settled on monochromatic plastic surfaces with slight reflection.

Screen shots of the modeling process show the complexity of the forms to be rendered.

The first step was to model the HVAC propeller objects using 3D software and to determine a rendering style—how the surfaces would be treated and reflect light. Deciding on a semi-reflective, plastic/metallic surface and a monochrome treatment, the team made tests of the renderings, developing a number of similar objects that would be animated. ▌ As the design team began to storyboard and build camera-moves in the animation software, they also turned their attention to the layout of the site. Unlike the earlier concept, more saturated color was to be used to contrast the animated

forms. The propeller animation, the team decided, would occupy one area of the site, while the other would contain the content. The A-levels were structured in a horizontal configuration, as type only, toward the upper right of the screen, and mouse-overs would activate fly-out menus for subnavigation. Directly beneath the navigational area, a space for content to expand allowed for long lists of the reference projects. ▌ The designers developed a system of animated lines that follows the cursor as it rolls over links; these lines expand like a tree structure around the selected

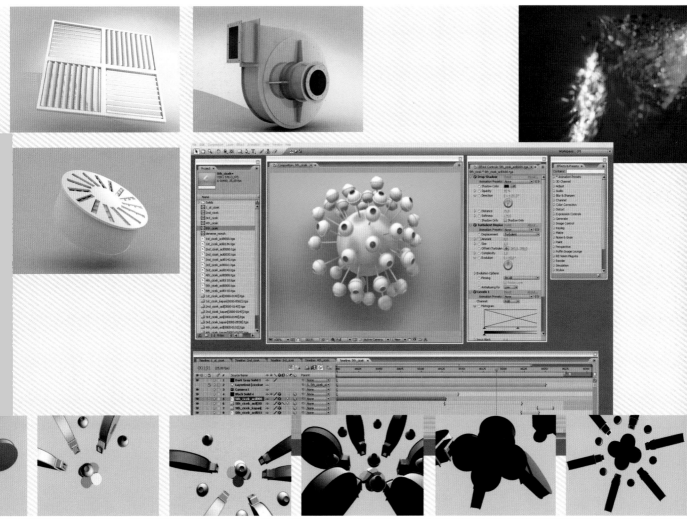

A field of dark blue was developed for the site environment, with a slight lighting effect, to provide contrast to the white machine forms. The navigation is clearly ordered at the top, with an area immediately below for content display.

link to reveal more detailed information. With the animations in the works, Bizer and his team were still looking for the "wow factor" they desired. They discovered it after an exhaustive search of animation effects in the software. "Dancing particles in the air," says Bizer, "particle animation." A kinetic flurry of chilly, snowlike particles, blown by a dramatic invisible wind, added just the degree of movement and excitement they desired.

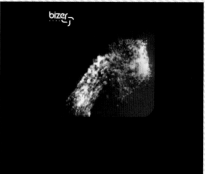
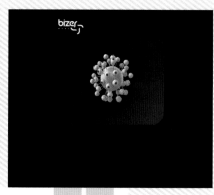

As a last component for the site, the designers developed a swirling explosion of snow particles for the site's launch transitions between navigable areas. Its movement across the frame of the site interfered with the navigation elements, so the screen was designed to contract to a smaller frame while the particles are in action, then expand outward. Animated linear elements act as indicators when mousing over a link.

> Particle animation in 3D was a real headache. The software was always crashing as the number of particles increased. So, we decided instead to create the particle intro in two dimensions.
>
> CanBurak Bizer, Creative Director

bizer

| PROFİL | HİZMETLER | PROJELER | İLETİŞİM |

TAKDİM

BIZER, YATIRIMCILAR İÇİN;
YÜKSEK TAKNOLOJİ VE BİLGİ BİRİKİMİ ÜRÜNÜ;
DÜŞÜK İŞLETME MALİYETLİ, YÜKSEK VERİMLİ;
ISITMA, HAVALANDIRMA, İKLİMLENDİRME (HVAC) VE MEKANİK TESİSAT
SİSTEM ÇÖZÜMLERİ ÜRETEN MÜHENDİSLİK FİRMASIDIR.

bizer

| PROFİL | HİZMETLER | PROJELER | İLETİŞİM |

PROJELER
TAMAMLANMIŞ PROJELERDEN SEÇMELER

KONAKLAMA

PERA ROSE HOTEL, THE
YAŞMAK SULTAN HOTEL
ST. SOPHIA HOTEL
VILLA ZURICH HOTEL
ROMANS HOTEL
SENATOR HOTEL

CITADEL HOTEL
1997_

ISITMA, SOĞUTMA, HAVALANDIRMA, SIHHİ TESİSAT, YANGIN TESİSATI
PROJESİ VE UYGULAMASI

AHIRKAPI, İSTANBUL

GRAND SAVUR HOTEL
MILPA TATİL KÖYÜ
TROYA HOTEL
ZURICH HOTEL
SED HOTEL
PRESIDENT HOTEL, THE

Secondary navigation is achieved with a drop-down menu that features a bright white box and dark blue type, which offers clarity and consistency, along with readability. Also, every time a box opens up, the graphic moves slightly, keeping the kinetic feeling alive.

The extensive menu of case studies is organized by industry sector in the main navigation up top. In the content area, the list of case studies within the selected industry expands and contracts to manage the volume of information. The movement of linear elements, along with the expansion and contraction, coordinates with the movement of elements elsewhere in the site. The three dimensional machine object tracks the movement of the cursor and rotates to follow it.

14

Beeline Honey Products Packaging
Kym Abrams Design | Chicago, Illinois; USA

It's an inventive idea, to be sure—exfelons making and selling honey to trendy, upscale shoppers. But it's this kind of thinking that makes for change in the world, and graphic design has a role to play. In this case, it was to develop the branding for Beeline—the honey products produced as a result of a program developed by North Lawndale Employment Network (NLEN)—that would help bridge the gap between prison and reintegration. NLEN is a nonprofit organization that creates innovative employment initiatives in distressed Chicago neighborhoods. Such was the charge given to Kym Abrams Design, a veteran Chicago studio steered by Abrams, and design associate Melissa DePasquale. | "The product was to launch in upscale farmers markets in Chicago," Abrams recounts. "It had to appeal to the clientele of a farmers market and jump off the shelves."

Getting a Little Buzz Going

The design process began with naming the product, so the designers developed word lists to crystallize ideas. Naming options, such as FreeBee, were conceived of to be simple, friendly, and clever regarding the source of the honey product—exfelons. Beeline won out as the most optimistic in its metaphor.

The initial sketch process, accomplished by hand, explored a variety of options, such as iconic imagery of honeycombs and bees, as well as strictly typographic ideas. The simplicity of icons reflected the immediacy and directness of the naming concept. Linear elements abstractly plot the flight path of a bee.

Abrams and DePasquale were involved with the naming of the project, from the ground up, an uncommon task for many graphic designers. It was important to keep the name simple and friendly, but the team was interested in developing a name that spoke to the context of the project and had some staying power. "We felt the name and branding should have a fresh, distinctly urban look and feel," DePasquale elaborates. ▌They explored a range of short and clever names that ranged from the clever—*FreeBee, worker bee, beelieve*—to the silly—*Honey, I Got a Job*—finally settling on Beeline for its directness and because it suggested the product's purpose: "Making a beeline to gainful employment," according to Abrams. Once the name was approved, the sketching began. ▌The two designers explored a variety of possibilities, from illustrative and iconic bee drawings to strictly typographic solutions. Several of the typographic ideas that would later merge to become the final design solution contained linear elements in combination with letters or bee icons, and Abrams and DePasquale mixed and matched various parts in their sketch process, even before turning from pencil to

> Right from the start it seemed that this logo should be primarily black and white. It was reflected in most of our early sketching and stuck throughout the process.

Melissa DePasquale, Designer

More refined digital sketches are based on the rough hand sketches. Even at this stage, the minimal approach to detailing and color is evident. Sans serif typefaces with uniform stroke weight are favored for their stripped-down, linear qualities. The designers also created concise combinations of type and line that focus attention on the idea within the word itself. The striped, lowercase B is a strong contender because the simple addition of yellow stripes allows it to represent the letter b, the word "bee," and the image of an actual bee. In another logotype, a broken line substitutes for the letter I, again referring to the insect's stripes.

computer. The sketches tended to share a similar quality—a lack of truly illustrative drawing in favor of iconic simplicity, limited color application, and sans serif type styles. "Beeline creates jobs for exoffenders in Chicago," DePasquale reiterates. "All the elements of the design were attempting to reflect a hard edge."

Other strong contenders at this stage of the design process play with the iconic form of the insect. The designers examined the symbol's interaction with patterns such as bar codes, simpler lines that could be interpreted as prison bars, and with letterforms. A refined version of the circular flight pattern concept incorporates the bee's silhouette and a sans serif setting of the two subwords in two colors. In this sketch, as in others, note the consistent contrast of sharp linear elements with more massive forms to create richness within simple configurations.

Three concepts ultimately made it to the client, each offering a very different message with a minimum of form. The top concept, in which "beeline" is handwritten in a broken line, is personal and approachable; the random quality of the writing suggests the bee's flight path or a path of searching. The striped lowercase *b*, shown in a condensed face to enhance its linearity, is clean and minimal. The third concept exploits the homey quality of a concrete illustration. The stroke contrast of the letterforms corresponds to the thick and thins in the drawing.

The nonprofit nature of the client meant no budget, and this dovetailed conveniently with the general aesthetic direction. "The client did not have a large budget for printing, so the limitation of black and white really contributed to the trendy, urban feel we were working toward," she continues. ▍Although Abrams and her team usually present only two or three concepts to their clients, in this case they were excited by four versions, and chose to show all of them. "We like to show the project on applications, so we sourced honey jars and lip balm tins on which to present the logos." And that

was that—the client approved the design that was implemented without any requests for changes. Abrams and DePasquale rapidly adapted the solution for various formats, integrating a serif face for secondary information on the back labels of jars, which are of a contemporary, cylindrical form that complements the simple lines of the identity. Abrams and DePasquale—and their clients—are ecstatic. "In its first season, Beeline sold out at several markets. Due to its great success, a number of employment opportunities have been created. Everybody is really happy about it."

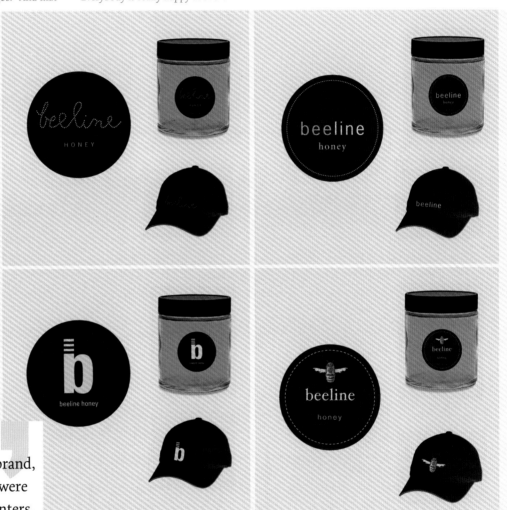

> With no budget for the brand, design and copywriting were donated. In sourcing printers, a very low–cost method was the only solution. Printing only black and one Pantone color brought the cost down significantly.

Kym Abrams, Principal

The designers made minor adjustments to sizing, spacing, and typeface selection for a second presentation. The refinements were presented on a baseball hat as well as on the jar to show the mark's potential for novelty application.

A fourth concept, shown here in the upper-right quadrant, was also presented. This approach was even more subtle than the others. Without the mass of the bee icon in the original sketch, this wordmark is visually more subdued in its degree of contrast, but very direct and still richly suggestive of its content.

It's a project that really stands out. Beeline products are 100 percent organic. The project is returning an empty city lot to productive use for honey harvesting, and it creates jobs for exoffenders.

Kym Abrams, Principal

beeline

body bar

fillmore apiary
chicago raised, chemical free

- - - - -

a project of the north lawndale
employment network

- - - - -

3726 west flournoy
chicago illinois 60624
www.nlen.org

beeline

honey

12 oz

a unique body moisturizer
massage directly onto dry skin

- - - - -

ingredients
chemical free beeswax
organic vegetable shortening
organic sweet almond oil
organic cocoa butter

- - - - -

a project of the north lawndale
employment network

- - - - -

3726 west flournoy
chicago illinois 60624
www.nlen.org

the buzz

beeline
honey scrub

beeline
honey
1 lb

beeline
lip balm

beeline
body bar

The final system of labels uses a supporting serif typeface to contrast the uniformity of the logotype, which shows the word "bee" in yellow. The same sans serif as the logotype is used for ingredient lists and supporting information on the labels.

The cylindrical bottle and matte tins complement the uniform stroke weight and linear detailing of the typography.

A slight adjustment was made to the frequency and spacing of the dashes in the line. Slightly longer dashes and an increase of space between them improved the directional quality of the line over the earlier version's more textural quality.

15

No More Gitmo!

The general public—and indeed, many graphic designers—think about the profession as an army of stylists and aesthetes working in the service of big corporations or promoting the glamour businesses of fashion, music, food, style, and art. They forget it's really about communicating. Graphic design is at its finest, however, when it takes to the streets to disseminate information on behalf of the public interest. Raising awareness about an unpopular and potentially sensitive subject, especially in America, this poster campaign attacks the imprisonment of detainees at a military base in Guantánamo, Cuba, and calls for public outcry against perceived human rights abuse.

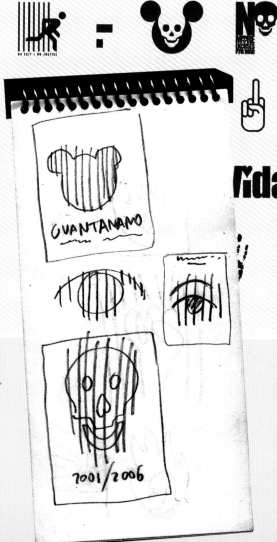

The five designers in the collective continuously build a library of icons, symbols, wordmarks, and supersigns they can call upon rapidly as the basis for their political work. The imagery cleverly combines universally understood content, such as a skulls and hands, with recognizable figures, such as Hitler and Che Guevara, with elements such as knives, thunderclouds, insects, religious symbols, and so on.

The project is similar to others produced by *Un Mundo Féliz* (UMF), a Spanish collective of graphic designers based in Madrid who initiate public awareness campaigns about political and social issues. Headed up by Gabriel Martínez and Sonia Díaz, of LSD (featured elsewhere in this book), this loose association of designers wields their extraordinary graphical skills as weapons in the fight for social justice. ▌For projects such as this one, initiated by Fundación Signes, a Barcelona promotional agency, UMF works from a collection of images they continuously generate

> We like to do our bit as designers and interested people to question public and social issues and state our opinions.

Sonia Díaz, Partner

Rough hand sketches show the pace at which this project was produced; the lines have an almost frantic energy. Combinations of selected forms from the library play with easily interpreted symbols to communicate quickly and provocatively: skull, flames, fist of power, heart, prison bars, eye, and a cartoon mouse. Combining two icons together can allude to more complex ideas—the overlap of the eye form with vertical lines suggests not simply imprisonment, but propaganda, disinformation, and news censorship.

tion of images they continuously generate and update. "We've been collecting these images for two years," Martínez says. Because the timetable for social and political work is so quick, it helps to have a library of relevant images on hand, from which to choose. He continues: "It requires a quick response. If we have a suitable image related to the message, we use it with minimal changes every time it is necessary. If we don't have it, we create it on the spot."

> We try to be conscious and objective, but sometimes the speed at which we work makes it impossible to control our design 100 percent.

Fernando Palmeiro, Designer

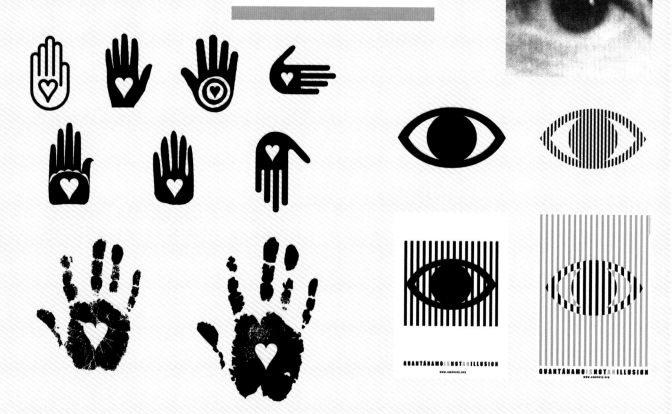

Comparison of hand/heart combinations reveals which form communicates most directly, as well as most deeply—and which deliver undesirable messages. The outline and solid iconic forms, with fingers together, is a gesture indicating "halt." The open-hand position articulates grasping or reaching. The sideways hand appears to offer or present the heart as a gift. The rough texture of the inked handprint brings a sense of pain to the image, but the relaxed attitude of the hand is too casual to seem urgent. The print texture of the selected hand is rougher, more broken, and feels menaced; the crisp white heart reversed from the palm suggests hope in the face of struggle.

The difference between the photographic and abstracted eye images is profound; while the photographic image seems relaxed or pensive, the iconic version appears aggressive or surprised. Although the photographic eye would prove useful, the designers investigated the iconic form more thoroughly, based on an early sketch. In the lower set of variations, the eye is combined with and interrupted by vertical lines. The blocking that occurs when negative lines cross the eye mass can be interpreted as a veil or other obstruction; fewer lines are more easily interpreted as prison bars.

The images are simple icons and typographic forms that can be rearranged, altered, combined, and added to in order to generate more complex conceptual messages. The directness of the images and their strong figure/ground contrast ensures visual impact and clear communication. ▌The group developed a series of provocative verbal messages and began to relate images selected from the 'library.' Phrases such as "Nightmare on Paradise" and "An Icon of Lawlessness" suggested more complex visual metaphors, while notions of incarceration and dissent meant including very clear, almost cliché images—prison bars, an eye, fists for fighting, and so on. ▌The designers explored image and text combinations over five days, working first in pencil and jumping rapidly to digital drawing software. For visual impact, as well as budgetary concerns, the color palette was kept high-contrast and minimal: black, white, and red. They edited variations as they went, settling at last on five images that were then produced in several media for free global distribution—as posters, postcards, and in a downloadable digital formats.

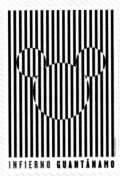

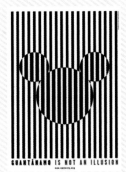

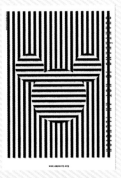

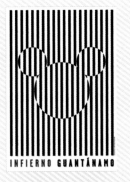

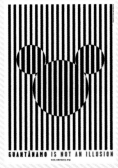

> Illustration allows us more graphic resources, but many times we start with photography.

Gabriel Martínez, Partner

Experiments with image combinations and manipulation for each card inform each other. Drawing from the manipulation of the eye image, the designers pursued the prison bars and optical linear effect with a skull and the powerful symbol of Mickey Mouse. In this series of studies, the designers tested the effect of changing the relationship of the lines outside the mouse form with those inside it. Depending on their orientation and density, the lines appear as prison bars or kaleidoscopic vibrations that obscure perception of the icon.

Another direction explores alterations and additions to a skull icon, among them the prison bar concept. Spatters of liquid evoke blood, suggesting violent death. Altering the eyes, adding a tear, and replacing the nose hole with an upturned heart suggest suffering, while the subtle effect of texture on the surface hints at abuse or squalor. The hooded version evokes the specter of the Grim Reaper, but also seems somehow glamorous, possibly playing a game with the idea of paradise and travel.

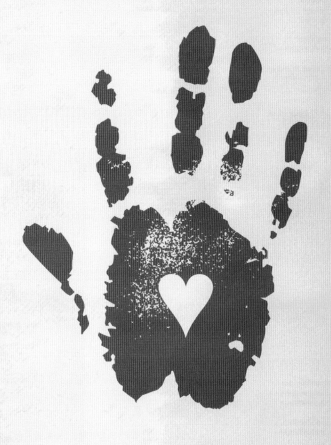

GUANTÁNAMO / END TORTURE NOW

SOONER OR LATER THERE WILL BE A NEED <u>TO CLOSE GUANTÁNAMO</u> HOPEFULLY AS SOON AS POSSIBLE

TARDE O TEMPRANO EXISTIRÁ LA NECESIDAD DE <u>CERRAR GUANTÁNAMO</u> ESPERAMOS QUE SEA LO ANTES POSIBLE

All five finished designs locate the image centrally, in a symmetrical relationship with the format's proportions. The designers masterfully avoid the static quality usually associated with symmetry by carefully sizing the material so that it is large enough to confront the format edges: the ears of the mouse, for example, create some tension with the left and right edges; the outer areas of the photographic eye image are a bit irregular, and their softer edges contrast the harsh vertical lines; the thumb of the hand icon performs the same function. The designers further enliven the symmetrical arrangements by altering spatial intervals between image and type.

Consistently applying a condensed, sans serif face unifies the series despite radically different image modes. In the context of the images with prison bars, the typesetting echoes the strong linear spacing of the vertical bars. In the hand and skull posters, it offers a rhythmic contrast to the irregular, organically textured qualities of the images.

GUANTÁNAMO

AN ICON OF LAWLESSNESS / UN SÍMBOLO DE INJUSTICIA

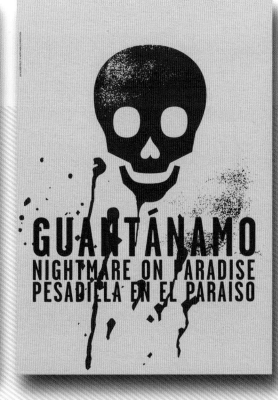

GUANTÁNAMO
NIGHTMARE ON PARADISE
PESADILLA EN EL PARAISO

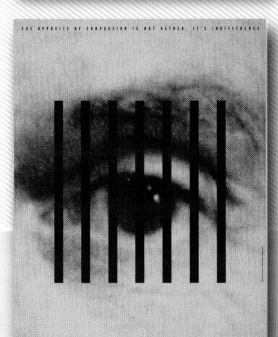

THE OPPOSITE OF COMPASSION IS NOT HATRED, IT'S INDIFFERENCE

LO OPUESTO A LA COMPASIÓN NO ES EL ODIO SINO
LA INDIFERENCIA

HUMAN RIGHTS WATCH / hrw.org

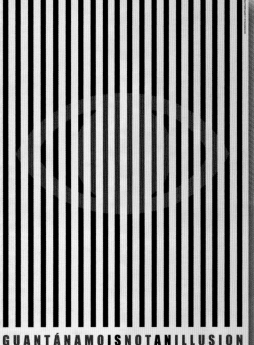

GUANTÁNAMOISNOTANILLUSION
www.amnesty.org

16

Tartini Music Conservatory Identity
Leonardo Sonnoli / Tassinari Vetta |
Rimini & Trieste, Italy

The Endless Permutation of Music

Abstract form and typography are often compared to the fluid system called music, precisely because of these attributes—their fluidity of form and their organic, systematic logic. It may come as no surprise, therefore, that a designer, looking for a visual language with which to represent a music conservatory, might very well gravitate toward a system of typographic symbols that can be infinitely recombined. ▌ It may come as less of a surprise to those familiar with the work of Leonardo Sonnoli that this is precisely the approach taken in developing the visual program for the *Conservatorio di Musica Giuseppe Tartini*, located in Trieste, Italy. The school's goal in enlisting Sonnoli and his associates at Tassinari/Vetta, a firm with offices in Trieste and Rimini, was to catalyze interest in the school and increase both enrollment and attendance at performances by developing a new identity.

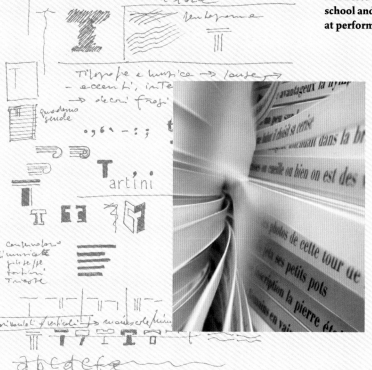

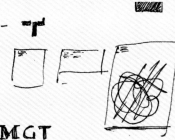

Rather than sketching by hand, as he often does, Sonnoli began the design process using drawing software after writing and reflecting on the client's brief. His affinity for the system-based identity work of Swiss design pioneer, Karl Gerstner, directed him toward the idea of variation within consist restraints, and this was corroborated by a chance encounter with a book of French poems—published cut apart, line by line, and therefore almost infinitely variable. Sonnoli perceived this idea as appropriate to the concept of music and began to explore sets of symbols that could be recombined to make a kind of variable logo. Unlike conventional thinking in corporate identity design, which invests unadulterated repetition of the logo form with absolute power, this method relies on the recognizability of the logo's components and the appreciation of the logic that organizes them. As long as the viewer sees the same kinds of elements, relating to each other in the same way, there is no less recognition and recall as compared to a traditional logo.

"forma" della musica -
onde sonore

Sonnoli is a veteran designer of identities for cultural institutions, as is his partner, Paolo Tassinari, so the project was something they could begin working on immediately, and without a great deal of preliminary sketching. Although Sonnoli does usually begin with pencil sketches, he notes that in this case, his starting point was to write some notes beside what he describes as "very simple and bad drawings," preferring to reflect on the problem and its context. ▌The notes and "bad drawings" resulted from Sonnoli's usual, conceptual approach to abstraction and typography, grounded in his reverence for modernism and his identification with conceptual thinkers in design and other humanities. ▌Among the former, the pioneering identity work of Swiss designer Karl Gerstner, exemplified in his book *Designing Programmes*, and always useful as a reference, seemed especially prominent in his thinking as the Tartini project began. Further, Sonnoli keeps an extensive library of visual and other subjects from which he can draw inspiration for well-rounded approaches with intellectual depth. ▌In thinking about music, visual language, and typography—an ever-present

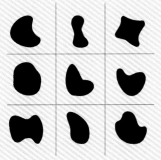

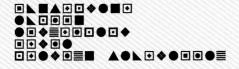

Sketches show the progression in design thinking. The first set features variations on a shape; these might have been too difficult to recall, while the lack of linear quality makes them a bit weak. In the next permutation, the shapes are made into a family and organized in a grid, which adds no meaning to the subject at hand. The forms are then made a bit more linear, colored, and simplified into a five-line structure related to a musical staff. A further alteration of the forms evokes the letters of the word "music." Another version investigates geometric, square-and-dot based forms that appear as toys or puzzle parts, which may be too childish in form.

love—Sonnoli meandered through some work by French typographer, poet, and writer Robert Massin, rediscovering not only Massin's unorthodox and indefinable approach to type, but a particular project for writer and poet Raymond Queneau. ▮ It was a book entitled *One Hundred Million Million Poems* (1961) that started the engine. The book contains ten sonnets in which each line is printed on a separated strip—like a heads/bodies/legs book. All ten sonnets share the same rhyme scheme and the same rhyme sounds, so any number of any poem's lines can be combined with the others from any other poem—resulting in 10¹⁴ possible poems. Reading for 200 million years without stopping, the average person would never read the same poem twice. ▮ Sonnoli recognized that this concept is similar to music—the same seven notes are recombined and resequenced without need of a repeat, creating an endlessly variable system. Over the course of the next week, he worked out a variety of abstract, amorphous forms as the basis of a visual language that could be just as flexible. The forms were organized in five lines as a reference to a musical staff; how many on each line and in what order they appeared remained flexible. This clustered system became Sonnoli's proposal for a logo. Prior to showing the concept to the client, however, he decided to investigate the same concept, but using an actual type form in place of the abstract form language. Something about the original concept struck him as not rigorous enough, maybe too decorative. Sonnoli developed a family of sans serif *T*s in five weights, and applied the same logic as he had employed in the first version. ▮ He introduced the two versions to the client, accompanied by conventional typographic

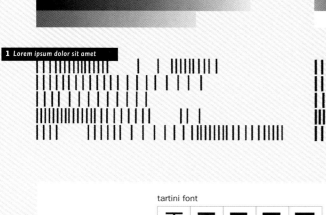

1 *Lorem ipsum dolor sit amet*

tartini font

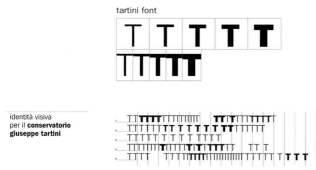

identità visiva
per il **conservatorio
giuseppe tartini**

Conservatorio
statale
di musica
Giuseppe
Tartini

Stripping the language down to lines, changing only in spacing, demonstrates not only how simple the language can be, but also that rhythm is an important consideration. Transforming the line idea into a single letter—that of the conservatory director's initial—adds the benefit of concrete

meaning. By changing the weight of the letter, the rhythmic quality of the spacing strategy is greatly enhanced.

After the client approved the concept, refinements were made to the mark's structure; the client's full name was added as a subordinate element in a single weight of a bold, sans serif typeface. A change in value within the type creates an internal hierarchy; the lighter words recede in importance.

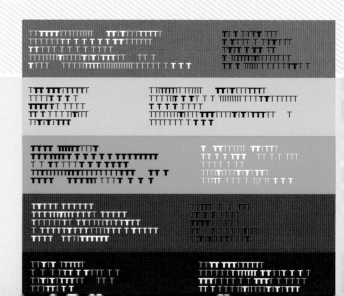

lockup, in environments of both solid-colored and photographic backgrounds. ▌ As a result of the conversation, Sonnoli and the client selected the concrete typographic logo system over that of the abstract shape system, for precisely the reasons that Sonnoli himself had developed it—it was more rigorous, more elemental, and the use of the *T* as a system component made an immediate connection with Tartini's name. The client made no request for changes to the concept. "If the client asks for changes, I prefer to restart from zero. … No compromises," Sonnoli states.

During a short refinement period to establish a grid for the publications and posters, and in deference to the elemental simplicity of the concept, Sonnoli eschewed imagery of any kind, relying instead on a simple color concept for variation—vibrant hues of a medium value that could accept black ink and allow for reversed white type without either option impairing legibility. ▌ This ensured some continuity despite the lack of formal color palette, and alleviated some cost concerns, as all the materials could be produced in two colors.

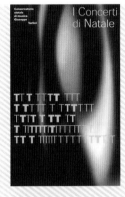

> I wanted to capture a kind of moving identity, to apply simply and in a variety of ways. There are five lines, like a music staff; it's a sort of typograhic music translation. And it's changed in each application. Like the music: always in motion and always changing.

Leonardo Sonnoli, Partner

In the next stage of development, Sonnoli investigated the use of imagery as a supporting language for collateral such as ads, posters, and concert programs. The restrained color palette mixes black and white with a secondary color, mostly for economic reasons.

The imagery in these studies is lyrical in its movement; the type elements respond to this compositional motion in their arrangement.

Conservatorio
statale
di musica
Giuseppe
Tartini

Nat King
Stravinskij

Il mondo della musica
ti offre più di una professione.

Vieni in un conservatorio
di respiro europeo
che vanta cento anni di esperienza
l'insegnamento di tutti gli strumenti
nuovi linguaggi musicali
video e musica informatica
l'esperienza dell'orchestra
borse di studio per l'estero
competenza ed entusiasmo.

Vieni a Trieste.

corsi inferiori
corsi triennali superiori
accessi per età differenziate
iscrizioni dall'1 al 30.4.2004

biennio di specializzazione
iscrizioni entro il 20.9.2004

Conservatorio Giuseppe Tartini
via Ghega 12, 34132 Trieste
tel 040 6724911 fax 040 370265

www.conservatorio.trieste.it

Conservatorio
statale
di musica
Giuseppe
Tartini

segreteria.didattica@conservatorio.trieste.it
segreteria.artistica@conservatorio.trieste.it
segreteria.amministrativa@conservatorio.trieste.it
biblioteca@conservatorio.trieste.it
www.conservatorio.trieste.it

Conservatorio
statale
di musica
Giuseppe
Tartini

Via Ghega 12
I - 34132
Trieste
t. +39 040 6724911
f. +39 040 370265

The letterhead is simply structured and positions type elements to activate space around the format. The business cards and envelope are equally spare and thoughtful in the size and positioning relationships among elements. The negative spaces respond to the proportions of the type elements.

The poster exploits tremendous scale change in the type, as well as enormous volumes of negative space. Clear alignment structures and use of weight change to develop hierarchy, as well as decisive proportions, contribute to the poster's simple dynamism and typographic color.

**Johann
Sebastian
Berio**

Ultimately, the designer discarded imagery as unnecessary. The typographic rhythm within the logo, along with that created by larger text elements and color relationships, was considered all that was needed. In this series of program covers, the horizontal banding created by the logo lockup and the titling text is very clear. Changes in contrast between type elements and the background color creates variation and perception of greater spatial depth.

17

Memorial Sloan-Ketterling Cancer Center 2005 Annual Report
Ideas On Purpose | New York; USA

Good Design Is In Its Genes

Annual reports for Fortune 500 corporations tend to focus on performance in terms of numbers, while those of medical or research institutions define it in human terms. Hence, the narrative of the report is of greater significance than the financial data—at least, for the purposes of outreach and fund-raising. These are, in fact, the purposes for this report, and why Memorial Sloan-Ketterling Cancer Center, a New York City research hospital, invested its creation with Ideas On Purpose (IOP) also located in New York. For IOP, the storytelling is by far the crux of designing such publications—it is, for them, an editorial endeavor. This approach defines the process for IOP's principals, Darren Namaye, Michelle Marks, and John Connolly, at every stage of the game. It's a collaborative, iterative approach that resulted here in a publication of depth and inspiration.

> We try to present a complete story, not just typical design spreads. We believe the story is an integral part of the design.
>
> John Connolly, Partner

The first proposed cover designs both grew directly from the interiors of their respective concepts. The "everyday" cover showed an unstudied, almost journalistic photograph whose cropping and slight blur suggested immediacy and real experience. The alternate cover showed very small images, combined with the DNA line language. A complete phrase excerpted from the mission statement replaces a conventional title.

Connolly outlines IOP's approach to the development of annual reports, which they have streamlined, out of necessity and through experience. "We begin by developing verbal concepts," he says, stressing their belief in the narrative aspect of the annual report as a document. "Then, we loosely map out or paginate our narrative ideas. From there, the design process begins with pencil thumbnail sketches, where we conceive formal ideas that are tied to the narrative. From these sketches, we develop full-size page layouts." ▌IOP generally presents three concepts to their clients, and this project was no exception—but in this case, they developed only two. The verbal concepts for this year's annual grew out of the designers' response to the hospital's mission statement and a story they were told they would need to feature—that of a new research fellow and his team, and his work analyzing DNA. ▌The designers were also aware of a need to carefully balance aspects related to patient care, research, and education across the institution—to some degree because of potential internal political repercussions, but mostly due to the hospital's desire to represent all three aspects from their

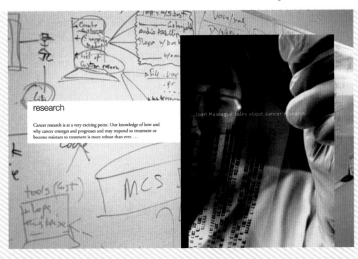

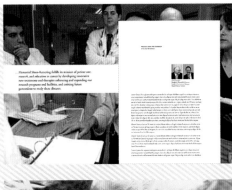

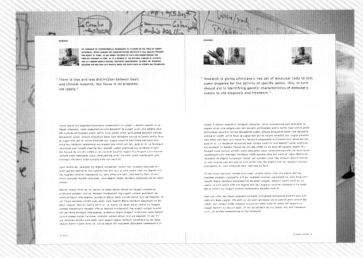

DESIGN EVOLUTION

Following initial discussions with the client, IOP developed two directions for the annual, both of which took elements of the hospital's mission statement as inspiration, defining three areas of focus: research, patient care, and education. The first concept developed a narrative based on exploring the daily efforts of hospital staff, researchers, and patients in their quests to defeat cancer. Each section opened with a full-bleed photograph surrounding a signature of smaller inset pages. These pages were treated differently for each section; in the Research section, for example, the smaller pages are textured with a graph-paper grid to convey a scientific feeling. The Patient Care section used black-and-white portraiture and warmer color to evoke the patient's personal story.

research

Peering inside breast cancer's 'toolbox,' Joan Massagué has identified a set of rogue genes that accelerate the spread of cancer to the bone and the lung.

Joan Massagué
Chairman, Cancer Biology and Genetics Program

mission statement as fully as possible. Of the two concepts presented, the one based directly on the hospital's mission statement stood out as the most desirable in accomplishing these goals. It had evolved with a formal concept that also grew out of the designers' inspiration in DNA sequencing they had seen. "We used vertical strips of image and text as a reference to that visualization. Within that basic formal structure, we injected as much differentiation in scale as possible to convey the sense of an energetic place." ▌Connolly notes that while the formal idea typically has a more direct con-

patient care

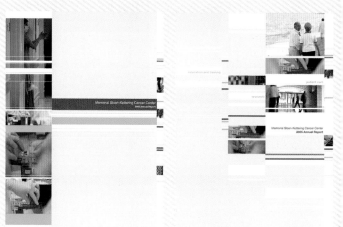

The second concept organized the narrative in a similar way, but the narrative was more directly tied to the mission statement and used an overall visual language inspired by the designers' visits to the research labs, where they encountered DNA visualizations. The designers abstracted these images down to a system of lines that varied in weight and length, moving in rhythmic progressions up and down across the pages. Narrower text columns continue the vertical movement established by the line rhythms.

Design changes to the selected concept were minimal and consisted mostly of content revisions, both editorial and in terms of the subject matter of photographs. One radical development was the freeing up of the text columns and callouts to more dramatically reflect the DNA line language. The designers worked with a very precise grid of fourteen columns, changing column widths and shifting elements up and down to accentuate the rhythm in the pages. This constant shifting intentionally imparts an energetic pace to the report.

nection with the narrative content, in this case the form relationship was more oblique, arising from a visual cue related to an aspect of the story. ▌The pacing, or pagination, of material, is derived in collaboration with the client's public affairs group, who writes the editorial content, but it's up to IOP to determine how to bring the text to life. "We interspersed stories with full-spread image combinations," Connolly says. "Then we wove in full-page images and played with the scale of the people when we photographed them."

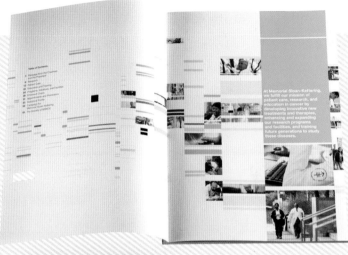

research
patient care
education

Memorial Sloan-Kettering Cancer Center
2005 Annual Report

The cover's phrase was replaced by a three-line distillation of the hospital's mission, corresponding to the three narrative sections within.

The opening spread and table of contents use the linear language to great effect. Images, as well as type, are integrated through their similarity in arrangement with the lines.

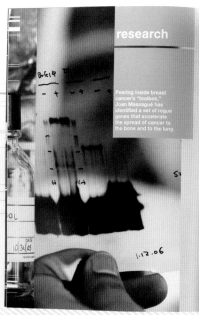

research

Peering inside breast cancer's "toolbox," Joan Massagué has identified a set of rogue genes that accelerate the spread of cancer to the bone and to the lung.

Joan Massagué
Chairman, Cancer Biology and Genetics Program

Dr. Massagué is internationally recognized as a leader in the fields of cancer metastasis and growth factors that regulate cell behavior. After leading the Sloan-Kettering Institute's Cell Biology Program for nearly 10 years, he was named Chairman of SKI's new Cancer Biology and Genetics Program in 2003. He is a member of the National Academy of Sciences and is a Howard Hughes Medical Institute investigator. In 2005, Dr. Massagué received the New York City Mayor's Award for Excellence in Science and Technology.

education and training

patient care

"We are at a special moment in time in oncologic research. After two-and-a-half decades of investment in basic research, and in the development of tools and technologies, we have accumulated a body of knowledge that tells us more than we have ever known about what makes a cancer cell a cancer cell," says Joan Massagué, Chairman of the Sloan-Kettering Institute's Cancer Biology and Genetics Program.

In describing the state of 21st-century cancer research, both at Memorial Sloan-Kettering Cancer Center and beyond its walls, he observes, "The distinctions between basic and clinical research are disappearing. Our focus is on problems, not labels. Interactions flow in many different directions at once."

A structural biologist, for example, can teach a cell biologist how two molecules are shaped in much a way that one fits into the "pocket" of another. And the cell biologist, trying to understand how cells "see" the world and react to it, uses the understanding of these molecule-to-molecule contacts to elucidate the chain of events that guides the way cells sense signals and make decisions. Meanwhile, the cell biologist may also identify for the molecular pharmacologist new targets for therapy, determining which molecules a tumor cell is utilizing to grow. And the pharmacologist, in turn, can develop new drugs or modify existing ones to block this process—drugs that clinical investigators will eventually employ to treat patients.

"The labels—'cancer biologist,' 'clinical investigator,' 'molecular pharmacologist'—don't matter so much any more," Dr. Massagué says. "Everyone is making essential contributions."

Progress has been accelerated by the Human Genome Project; by technological advances such as microarrays, which give investigators the ability

to detect the activity of thousands of different genes; and by new imaging techniques that "let us 'spy' on tumor cells as they do their deeds," Dr. Massagué explains. "And these are just some of the tools that enable research activities to flourish."

MSKCC's rich and longstanding tissue bank allows researchers to take samples from a single patient's tumor, or from a group of patients with the same type of cancer, and apply new technologies to learn how disease progression correlates with certain gene mutations and gene activity levels. "Over many years, we have developed a tremendous resource of molecular characterization of tumors: molecular which researchers can develop and pursue hypotheses," says Dr. Massagué.

And no longer are these investigations confined to cultured cells in vitro. "Such cells may have been derived from a tumor," he says, "but can look very different

from the original tumor cells and be located in a distant site in the body," Investigators are increasingly disease-focused; modeling cancer in mice has become a central area of research. Because tumors develop in mice through the same pathways as those in humans, mouse models are vital for understanding cancer biology and genetics. "Metastasis, for example—tumor cells traveling to a specific organ—is an activity that can only be studied in a test animal," Dr. Massagué notes. "You can't duplicate the process of metastasis in a test tube."

In his own research, Dr. Massagué and his colleagues are uncovering the genes that drive metastatic breast cancer. In a paper in Nature in July 2005, his group described a set of genes in early stage breast tumors whose presence appears to predict if the disease will spread to the lungs and, once there, how virulent the cancer may become. That study followed their 2003 report in the journal Cancer Cell on a cluster of genes a breast tumor's whose expression results in tumors migrating to the bone. "Our work shows that the ability of a tumor to form metastases depends on the combined action of multiple genes—and a different set of genes is required for each organ the tumor spreads to. Dr. Massagué explains. "Based on these insights, we are seeking genes for metastasis by other tumors and to other organs."

"Our work shows that the ability of a tumor to form metastases depends on the combined action of multiple genes—and a different set of genes is required for each organ the tumor spreads to."
—Joan Massagué

The section openers are defined by wide, blue-green columns of color that cross a full-bleed image top to bottom. This treatment distinguishes the opening spreads from their corresponding text spreads, acting as a clear signal that the narrative is about to change direction.

Using only one sans-serif typeface, Helvetica, throughout, and changing only weight and size provides visual consistency and prevents the active typography from distracting the reader from the content. Helvetica's curved forms are more rounded than those of other sans-serif families, such as Univers, and feel more organic in this context.

Photography is an important aspect of the narrative approach, but especially in this case because the report is telling a human story. IOP selected and hired the photographer and art directed the shoots. ▌According to Connolly, their goal was "to generate real-life environmental portraits to reinforce this human story. We would spend a day or a half-day with each subject to fully understand them and capture that on film—or, digital as the case was." They reviewed thousands of frames with the client's public affairs staff, collaborating again on the final image selection.

"After the shoot, we found our idea of vertical stripes challenging to work with," Connolly grimaces. "It was hard to make [the subjects] not look as though they were forced into a layout." IOP's designers used a grid, but in a kinetic way, playing with the verticality on the pages. Different column widths—all derived from a tighter, master grid—were combined and subdivided. This flexibility allowed the designers to redesign a few sections so that the image content would feel appropriate to the constraints of the pages.

Helvetica's legibility at smaller sizes, and in complex contexts, such as the financial section, is due to its large x-height and optimal spacing.

Cool blue-greens were selected to suggest the interiors of hospitals; the contrasting olive brown was paired to create an unexpected color harmony. The two colors are near complements of each other.

18

Scheufelen Paper Promotional Desk Calendar
Strichpunkt | Stuttgart, Germany

Free to Be You and Me... and Paper

Paper promotions are usually fun. But it's not often that they become a literary and conceptual experience. In the spirit of maverick paper company Scheufelen, German design firm Strichpunkt developed just such an experience. In the course of demonstrating the capabilities of a premium paper stock, they created a biography of the ways in which people experience freedom and independence—from birth to eternity. Through photographs and text, the *Book of Independence* illustrates the various stages of life, and a special calendar begins whenever the reader wants it to—with stickers to mark off the dates and to highlight personal celebrations of freedom.

"I'M THE ONE THAT HAS TO DIE WHEN IT'S TIME FOR ME TO DIE, SO LET ME LIVE MY LIFE, THE WAY I WANT TO"
(JIMMY HENDRIX)

'Excuse me while I kiss the sky.'

NO LOGO

1 Lorem ipsum dolor sit amet

Be Independent

Be Premium
Be Special
Be Different
Be Independent

One of the important considerations was the audience. "Well, it's mainly people like ourselves we had to design for. Sounds easy, but it makes it more difficult to get an objective view," Jochen Rädeker, Strichpunkt's creative director, says wryly. ▌Constant discussion took place about the project, almost daily, because it was part of a larger initiative to communicate Scheufelen's core values to the market. Independence is the company's most cherished core value because of the founder's run-in with the law back in the 1880s. Strichpunkt conceived of a day planner or calendar book

> "It's an enjoyable process: first, thinking (a lot of thinking!); then creating a clear strategy; and then closing the mind, opening the heart, and doing the best possible design to express what we and the client want to say.
>
> Jochen Rädeker, Creative Director

Notes, photographic research, and drawings seek out images and ideas to represent independence. Iconic images, such as those of 1970s rock stars Janis Jopln and Jimi Hendrix, share space with handwritten declarations and drawn images related to punk, flags, and so on.

The slogans, in particular, carry a provocative and independent spirit that feels immediate and authentic. References from bumper stickers, ads, and other ephemera bring typographic variation into the mix.

The team presented a preliminary version of the evolutionary concept in the form of color laser-printed pages. A die-cut hole in the first page suggests a baby's view as it enters the world at birth.

Designing is always discarding, pursuing, and a mix of things in your mind and on your desktop. To be honest, I think there is no straight creative way to a straight project.

Jochen Rädeker, Creative Director

with the intention of making it much more than that. Twelve chapters later, they had. █ A team of seven people at Strichpunkt— five of them designers—worked for about four months developing the concept. Sketching first by hand, informally with each other and during repeated meetings with the client, the designers built the idea to a point where they could give it a cleaner— although still unresolved—form for an "official" presentation. █ Similar to some other design studios in this book, Rädeker and his team present only one concept to their clients,

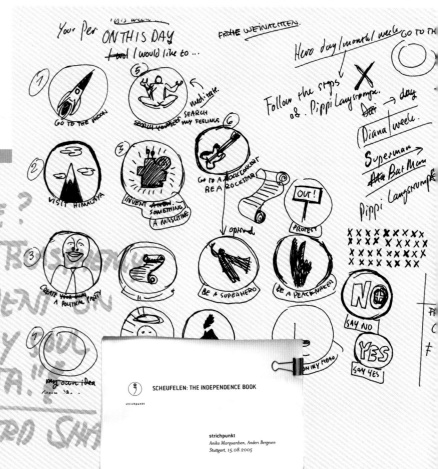

Handwritten notations were scanned for use in the calendar pages.

As the concept evolves, ideas from different stages in the sketch process combine to form ideas for new sections, as well as enhancements for image pages. Developing several sections, each with a different narrative and treatment, allows the designers to showcase the paper stock's qualities in more complex ways. It also makes the overall experience more editorial. The sequence of material becomes an important aspect of the editorial sections.

KALENDARIUMSENTWÜRFE _TEIL 1

– Entwurf 1: Gestalterische Anlehnung an ein Flugticket, *fly away and get free with scheufelen!*
– Entwurf 2: Illustrative Herangehensweise, freie und ungezwungene Gestaltung
– Entwurf 3: Typografisch feine und auf Scheufelen abgestimmte Gestaltung inklusive Entwurf der einzuklebenden Marken, *mark your day with scheufelen!*
– Entwurf 4: Highway life, das Leben ist eine Reise auf einem langen Highway …
– Entwurf 5 und 6: Dein "Independence-Wert" wird gemessen

A descriptive page from the second presentation of a more refined concept defines the sections to be implemented. Additional pages show more refined typography, mixing weights and styles with linear elements, and evolving image pages for the various sections.

whether they've established a track record on previous projects or not. "It's a matter of principle. It's part of the job of a strategic thinking agency to present a solution, not options for possible solutions," he explains. ▌Because the client had been a part of the discussions as the concept was developing, there weren't any surprises. The only change the client requested was to edit out a few topless shots for the American market. ▌The book is an exact analogy between form and function: it's a calendar without fixed dates for becoming independent. This disconnect is also seemingly apparent in

what appear to be unrelated parts. "Our aim was to feature as many aspects of independence as possible . . . We wanted to showcase the printing possibilities on the PhoenXmotion stock—after all, it's a book of independence, but mainly a paper sample," he continues. "This is the same reason we used different kinds of photography: showing light and dark shades, gradients, skin tones, and so on." It's the consistent combination of full-page photos with fine graphic elements, two corporate typefaces, and a distinct red that creates a recognizable corporate visual language repre-

senting Scheufelen. ▌Refinements to the spreads they had created were ongoing, and continued as Rädeker and the other designers were creating new ones. These refinements consisted mostly of fine-tuning the typography, adjusting color balance in the photography, and overseeing the production issues by coordinating closely with the book's printers. Along the way, they showed their clients at Scheufelen the book as work-in-progress twice, which Rädeker says was fine for them, as the production schedule was extremely tight. Preparation time for the final layouts was

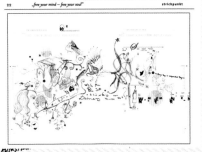

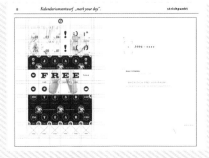

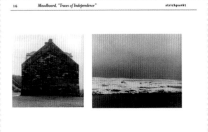

Photographic images begin to suggest an overall direction for one of the sections in the diary, an exploration of life stages (from birth to death) and the exercising of independence at each stage. Photographs are selected for consideration based on their unusual, quirky subject matter, composition, unexpected color, and conceptual connection to the idea of independence—the nude couple trimming the hedges, for example, and the lone shack on the seashore.

In looking at treatments for the daily calendar, the designers investigated the idea of personalizing it from the outset. Here, hand-drawn illustrations make each page individual. In another concept the calendar asks the user to mark their day. This idea led to the notion of the calendar having no beginning and no end, completely defined by the user. To make the experience more fun, the designers conceived of stickers that could mark months, days, and times, as well as other kinds of ideas, based on slogans and ephemera from their research.

compressed into four weeks, with printing and binding eating up another six. ▌"Most paper promos are just eye candy. This book tells a story, it leads you through your life from chapter to chapter," says Rädeker. "It's interactive by challenging the user to create his own calendar. And it goes along with the client's core messages without being too close-minded. It gives hints without being schoolmasterly."

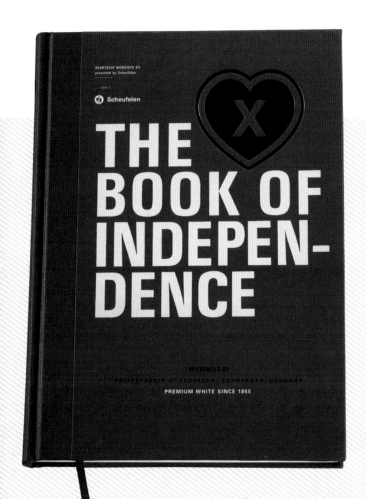

The final cover is bound in vivid, matte red and foil-stamped.

The opening sequence introduces readers to the concept and the paper stock with iconic images and short, well-typeset texts.

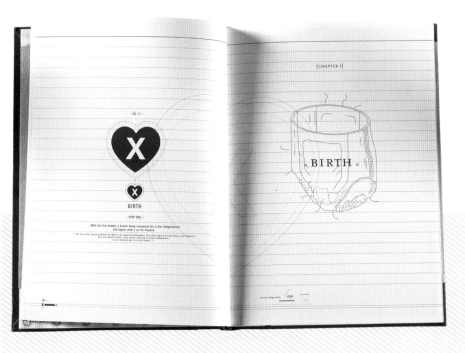

Photographic spreads are connected through a repeated headline, located at lower right, that enumerates ways of gaining independence from various entities or states of mind. The images are shot directly straight-on, whether of people, objects, or scenes, giving them an objective, journalistic quality. Their color and detail are rich and tonal.

Symbols, notations, statistical figures, and diagrams overlay the images to create a complex narrative the reader can explore.

This spread, the first in the life stages section, shows all the elements that appear on such opening spreads consistently among the sections. Iconography, illustration, and typography combine with notebook lines to evoke an academic feeling.

Some images are staged or altered to bring branded and conceptual content directly into the scene, as is the case in this spread showing a class-room environment. Note the images and writing on the blackboards.

> The basic idea is very serious and tightly linked to the company's values; the design and the tool itself is fun. So it is with our business: Taking it serious means having a lot of fun with it.

Jochen Rädeker, Creative Director

As a vehicle for demonstrating printing techniques on the client's paper, the designers use various methods, including varnishes and metallic foil-stamping, to enrich the textural qualities of the pages.

A photographic essay details the lives of truckers who spend long portions of the year on the road. The images are shot in an exaggerated, almost surreal, photojournalistic style that contrasts the directness of the earlier section.

The ever-changing visual and conceptual experience is held together by an organic mixture that relies on the client's corporate color red, the use of specific typographic treatments, and thematic consistency.

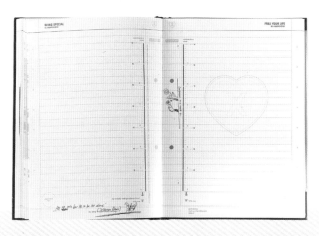

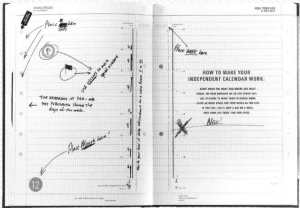

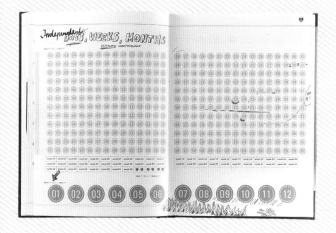

The opening spread features handwritten instructions. The combination of crisp, linear typography, icon details, and rough, scattershot handwriting continues the variation of visual language.

Stickers allow users to customize the calendar and help set goals that run from personal to world-changing. A sticker that suggests using only the company's paper reinforces

the brand message, but with a sense of humor and self-awareness.

19

Heide Museum of Art Exhibition Catalog Cover
GollingsPidgeon | Melbourne, Australia

The Heide Museum of Modern Art in Melbourne has long been a client of design firm GollingsPidgeon, who was responsible for developing their identity and wayfinding signage. The design firm also handles a multitude of publication projects related to the museum's exhibitions, including the catalogues. The museum needed to create a catalogue for *Living in landscape: Heide and houses by McGlashan and Everist,* an exhibition featuring the work of two award-winning architects who were responsible for designing one of the houses on the museum property, which has now become a gallery space. **|** "We wanted to differentiate this catalogue from those that simply use an image as a cover," says principal David Pidgeon. The exhibition catalogue highlights the importance of influences such as German architect Ludwig Mies van der Rohe and de Stijl artist Theo van Doesburg on the architecture of McGlashan and Everist. This influence, which is illustrated by the abstract nature of the floorplans, was the inspiration for both the text and cover design.

The Architecture of Book Covers

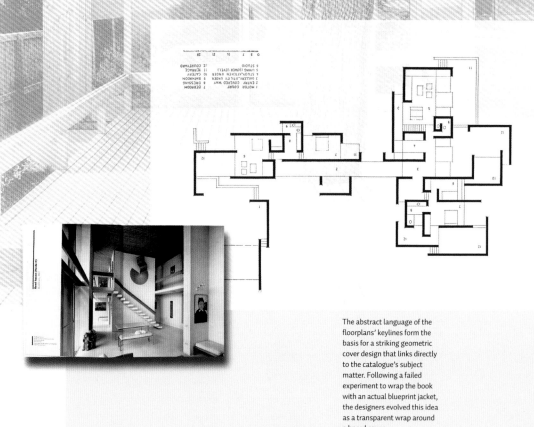

The abstract language of the floorplans' keylines form the basis for a striking geometric cover design that links directly to the catalogue's subject matter. Following a failed experiment to wrap the book with an actual blueprint jacket, the designers evolved this idea as a transparent wrap around a board cover.

Pidgeon and lead designer, Kate Rogers, developed an initial concept to print a blueprint floorplan of Heide II that would wrap in on itself and around the cover like a dust jacket. This approach wasn't pursued because the floorplan didn't suit this type of treatment and because of the associated costs. However, because of its significance to the project, Rogers continued developing the concept of using the Heide II floorplan as the basis for the cover. Investigating further, she proposed using a thick keyline composition, abstracted from the Heide II floorplan. ▌Pidgeon and

Rogers conceived of printing the floorplan on a translucent outer sheet that would wrap the cover. Preliminary versions, in which only the external walls were included, were more abstract and closer to the de Stijl style than the final version. More detail, such as windows and staircases, were added in a thinner keyline to ensure that the relationship between the Heide II floorplan and the composition wasn't lost. During the evolution, it was decided to print the title type on the board cover underneath, and die-cut the wrapper to let the type peek through. Rogers chose Grotesque for the head-

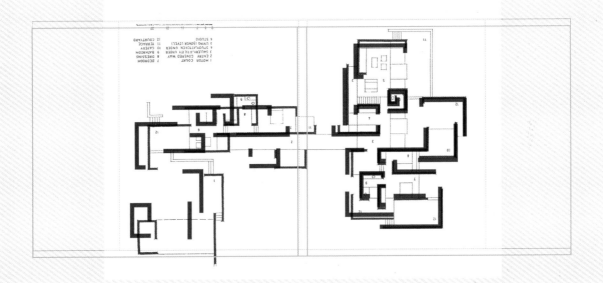

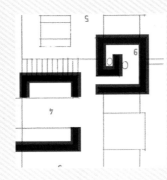

The floorplan drawing itself proved too delicate, needing thicker lines. The floorplan was re-created using drawing software so that global changes to line weights could be made more efficiently as needed.

I try to present one concept only; however, we often present the thinking process that led there, which may include alternate solutions from along the way. We still end up with one clear recommendation.

David Pigeon, Principal

DESIGN EVOLUTION

ings because it was sympathetic to the modernist style without being too obvious, as a face such as Akzidenz Grotesk might have been. ▌ "We briefly considered printing the inner cover fluorescent green so that the transparent line-work on the outer cover would add color to an otherwise monotone catalogue," Pidgeon relates. The client opted for a gray version of the cover instead because they felt this better suited the internal color palette. ▌ The cover design caused some production issues. To ensure that the catalogue title was legible, the transparent line-work on

the vinyl outer cover needed to register almost exactly with the type printed on the inner cover. ▌ Due to time restraints, the two elements had to be produced by different suppliers simultaneously, which meant there was no guarantee they would match up. The designers compromised by expanding the line-work slightly and hoping that the registration would be accurate.

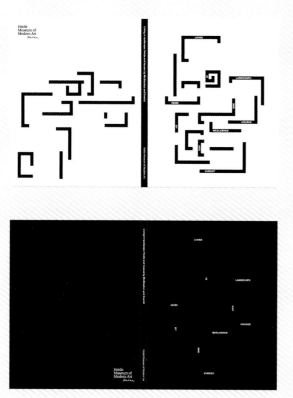

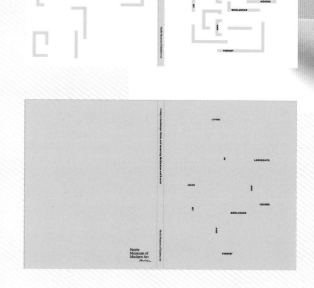

The designers experimented with the transparency of the outer wrap, eventually deciding the wrap would be more interesting if printed with an opaque white ink to allow hints of the book cover underneath to show through. This led them to consider a vivid green binding so that this color would glow through the floorplan's thin keyline openings.

The final cover, printed with white opaque ink, still retains some translucence, which adds dimension to the experience when in contact with the cover underneath.

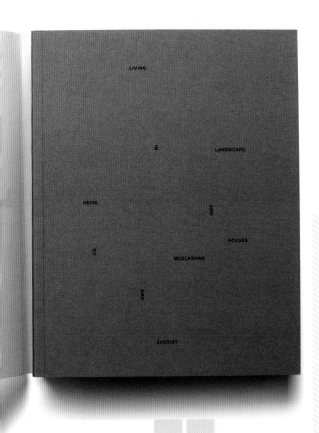

> By printing the cover in two parts, the outer a clear vinyl wrap screenprinted white to create transparent linework, the inner printed with solid color and type, we have transformed a flat, one-dimensional graphic composition into something that is reflective, textural, and interactive.

David Pigeon, Principal

The cover itself is printed with the exhibition's name in Grotesk as a nod to sans serif typefaces of the period referenced by the architect's work, and used throughout the interior of the catalog. Careful attention to positioning allows the individual words to lead the eye from one to the other, aided by the linear elements of the floorplan when the outer wrap is applied.

The cover's keylines echo those used within the page spreads as content dividers.

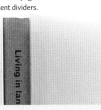

DESIGN EVOLUTION

20

American Players Theatre
2007 Summer Program Branding
Planet Propaganda | Madison, Wisconsin, USA

A Class Act,
A Lincout Above

What could be more fun than walking into the woods on a hazy summer evening to discover Julius Caesar, dappled with moonlight and leaf shadow? Such is the context of this project, developed for the American Players Theatre, a classical outdoor repertory theater company in Spring Green, Wisconsin. The drama of great performance, grand themes, color, costumes, and fresh night air come together in the expressively rustic print collateral created for the client's 2007 season by Planet Propaganda. The task for the designers is to develop an overall visual idea to promote the new season and attract theatergoers.

As a starting point in developing an illustration style for the season, themed to emphasize the outdoor aspect of the theatergoing experience, the designers pulled reference images from a variety of sources. Textural hand-drawn and woodcut images captured the rustic outdoor idea, as well as the human quality of the season's plays. Painterly images from the Polish poster tradition appealed for their dramatic sensibility.

While investigating illustrative style, the designers began to develop images for the various plays. These hand-drawn sketches show an emphasis on mythic, iconic, and elemental images—kings, fire, rockets, swords, crowns, the Moon, masks—as well as natural images—trees, leaves, birds, squirrels, and other forest dwellers. The clarity of the drawings makes a good record for the designer, as well as a way of communicating concepts with the client. Notations mark selected concepts to pursue further for individual plays.

Even from the start, without a thematic direction, the likelihood of an illustrative direction is good. "We've done APT for sixteen years," says Dana Lytle, one of Planet Propaganda's creative directors, "and have chosen illustration over photography all but one of those years. When we start work on the brochure, the APT season is still in flux. Illustration is a malleable medium that allows us to make adjustments based on the evolution of each play and of the season as a whole." ▌ This year, APT and Planet Propaganda decided to emphasize the fact that theatergoers attend the performances outside in the woods, itself an exciting and dramatic experience. APT began to adjust the season's lineup with intriguing selections of repertoire that seemed to emphasize the earthy and elemental. As the theme developed, the designers began to consider illustration styles that would complement these messages. ▌ They were drawn to historical woodcut illustrations, because of their handcrafted quality, and to Polish theater posters, which feature vibrant, surreal images and feel very dramatic. Taking this into account, the designers began sketching images that would lend themselves to the

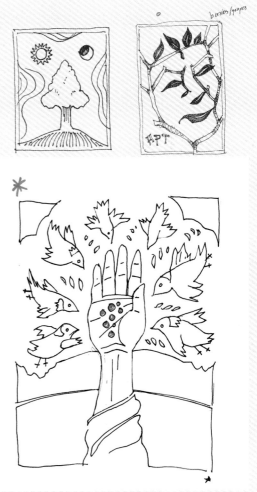

A general image for the season centered on the idea of a tree as a stage and birds as actors or audience. The naturalistic subject alluded to the elemental nature of that season's plays, as well as directly evoked the wooded venue outdoors.

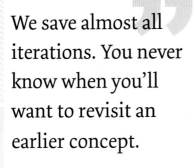

We save almost all iterations. You never know when you'll want to revisit an earlier concept.

Dana Lytle, Creative Director

theatrical subject matter. At a relatively early stage, these drawings were presented to the client, with examples of the kind of illustration they were intending to pursue—linoleum block prints. ▌Lytle clarifies this strategy: "Presenting one concept is unusual. But APT is an atypical client—the development of each season's materials is a very collaborative process… So while we may not offer them a choice of initial concepts, we rely heavily on their input throughout the creative process."

> There are no easy do-overs in linoleum block. One unfortunate slip of the knife or choice of line, and it's onto a fresh block.

Dana Lytle, Creative Director

Once the grand tree theme was paired with an illustration style—color linoleum cut prints—each play in the series underwent a similar evolution from initial sketches. This sequence shows the evolution of the image used to illustrate Thornton Wilder's *The Matchmaker*. Smaller conceptual thumbnails segue into larger, more detailed pencil drawings. Here, the illustrator investigates combining various image components related to the play's subject and incorporating the bird and tree images.

The bird becomes the title protagonist, occupying center stage. Objects such as wine goblets, figures, and fish replace trees; in another iteration, the field over which the central bird flies becomes a texture of other birds. Much of the process focuses on simplifying the number of elements and concentrating focus on the central character.

Subtle changes add and delete symbolic content. The shape of the bird's wing transforms from something naturalistic to a shape reminiscent of a hand. These kinds of details are more theatrical and help pack more information into the image using fewer elements.

The client signed off on the general direction, and the designers continued to develop subject matter for the illustrations, generating images showing grand, symbolic content and unconventional scale relationships. The images presented elemental characters in forest settings. A strong central tree image evokes the forest but also serves as a metaphor for the stage—a structure where nature's drama takes place—and birds populate the collateral as protagonists. ▮ Objects and secondary characters, symbolic of the individual plays' subjects, share in the spotlight. There is an odd, fairy-tale quality to the images that enhances their connection to the theater and the outdoor experience. ▮ Over the course of a few months, the drawings were refined, transferred to linoleum, and then cut for printing. Refinements were presented more as works in progress as they transpired in preparation for printing. "It's a gradual evolution, with the client involved every step of the way, rather than the more usual series of milestones and revisions," Lytle explains.

The final inked drawing is transferred to a linoleum block, which is cut in relief for inking.

The printed images were scanned and separated for four-color printing; the designers adjusted the color separations to maintain the freshness of the block-printed inks.

MA

D

Our knock-your-socks-
A big-hearted comedy
The world's one ripe an
Have a grand time adve

Off we go on a fast-pace
characters we're traveli
a lot of heart and spicy

Meet the charismaticall
guessed it. This is the c
was adapted.) She's pla
hilarity to Brian Rober
Vandergelder. He's out
over his household. Fre

Talk about romantic in
being conjured in our r
identities and twists an
their mitts on this. Wit
Paul Bentzen whipped

One of those great feel-
of that kind of magic t
and leap outside of tha
hours. ❀ OPENS JUNE

THE MATCHMAKER · ROMEO AND JULIET · MEASURE FOR MEASURE · ARMS AND THE MAN · JUL

AMERICAN PLAYERS THEATRE
2006

It's a classic design paradox: the more organic and seemingly unstructured the aesthetic, the more careful editing is required to pull it off successfully. At the same time, we trusted our gut.

Dana Lytle, Creative Director

Alongside the continued evolution of the illustrations, the designers introduced equally rustic typography, with an eclectic mixture of hand-cut letters, decorative elements and slab serifs. ▌The illustration style called out for a strong, elemental palette—as did the fact that the marketing push reaches Wisconsin theatergoers in late winter, when the landscape is at its grayest and dreariest. The vibrant, summery color is a welcome part of the sales pitch.

In the main season poster, the tree image has pride of place, growing up from the bottom of the format and branching outward. An iconic sword communicates passion and danger; droplets of blood drip down its blade into the elemental earth, feeding the roots of the mythic tree. A delicate bird perches among the leaves, while a

decrepit-looking raven approaches. A palette of browns, green, gold, red, and blue—subdued for richness to avoid a cheap, carnival-like quality—support the rugged strength of the image. Their chromatic simplicity—primary hues that are more simple to understand—evokes the elemental quality of the plays.

Print collateral adopts a direct, somewhat casual, sometimes irreverent tone in the writing that complements the images and rough-hewn type. The collateral system—program, ticketing guide, schedule—avoid complication in the typography, relying instead on centered structure, a bookish serif, and an assortment of wood-type gothics and slab serifs. The casual nature of the headlines contrast with the quiet text settings.

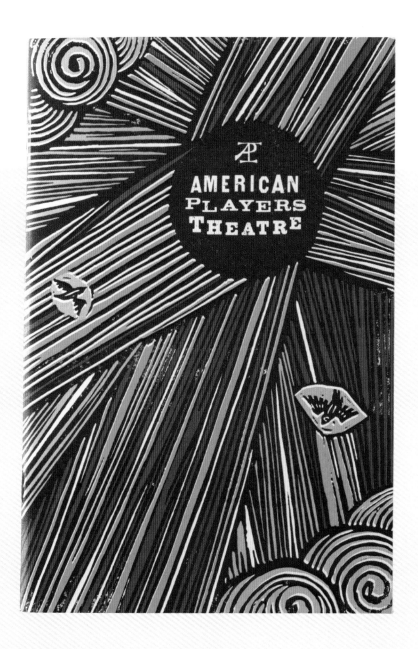

Supporting graphic details, also cut from linoleum block and printed, are used to support the major images throughout the collateral. Even simple pieces are made richer and more clearly a part of the program with these additions.

ARMS AND THE MAN

by GEORGE BERNARD SHAW
Directed by JAMES BOHNEN

A young woman alone in a dark bedroom. Gunfire explodes in the streets below. As she cringes in fear, the shutters slowly pull open and the figure of a man clambers inside.

Thus begins one delightful comedy on the absurdities of love and war. Opened to raves in London, 1894. Hugely popular to this day. Welcome aboard. You're in for quite a treat as our acting company sinks its talents into a world famous show.

Colleen Madden plays Raina, the woman above, whose romantic notion of love (and war) is stood on its head when a desperate, beaten soldier on the run climbs in through that bedroom window. What fun. Tricky part is, her fiancé fights for the other side. That's Jim DeVita. A ridiculously courageous cavalryman. Preening peacock besides.

You'll have an ache in your side, bursting with mirth as this threesome entangles itself in Raina's lovably dysfunctional family. Sarah Day is her snob of a mom. Paul Bentzen's the dad, a Major who's majorly befuddled. Their maid is a volatile volcano. She's craved by the pragmatic valet.

Shaw's a play writing genius for sure. His work lyric with wisdom, hilarity and charm. The repartee zings. In laughter your spirit will wing. Leaving you feeling so light on your feet, you just might glide down the hill to the parking lot after. OPENS AUGUST 12

THE PLAYS

"WHAT HAPPENS UP THE HILL ON THAT STAGE LEAVES ME AMAZED. FOR DAYS."

THE MATCHMAKER

by THORNTON WILDER
Directed by WILLIAM BROWN

MEASURE FOR MEASURE

by WILLIAM SHAKESPEARE
Directed by KENNETH ALBERS

In this outrageous comedy, the arrogance of power runs amok among the affairs of church and state. Neither which escapes Shakespeare's engaging, scathing satire enlivened by a rowdy bunch of characters unlike any other in the world of Bard-dom.

Vienna's become a Sin City of moral decay and decadence. The ruling Duke's lost control, so he puts his Deputy in charge to clean up the mess, and then skips town. At least that's what everyone thinks. The Duke actually stays around in a monk's disguise, spends the play pulling strings in the wings.

Meanwhile, the vice squad is unleashed to purge iniquity's dens. Problem is, the new ruling Deputy can't seem to control his own illicit desires. He agrees to pardon the condemned brother of a nun provided she agrees to jump into bed. That's when the fireworks begin. By the end, we've got a severely severed head, a bedroom switcheroo and enough power abuse to cook that Deputy's goose.

What bark. What bite. This play's got fantastical powers to incite. With Jim DeVita as the Deputy taking a run at Colleen Madden the nun, while Brian Robert Mani looks on as the Duke in disguise. Sarah Day plays the Madame of Tarts with a tongue that's sharp and Paul Bentzen's a revered advisor worth listening to. Grabbing great seats now is definitely the thing to do. OPENS JUNE 29

YOUR MASSIVE SAVINGS

"WHEN I BUY MY TICKETS NOW I FEEL LIKE A MILLION BUCKS. AND SAVE ALMOST AS MUCH."

20% OFF
every single ticket for any show on any date. Its that simple. That complete. Save 20% on every seat.

30% OFF
September and October shows when added at the same time as your summer show order. On the joy of your fall comeback at incredible savings.

BONUS BENEFIT! FREE TICKET EXCHANGE.

BEAT THE DEADLINE OF
JUNE 9, 2006.

YOUR CALL TO ACTION
LOUD AND CLEAR.

How does the trumpet sound from ramparts o'er this forest land. Summoning you to the Theatre in the woods.

To smash the icy grip of old man winter. And awaken gentle summer from her slumber.

ACROSS THE NATION HEADLINES BLARE.

"APT THE BEST, BARD NONE."
Across the Chicago Tribune

"The curtain level of classical work here is without self-evident Midwestern peer."
The Wall Street Journal agrees.

"APT fills its naturally beautiful performing space with simply staged classics that I might call.

"BROADWAY QUALITY"
APT sees a Broadway revival lately that was half so good."
Milwaukee Journal Sentinel is pleased.

"A REMARKABLE YEAR FOR APT.
The company produced the best work in its 36 outstanding seasons."

JULIUS CAESAR

by WILLIAM SHAKESPEARE
Directed by SANFORD ROBBINS

Thrill to the action up the hill. Its fervid pulse beats. The pounding of destiny beneath your feet. This gripping political thriller spins such a web, you're totally immersed in a mesmerizing spectacle.

Find yourself among cheering, enthusiastic crowds welcoming mighty Caesar home to Rome in triumph. Feel the knot of a deadly plot tighten as conspirators coalesce around Brutus and Cassius. Recoil in shock and awe as those assassins converge upon the Emperor, slashing him open.

Spellbound, you witness Mark Antony pouring his heart out over Caesar's dead body. Incites the mob to murderous riot, hell-bent on revenge. You're swept along to barren battlefields where murderers meet an ignominious end. Their ideals could never justify that single act of savagery. Indeed, from ancient Rome to now, this is a work for our time, for all time. In a world where history continues to be written in blood.

The rock solid core of our acting company has been cast. Brian Robert Mani plays Caesar. David Daniel is Mark Antony and Jonathan Smoots the conflicted Brutus, paired with Tracy Michelle Arnold as his wife Portia.

From the beautiful soaring of its language to the profound psychological ache embedded in its soul, this is one powerful show. OPENS AUGUST 10

Careful attention to vertical spacing intervals, column widths, and cross-gutter alignments helps enliven the symmetrical page arrangements.

Color and type contrast is managed to enhance hierarchies and ensure legibility.

21

Toronto Film Studios
Identity and Website
Compass 360, Inc. | Toronto, Canada

"Film studios are often marketed as just big boxes for rent," says Compass 360 founder and creative director, Karl Thomson. "We've given Toronto Film Studios a distinct identity that is unique in the industry. All of the elements are refined, and yet the tone of our advertising copy is typically Canadian in its humor. It's managed to raise their profile in the entertainment world, and has put them front-and-center in the Toronto market." And despite its seeming simplicity, it offers a good degree of conceptual depth, and practically designed the website itself. Plus, it's red.

Four Squares and a Hot Red: That's a Wrap

It's important that the client is in the right frame of mind to review creative material, and we work hard to ensure good grounding in the options we're presenting. We encourage discussion as we're presenting, and our clients most always find themselves engaged by the time we've presented our first ideas.

Karl Thomson, Creative Director

The designers worked directly on the computer to explore typographic concepts for the logo, focusing on a generally neutral approach with very subtle references to the idea of film.

Line elements separating a horizontal configuration of letters to suggest film frames. The substitution of the letter *i* with four squares, representing the four lots of TFS property, creates a vertical filmstrip; the radial-cornered box evokes a screen. The vertical lines separate the type forms into a ticket.

Stacking the three words in the box configuration alludes to the clacker.

The process leading up to the launch of Toronto Film Studios' award-winning website began with the development of the identity. The client had approached Compass 360 to help position them as the premiere Canadian studio facility, and part of that positioning was rebranding them. ▌The initial logo development phase, a month-long endeavor, began almost immediately on the computer, although some sketch. "It depends on the designer," says Karl. "But working in black and white on our computers is helpful simply because it allows us to see the core idea unhindered by the visual distraction of color." ▌These core ideas focused on typographic studies, many of which highlighted the word FILM and, with subtle treatments of configuration or linear detail, referred to filmstrips and other industry symbols. After several rounds internally, Compass 360 presented a single concept to their client, one in which the word FILM is separated into four quadrant boxes that represent a map of the building lots where the studios are located. ▌"For identities, we'll show between three and five [concepts]... In the case of TFS, because the advertising is a direct extension of the brand,

Among the candidates the team considered in the exploration was the version presented to the client: the word "FILM" configured in four quadrants, with the remaining type situated above and below. It's a subtle reference,

as is the four-square *i* in another concept, to the four building lots occupied by the client, and where their shooting and service facilities are located.

> "Red is dynamic, it's arresting, and it works really well in an environment cursed with visual clutter. There is one huge wall of a building on the TFS lot that faces a high-traffic road in downtown Toronto. That wall is painted with the eye-searing solid red with the words "Now Playing" in white type aside the TFS logo.
>
> Karl Thomson, Creative Director

The serif face was discarded in favor of unifying all the type elements within one style. The black type elements are sized so that their stroke weights are optically equal to those of the red squares. The word "FILM," set larger, separates itself through bolder weight.

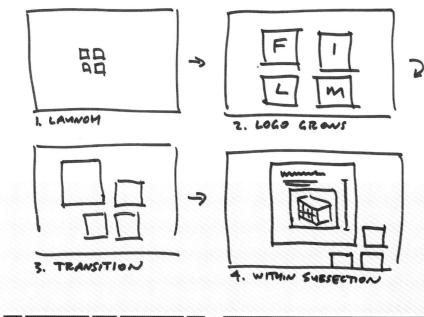

1. LAUNCH

2. LOGO GROWS

3. TRANSITION

4. WITHIN SUBSECTION

> Although we've learned to trust our instincts, very little of our design process is unconscious. Each and every aspect of every design is carefully considered.

Karl Thomson, Creative Director

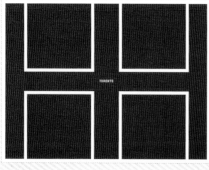

The website nearly designed itself. Given the maplike quality of the four logo squares, dividing the limited content into four major categories was intuitive. This sketch captures, in a few quick strokes, what the site would become.

The site's launch sequence, in its original and current forms, shows slight variation on the same concept: the creation of four squares that contain content, arranged in quadrant formation. Interestingly, the complete logo occurs nowhere on the site. Only the word "FILM," appearing in this sequence, is ever seen.

we presented a single visual design with a variety of copy directions for the headlines," he continues. ▌The TFS management group understood Compass 360's creative direction and approved it with virtually no changes needed. Karl and company moved onto designing the stationery, which took about three weeks. "The TFS logo represents the very essence of what the facility provides," says Karl excitedly. "The magic of movies are created within the four little blocks, the sound stages, and other buildings on the TFS lot." Given the clarity of the identity and the ease with which

its grid-based form helped articulate the stationery, it's not surprising that the website was nearly complete in its conception after a single sketch. ▌Again, the architectural underpinning of the logo directed the vision of the site's organization—navigating among the quadrants—and the possibility of vector animation meant being able to do so interactively. Thompson and Buchner showed the client the sketch and a sample screen shot, generated digitally… and they were off and running. The site opens with a quick, spatial animation of the FILM squares that sets up the quadrant-based

navigation. The user moves among the four "lots" of the virtual studio quadrants to access simply structured pages with pertinent information. B-level navigation within these areas happens through typographic buttons.

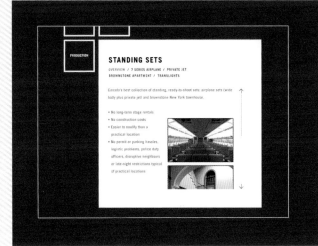

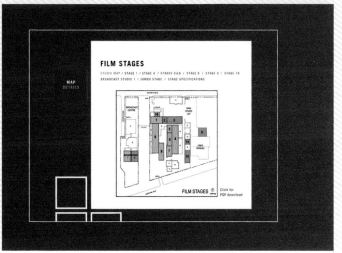

Each quadrant enlarges and fills white to support content. An austere, single-line navigation system for sublevel content within the selected A-level presents a clear and scalable option should these links be changed or added to in the future. Content appears in the lower portion of the white field, with supporting text to the right or left as needed.

The remaining A-level quadrants display their links on mouse over.

Transitions between each quadrant are quick and fluid, connoting efficiency, purpose, and attention to detail. Custom scrollbars add to the sense of detail.

22

Henry's Drive Vignerons Branding and Packaging Program
Parallax Design | Adelaide, Australia

Something to Write Home About

Viniculture is a rich and storied human endeavor, dating back thousands of years. The foundations of a wine's quality and character are the lands on which the vineyard rests, the regional climate, and the philosophy of winemaking the vintner brings. With such profound ties to the land and to the people that live there, local history is a rich source for identification and narrative—it's what breathes life into the wine brand. Matthew Remphrey of Parallax Design captures this history in branding Henry's Drive Vignerons, a South Australian winery. During the nineteenth century, the driver of the mail coach from Adelaide to Melbourne, in South Australia, rested his horses on the land now owned by Remphrey's client. The proprietor of the mail coach service, Henry Hill, became the vineyard's namesake, and the romantic notion of the postal service the basis for the brand exploration Remphrey undertook.

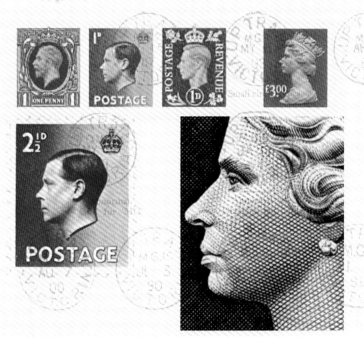

While some rough hand-sketching preceded full-blown development, Remphrey moved very quickly into creating artwork for the various elements of the identity after showing the image research that supported his central idea—nineteenth century postage and related ephemera. This direction, and the vineyard's name, stemmed from the fact that a local mail carrier rested his horses on the property before it became a vineyard.

Cancellation stamps, mailing stamps, postal tickets, and the surfaces of letterboxes all contribute possibilities toward a varied, textural environment.

"Our goal was to develop a strong and relevant brand that separates Henry's Drive Vignerons from its competition and gives the consumer a reason to connect with it," Remphrey says. He continues, "Henry's Drive's customers are experienced wine consumers—collectors, aficionados, sommeliers and restaurateurs. We developed the brand based on this criteria." ▌Remphrey always begins sketching, both by hand and using a photocopier, to acquire a sense of scale and texture in a physical way. This initial process took roughly four weeks before a first presentation. At that stage, it's

A collection of stamp samples combines with the designer's hand sketches, investigating what will eventually become the vineyard's "logo." The drawn stamp detail is the birth of the letterhead concept— stamp images representing the owners, hand-cancelled with a custom rubber stamp. This early on, Remphrey is also thinking ahead to product con- cepts. This sketch for the Pillar Box Red varietal—named after a letter-drop box—presages the variety of approaches the branding will assimilate.

The wine industry is extremely fragmented and unlike most other indus- tries. If you want to buy a $20 bottle of Australian shiraz, you have literally hundreds of choices. Most of these look generic—like the category—and fail to engage the consumer at all.

Matthew Remphrey, Principal

customary for Remphrey to show sketches and fragments, rather than finished-looking executions, inviting the client into the discussion of the concepts Remphrey feels are most viable. "Sometimes we may only hone our thoughts down to one direction. It depends on feedback at the early stage and the solutions we begin to develop. I rarely present three ideas, and never more." Aside from the discussion, there's nothing special Remphrey and his team do for presentation, other than "Listen, and include them." ▌From that conversation, the client entrusted Parallax with pursuing a central idea: the romantic feeling of nineteenth-century postage. "We looked for authentic expressions. Illustration style, printing techniques, paper stock, and color are influenced by the ephemera of the period." ▌In particular, Remphrey gathered samples of stamps and cancellation marks to devise a logo that could be cleverly altered. For the client and his wife, the co-owner of the vineyard, Remphrey commissioned profile portraits based on engraved stamps, which are printed on the letterheads and then cancelled—by hand—with a custom-made stamp. The stamp acts as a logo of sorts,

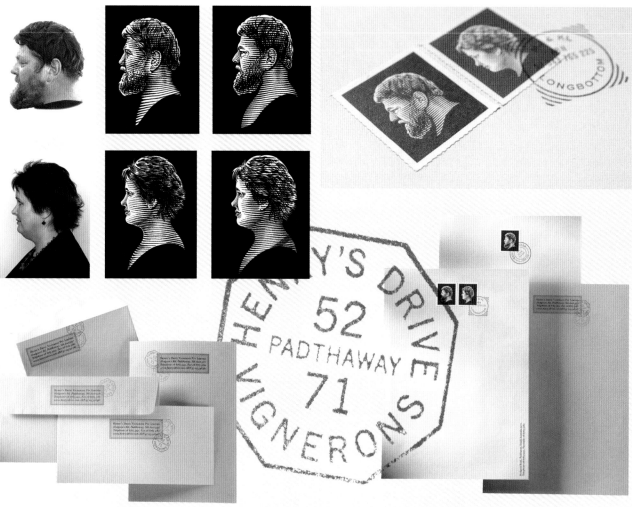

From photographic reference, an illustrator executes Remphrey's engraved-stamp portraits of the client and his co-owner wife in black-and-white ink. The progression results in a finely wrought period-style illustration that is traced and finessed using drawing software.

The rubber stamp for the cancellation was custom made using drawing software, cast in rubber, then physically stamped onto letterhead.

The stationery suite expands the postal concept with paper stock of varied colors and the inventive use of a mail-bag tie-tag as a business card. This mix of three-dimensional forms and abstracted symbolic elements creates a rich, romantic, metaphorical experience.

but it easily acts as an image—as a repeated texture on promotional mailers, for instance. This individuality to of the various projects covered by the identity—promotions, bottling, media kits, and so on—creates an opportunity to be specific with image messages and to vary the mix of illustration, typography, and symbolism throughout. ▌The authenticity of the concept is the guiding force, "But," as Remphrey says, "we aim to include a twist with the execution or of individual concepts to make them relevant to a contemporary audience." Old-World letterpress printing techniques, for

example, meld with bright colors and unusual labeling applications, such as the rubber band that secures a label card and "letter" to the magnum bottle. For business cards, a mail-bag's tag is cunningly printed with the vine-yard's information, and can be used as a closure device for the folder, whose shape is derived from a letter-carrier's pouch and printed inside with enormous handwriting. The historical metaphor is lifted from being a merely literal derivative and given life through unusual scale changes, color, and intermixing of effects.

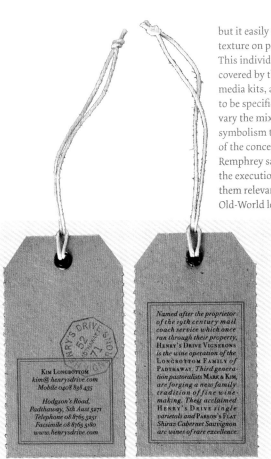

The idea of the written letter is abstracted through scale change in this flapped folder, fashioned after a letter-carrier's folio.

> I spend a lot of effort on refinement. The Henry's Drive magnum is a good example of this, with its handmade envelope enclosing the postcard and ticket.

Matthew Remphrey, Principal

No amount of reworking or refinement could improve this quickly scrawled mark that became the brand for the varietal known as Dead Letter Office. Clever manipulation—the crossed pens, the double stamps, and the downturned envelope flap—transforms these mundane postal elements into a skull-and-crossbones symbol.

The label for Dead Letter Office shows how decisive sizing and placement yields a sense of loose spontaneity. The visual push and pull between the envelope-symbol rectangle (darker and smaller) and the red stamp (larger, lighter, and irregular), along with the off-set type (note the alignment between the initial capital and the center axis of the crossed pens) all contribute to the layout's unfussy presentation.

The bottling and other product packaging continually evolves the postage theme in various directions. Mixing and matching the individual elements from the brand's varied assets—handwriting, stamps, postcards, labeling, tickets, engraving—creates an organic system not hampered by con-

ventional branding concepts. The Reserve Shiraz bottle plays with dimensionality by printing the handwritten texture on the bottle surface, but holding the trompe l'oeil postcards label on with a letter carrier's rubber band.

Writing makes another appearance on the small portfolio that carries a set of promotional postcards (appropriately enough). Each card is designed individually to reflect its individualized brand. Pillar Box Red's card, for instance, employs a die-cut as a letter slot.

23

Adobe Systems, Inc. Design Conference and Trade Show Environment
AdamsMorioka, Inc. | Beverly Hills, California, USA

What's Your Big, Bedazzling Idea?

For the past twenty years, Adobe Systems has been the industry leader in developing software tools for design visualization and production; there is no graphic designer working today who doesn't interact with an Adobe product. The company has been helping the design community do what it does for so long, it's difficult to imagine why a trade show presence would be necessary at all. "We feel that especially for larger companies it is crucial to stay in touch with their consumers, being approachable and true to their core brand promise," says Sean Adams, principal of the design studio charged with creating just such an exhibit.

AdamsMorioka developed an overall convention floor presence, including the print collateral that accompanied the booth. Conceptual development, however, began focused on the booth experience itself, and in digital form. These pages from the preliminary presentation explore the team's ideas about engaging the attendee—and making them feel as though they're the important part of the equation.

This concept presented a wall of rhythmically animated lightbulbs, supported by an LED ticker displaying text generated on laptops in the booth area. The lightbulbs were considered a safety hazard because of the heat they would generate, but their pixel-like quality was something that stuck with the designers.

"We wanted Adobe to make their audience feel that they are being understood." There is, after all, a sea of competitors, and designers will jump on the next best thing when it comes along. And the best way to do that, of course, is to be the next thing. ▮ Along with partner Noreen Morioka, Adams and the studio team accomplished that with a vibrant environmental display for the company at the HOW Design Conference that captures the responsive, forward-looking aspirations of the design community's technological partner. ▮ "Since we're part of the target audience of creative

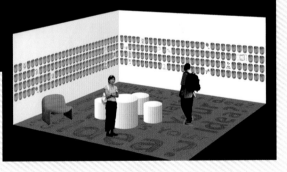

We never talk about design with clients. We talk about message and results. And we listen. Certain clients aren't articulate with design language; it's our job to translate what they are saying, getting to the core of their issues.

Noreen Morioka, Principal

These concepts showed video presentation that could be updated by conference attendees; this interaction put the visual aspects of the display in the hands of the audience.

This concept showed walls of fans that hid ideas, drawn on the surfaces underneath. The carpet in this concept was intended to be woven or printed with the slogan "What's Your Big Idea?"

> Design that seems extremely simple is very carefully crafted. The trick is to make it seem effortless and natural.

Monica Schlaug, Designer

professionals, we simply asked ourselves "How would we want to experience Adobe at these events?"" Morioka shrugs. So rather than running to the drawing board or mouse, the designers—Volker Dürre, acting as art director, along with Christopher Taillon and Monica Schlaug—started by discussing the experience they wanted to create for the audience, sketching out rough ideas in a way Morioka describes as 'whacky.' ▌ "We draw in such a basic way that it is indistinguishable from bad handwriting. In fact, the two go hand in hand at AdamsMorioka," she jokes. The designers focused on a perceived

need for designers to feel appreciated. "They want a platform to voice their perspective," says Volker Dürre. ▌ The team felt it important to reposition Adobe as an integral part of the design community, having reinvented itself as more than a mere software company. "Adobe understands the creative community and wants to highlight achievements in creative expression," says Adams. "It's not about tools, it's about the mindset." ▌ The six concepts AdamsMorioka first showed Adobe revolved around dynamic, illuminated visual displays. One concept proposed 2,000 lightbulbs that

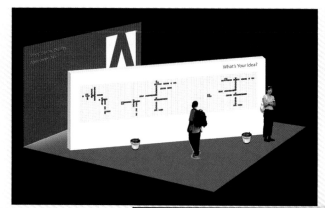

Top: Another way to engage visitors, this concept presented a whiteboard wall with markers and a crossword puzzle–like grid where messages could be written.

could be animated—one for each conference attendee—but with further investigation, it was abandoned as a safety risk. Another concept proposed a digital ticker displaying changing conceptual mantras. Another allowed attendees to interactively add images and text to a video wall display. This concept seemed to work well with another that was shown, a giant whiteboard that attendees could use to make their ideas known. ▌These rough ideas all fed on a direct, written challenge that clarified Adobe's role and positioned the audience first and foremost: "Everything but the idea. What's yours?"

Based on Adobe's enthusiasm, the designers explored ways of making it happen. "Once we greenlight a direction," Morioka says, "we look at it with fresh eyes, trying to find other expressions that can be utilized for the context." This strategy led them to locating another technology that could replace the video wall and lightbulbs—which seemed appropriately pixel-like—and to investigate the interactivity aspect with greater depth. ▌The discovery of a modular cell lightwall thrilled them, and they decided to create an animation for the wall to add color to the space. 1920s fabric designs

from the Bauhaus somehow entered their consciousness. "What would these look like if they had been designed on a computer?" they asked themselves. ▌The aesthetic and the color scheme for the animation derived from this idea, and it was executed in-house. "Amazingly," remarks Schlaug, "one pixel of the animation exactly mapped one unit on the lightwall. So the QuickTime movie playing was a tiny 25 x 65 pixels." On the reverse of the lightwall, the designers set up a giant blackboard wall that conference attendees could use to write or draw on—to express the creativity that is at he heart

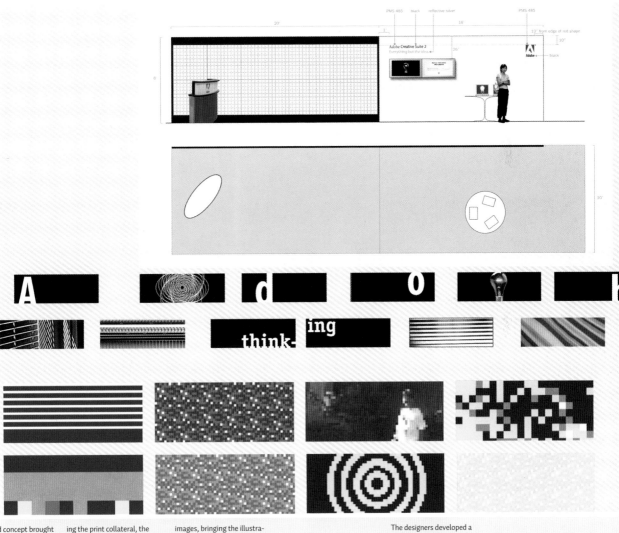

The approved concept brought together the idea of the video wall, visitor input and another positioning statement: "Everything but the idea. What's yours?" Looking for ways to solve the hot lightbulb dilemma, the designers came upon a video wall technology that replicated the pixel-like quality of the lightbulbs. During the process of design-

ing the print collateral, the writers introduced the designers to illustrator Peter Arkle, whose quirky drawings added a human element—the idea— to the cleanly organized layouts. The design team decided to install a giant blackboard on the backside of the video wall. Arkle's opening drawing would invite visitors to participate with their own words and

images, bringing the illustrative quality—and an ancient form of community communication—into the modern context of the floorplan. The choice of medium for both old and new is directly, almost literally, related to the historical development of writing and image making.

The designers developed a looping animation for the video wall. They discovered, by chance, that the cells in the wall would display the pixels in the animation one-to-one, no matter how large—the animation file was extremely small, as the selected frames here show.

of Adobe's core mission. Bringing this human element into printed materials meant sourcing an illustrator; the writer taking care of the conference literature introduced the team to Peter Arkle. ▌ "The illustrations that Peter Arkle did for us were a wonderful contrast to the rest of the design elements, resulting in a high-tech / low-tech juxtaposition that many people immediately understood and appreciated." Arkle started the drawings on the wall at the conference, encouraging attendees to take over. The project underwent six weeks of design refinement and sourcing of viable

manufacturing, and then several months as individual deliverables were needed. The date of the actual events set a very specific timetable that could not be negotiated. To simplify the booth and contrast the activity of both sides of the wall, white walls and a cool gray carpet were all that were added to the space.

The form-making may be the result of happy accidents and deliberate actions, but nothing is on the page or screen that doesn't have a reason to be.

Sean Adams, Principal

Print collateral, with its grid-structured organization of square-cropped images, text columns, and Arkle's illustration, merged seamlessly with similar elements in the three-dimensional booth.

Arkle begins the illustration on the community blackboard wall.

The illumination of the space attracted crowds from across the convention hall.

> Most trade show venues feature dim lights and unattractive carpets. The sheer impact of the lightwall was startling. It had a warm glow that could be seen from the other end of the hall. Visitors flocked to it like moths to the flame.

Volker Dürre, Art Director

24

Kohn Pederson Fox Architects Website
Firstborn | New York and Los Angeles, USA

The notion of architecture as an idea has been part of graphic design practice for many years. The Swiss Modernist Josef Müller-Brockmann spoke of typography in terms of its architectural qualities; Richard Saul Wurman invented the notion of "information architect." Guiding an audience through visual/verbal experience in print is very much like establishing flow through three-dimensional space, governed by—as architects themselves like to say—a "program": a specific usage concept. When the two disciplines met in the new spatial frontier—the Internet—Web developers Firstborn built an organized site for award-winning firm Kohn Pederson Fox Architects that shows exactly what architecture is all about.

Into Space and Guided through Structure

The new KPF.com is about presenting the company in a visual manner, to tell the story of the company and the complexity in each of its buildings.

Luba Shekhter, Producer

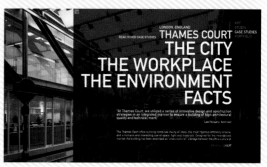

One of the preliminary concepts presented to the client exploited the rich photography in full-screen form. A darkened, transparent frame containing typographic navigation links, expanded and contracted—as did the type itself—as the user browsed among the links.

Clear changes in size and value among the type elements—i.e., larger and brighter when selected—established a clear hierarchy.

The design team started off "on a very high note," recalls then-creative director Vas Sloutchevsky. "This was a project we really wanted to sink our teeth into," adds Jeremy Berg, executive producer for the project. "We were thrilled to be working on an architecture site…. We saw eye to eye with this client." This initial excitement, while never flagging, was tempered by the early realization of the project's enormous complexity. First, the client maintains two offices—one in New York, and the other in London—and the difference of opinion

This concept presented the building images as a backdrop, set into a white frame and overlapped by a small box containing the navigation. Color change, rather than size, indicated activity on mouse over, and a click expanded the box to display the selected link's B-level, or subpage, navigation. The same logic applied through deeper and deeper levels as the user drilled down into the content.

The third concept presented a single image, enclosed in a white frame and disrupted by a lightly textured grid. The grid panes were labeled for content, and indicated their active state with a "smart box" on mouse over. Clicking zoomed the user inward to another structure and then deeper still into case studies. The lower-level navigation was hidden in a pull-down menu accessed from the top of the page.

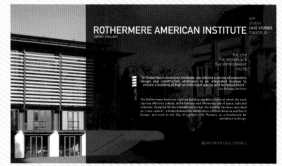

The client asked to have two concepts developed further. The navigation in the concept shown above was simplified without losing the kinetic energy. The size difference between the smallest (not accessed) and largest, (selected) A-level type was dramatically increased, and fewer A-levels remained visible as the user drills down into the site. Some supporting detail information was also deleted to open space and simplify texture. In spite of these improvements, this concept was not chosen.

between the two resulted in the Firstborn team having to conduct dozens of interviews with key personnel to establish some commonality in desired approach. ▌ Adding to the scope of variables to consider was KPF's beginnings as a boutique firm; having grown into a global player, they were often perceived as a commercial conglomerate despite remaining a small firm, and they still considered themselves "boutique." Last was the overwhelming breadth of material—years' worth of award-winning structures, industry accolades, important articles. All these made for a daunting task.

After two weeks of intense work, the eight-person team presented three concepts, distilled from dozens—each a search for a precise, tactile, and engaging way of expressing KPF's forward-thinking approach to architecture. The concept that engaged the client immediately presented the content through a navigation structure that resembled floors with stairwells between them, which they considered "explorative." ▌ A tidy grid-based structure overlayed on the images permitted users to "zoom into" more in-depth information, making each page a kind of individuated case study. One of the

benefits of this concept was that it communicated the method of accessing complex levels of information intuitively and architecturally. ▌ Having secured approval for the design direction, a period of refinement began. One huge task—developing a back end content management system for the client to be able to update the site's content—ran parallel to the task of visually refining the site. Font styles, supporting details, and the flow of interactive transitions, were all in an ongoing state of flux for three months: the "pixel-pushing," as Berg refers to it. "Font-changing, bounding-box

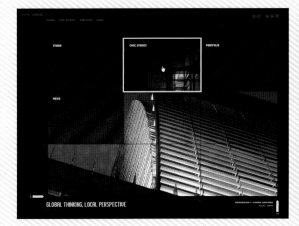

> We had video conferences across the Atlantic to discuss little things like the thickness of the "smart frame" in pixels. I remember it took us a while to agree on a thickness of three pixels.

Vas Sloutchevsky, Project Creative Director

The first thing to change in this concept's evolution toward launch was to place the full navigation as a stepped series of links across the top of the image frame, instead of hiding them in a pull-down. The horizontal structure allowed for more B-level links to be listed, so that each vertical line could be devoted to A-levels. Supporting text and links to more detailed content in the case studies was shifted to locations around the outer frame, and the frame itself changed shape to accommodate buildings of differing proportions and varied amounts of text.

pixel-width shrinking, endless e-mails explaining what a pixel font was … and why the point size could not be enlarged," he intones. Plus, the sheer size of the job converting images of the architecture was enormous. "There are about 900 different images of buildings. Each image has four different dimensions: high resolution, large, medium, and thumbnail size," Berg continues. The multiple image sizes reflects the user's ability to enlarge images as they see fit—an outgrowth of the grid-based zoom-in navigation idea, and the "big-ticket" item in terms of interactivity, according to

Berg. "This effect is particularly rewarding on a large monitor with high resolution. Clicking on an image will fill the screen as much as possible, which is cool when viewing panoramic images." Another feature that some consider special is the sudden change of screen background from black to white. "It's such a simple effect," says Luba Shekhter, another producer on the project, "but the results are dramatic." ▌Both the team and the client were happy with the results. One of the original goals KPF expressed in their brief to Firstborn was that it should appeal to the general public—that peo-

ple would send the URL to friends with a note: CHECK THIS OUT. Says Berg proudly: "Mission accomplished."

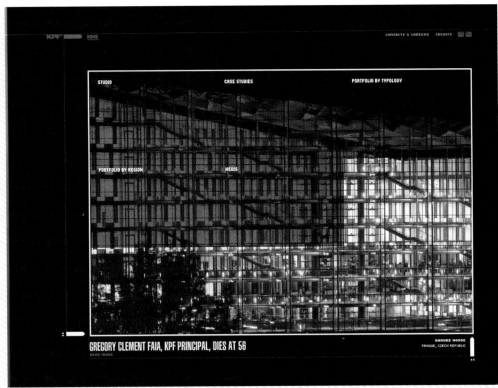

Despite the intimidating appearance of the sharp, linear grid and deep, black field, the navigation is intuitive and easy to use. This sequence shows the interactivity of the "smart box" that travels with the cursor as it mouses over the panes in the grid. The smart box snaps into position as it highlights a selected A-level.

Site development amounted to roughly fourteen weeks, but it took closer to nine months for the site to go live. After what seemed like a never-ending project, we launched a site that was as close to perfect as we could have made it. And you know what? We love it, imperfections and all.

Jeremy Berg, Executive Producer

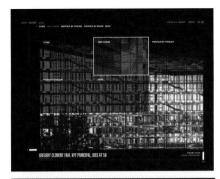

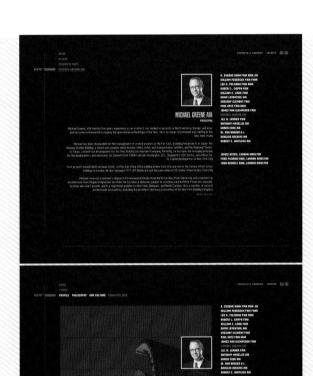

The typographic links at the top are aliased and well-spaced to accommodate the coarse resolution of the screen, and the resulting mechanical feeling corresponds to the geometry and precision of the architecture and other graphic details.

A sliding bar at the left locates the user within the stack of A-levels for quick reference. A color change from white to red indicates the selected B-level.

The company profile area follows the same logic as the remainder of the site, using a smaller-module grid for architects' portraits.

25

Moonlight Cinema 2007 Identity
Studio Pip & Company | Melbourne, Australia

The very word "moonlight" conjures an array of feelings and emotions, from shivery fear to surreal passion, and everything in between. The night is a time for mystery and a little madness—and a whole lot of fun, especially if there's a movie involved. Moonlight Cinema is a nation-wide, outdoor cinema concern in Australia, operating public outdoor theaters in five Australian cities from Melbourne to Sydney. Studio Pip & Company's principal Andrew Ashton succeeded in creating a vivid pictorial experience to promote the theater chain that could safely be described as "kooky." The surreal, urban fairy-tale quality of the images communicates powerfully for the client, and highlights the filmic, experiential process informing Ashton's working method.

Summer Blockbuster

BLINDED BY THE LIGHT
faces as icons / moon as spotlight /
summer colours / fading into the
light /

MOONSTRUCK
transformation when the moon
rises / vampires and werewolf /
shadows / people turning into
animals in the moonlight /

SUMMER MOON
celebration / summer feeling /
euphoria / light /

Moonlight Cinema 06/07

MOONLIGHT GARDEN
people wandering / garden /
shadows / people becoming part
of or blending into the garden /

G
geometric shapes / patterns /
fluoro colours / energy / chaos /
people blending into patterns

MOONSHINE
airbrush / fantasy / glitter-glamour
world / dreamscapes / space-like
landscape

Moonlight Cinema 2006/2007 concepts
Prepared by Studio Pip and Co. in Melbourne
for Moonlight Cinemas. July 2006

Studio Pip's development process begins as a set of caption-like notes that outlines principal Ashton's initial thinking, presented as pages like this one and supported by his selections of visual reference from an extensive library. The function of these images is to help conjure feelings and promote discussion with the client, who is very involved in defining the direction Ashton will explore.

> We like our clients to understand the process; it helps them understand why we have come to the recommended direction. However, some clients are overwhelmed by choice, so we'll present three directions only.
>
> Andrew Ashton, Principal

Ashton describes his organic process that brings experience and ideation together in his studio: "I carry a sketchbook or camera with me everywhere. There was a period early in my work life that I would madly record everything I experienced. As time passed, I got to the point where I was seeing and experiencing similar ideas, only the circumstances had changed. I still carry the sketchbook and pen; however, it takes a unique situation to bring it out. ▌ "We will often be thinking about other problems and incidences and come up with ideas that we'll save for the appropriate project," he continues, "a little like an idea library. I also have an extensive personal photographic library." ▌ The Moonlight Cinema experience is fun, Ashton says, and the client wanted to emphasize the idea of seeing great films in a unique setting: "Bring a picnic, enjoy a beautiful garden setting, and see a film." Ashton explored a wide range of ideas verbally and visually, preparing his trademark presentation: captions and found images that allow the client to participate in what is, at this early stage, an open-ended, egalitarian discussion about possibilities. Many of the concepts riffed on

Quick studies with some stock imagery and an older logotype help Ashton explore concepts, including some that become important relative to the eventual, more refined direction. Among these are figures situated in a park setting, geometric patterns, figures and transparent color, and mysterious images related to the night.

The exploration became more involved, the imagery became more complex, involving flat, photographic, diagrammatic, and geometric content in collage-like arrangements. At this stage, Ashton envisioned people with "tree hair," resulting from poorly framed snapshots where the subject appears to have a tree growing out of their head. Expanding on this idea, especially because it captured the fun aspect of the outdoor movie experience, Ashton evolved the concept to become "tree people." Two illustrators were commissioned to submit roughs based on Ashton's direction.

moonlight ideas—transformation, forest spirits, outer space, shadows in the garden, and so on. ▌Among these concepts, an idea about "tree people" surfaced from an image that sparked a memory about taking pictures. "In a park, it's very easy to frame a person in front of a tree so they look like they have tree hair. We pushed the approach."

We cannot begin to predict the visual outcome before the work is commissioned. Illustration, photography, and writing will often transform a project with a special outcome. During the concept stage, we suggest ideas; however, we never prescribe what the selected idea will be prior to commissioning the writer, illustrator, or photographer.

Andrew Ashton, Principal

These explorations of vector-based image were an interesting direction, but seemed too stiff and cold for Ashton's vision. More photographic roughs submitted by the illustrator were met with instant approval. The mixture of high-contrast tecture, collage-like elements, and intensely colored graphic patterns presents the eclectic, spontaneous, and surreal associations Ashton wished to evoke for his client.

After the discussion, Ashton and his associates developed the "tree people" concept, plus another, to a relatively finished state, appropriate for a promotional postcard. The tree people concept won. "At the sign-off, we commissioned two illustrators to interpret the concept. After seven days, the first illustrator failed to understand the brief. After 12 hours, the second illustrator sent concept illustrations. The client approved the concepts instantly. ▌From there, the process ran like a machine. "The client approved the talent, colors, and props. The client then approved six individual characters.

Configurations of these characters were then approved and applied to postcards and posters." Moonlight has over five hundred applications and an event type suite ensured the event has a unique image. Ashton chose the Sauna family by Underware. "Sauna had a range of weights and its design is rigorous and memorable," he opines. "It is also kooky-looking as well."

The photo shoot yielded a number of figures, each of different gesture. As part of the refinement process, Ashton spent time considering their combination and arrangement, incorporating other approaches, like flat vector tracing and landscape scenes, from earlier sketches.

Extreme scale changes and vibrant color create dynamic compositions within the poster formats. The unnatural color heightens the viewer's sense of an unexpected and fun experience.

Royal Botanic Gardens Melbourne

SUMMER 2006/07
moonlight.com.au

The mix of photographic and illustrative textures provides for a more inventive and, therefore, more distinctive and memorable visual language on behalf of the client.

Extreme scale changes and vibrant color create dynamic compositions within the poster formats. The unnatural color heightens the viewer's sense of an unexpected and fun experience.

Royal Botanic Gardens Melbourne

SUMMER 2006/07
moonlight.com.au

Moonlight is a fun event that warranted a fun typeface. A great deal of contemporary design zealously uses a restrained sans-serif suite as a design cue. We like to question these idioms and present alternatives.

Andrew Ashton, Principal

Free

A guide to Summer 2006/07. Cillian Murphy, Picnic do's and don't's. Breakfast Club vs. Robin Cloft. Film reviews and more...

Moonlight Magazine
summer 2006/07

In interviews over the previous three days in a whirlwind publicity tour to promote the Wind that Shakes the Barley. Needless to say, Cheekbones was looking a little tired. Tired enough that all the light-hearted questions I had planned somehow transported themselves out of the repetitively curtained window of the hotel room high above Melbourne where we sat, with Cillian struggling to stay vertical in his chair.

Add this to the mysterious non-performance of my dictaphone (later diagnosed as batteries insertia – commonly known as putting the batteries in the wrong way, you dickhead) and the actor's habit of checking the time every thirty seconds, so let's just say that the mood was tense. A challenge for even the most resolute non-professional journalist pretending to be a seasoned professional. Luckily I came prepared with a heavy arsenal of self-deprecating small talk, and incisive questions about the nature of publicity teams. In a stock Irish accent, Cheekbones talked...

Three days later, having seen and immensely enjoyed two films starring Cheekbones himself, I was converted. Now could one actor sit so gracefully inside the characters of both troubled transvestite (Breakfast on Pluto) and moralistic freedom fighter (The Wind that Shakes the Barley) that you forget you are watching a performance? How does an actor cope with the emotional load of the characters he plays? How does it feel for a man to make such a damn fine-looking woman?

Upon arrival at the flash hotel where the encounter was to take place, I discovered that I was the last of what was probably

How if I'd ever get to Melbourne other than with this film, and I really like this city." A breakthrough! Some more talk about the virtues of Melbourne, and Cheekbones was warming up, I/or should I say thawing out. "Someone famous said, it's not the acting you're paid for, it's the waiting around. It's true. But when the camera is rolling and it's a good scene, being well directed, yeah it's when I'm at my happiest. If you're involved in something worthwhile it's very satisfying."

How does it feel for a man to make such a damn fine — looking woman?

The Wind that Shakes the Barley is a moving film. Directed by Ken Loach and winner of the Palm d'Or at the 2006 Cannes Film Festival, the story revolves around a community in 1920s Ireland and its struggle for independence against the savage occupying British forces. It is essentially a document of the transition of one community from solidarity to chaos in the face of state-sanctioned terrorism designed to kill off Irish culture. Like all Loach films, the actors do not see the whole script before filming begins, so know nothing about the ensuing plot turns or the ultimate fate of their characters. It is a formula that has produced exceptionally raw and revealing performances, often from non-actors. This film and Murphy's performance are no exception.

The privileges of being an actor are not lost on Murphy, nor the responsibilities, and despite his habit of time-checking and wriggling around in his chair like a teenage

Cillian, Cillian, dear it was really nothing...

PJ Carroll interviews Cillian Murphy

I have to admit that I hadn't really thought twice about Cillian (pronounced Kil- yan) Murphy before the opportunity arose to interview him. Vague recollections of him snorted in apocalyptic grime in 28 Days Later merged with the disturbingly convincing psychopath he played in Red Eye. If anything, my most enduring memory was of a strangely shaped face with vaguely extra-terrestrial qualities.

But my interest spiked with the news of the irreverent interview or, more specifically, with a female friend's endless gushing and professions of jealousy at my opportunity to meet Mr Murphy –

hereafter known as 'Cheekbones' – face to face. So armed with a hastily scanned press kit and a newfound appreciation that one woman's ET is another woman's perfect ten, I dipped my toe into the Cillian Murphy appreciation society.

"I hate actors who give out and say they are tired and exhausted, we're so lucky I hate actors who moan about things like that. And we get to travel, I mean I don't

The high-contrast base of the montage images translates well into less sophisticated applications, such as the promotional T-shirt, printed economically in two colors.

26

Zapp Visual Identity
Hesse Design | Düsseldorf, Germany

Direct and to the point: business people pride themselves on clarity and decisiveness. These two characteristics are remarkable emissaries in business-to-business communications, connoting reliability and honesty. For clients whose livelihoods depend on such communications, design that also speaks this language is at the core of their ability to make a profit. Of equal importance is establishing a visual voice that is timely and relevant within a given industry. For Zapp, a leading supplier of semifinished metal goods for complex industrial applications, clarity, decisiveness, timeliness, and relevancy came in the form of a new identity, developed by German studio Hesse Design.

Visualizing High-Tech Competence

Even though Zapp's production is mostly automated, it still involves working people, who we like to show.

Klaus Hesse, Principal

Located in Düsseldorf and presided over by Klaus and Christine Hesse, the studio's sleek, highly edited aesthetic delivers the cool, machined precision Zapp needed. When Zapp approached Hesse Design for a new identity, the company was taking a step into untested waters—for its management. "Most medium-sized companies in the same genre don't have a modern and consistent corporate design," says Christine Hesse. Zapp was about to find out that Hesse Design's modern approach is the definition of consistency—not repetitive or formulaic, as is the work of many who attempt to impose a specific style—but a measured response that is holistic and purposeful. There is always a grid. The typefaces are always chosen for legibility. Color is used for a reason. Their goal appears to be "fix it good"—once the Hesse team is done, it will run for the next thousand years. ▎Despite this clarity of vision, one need only investigate their portfolio to determine that each project breathes with its own voice. The structural integrity Hesse imparts never diminishes the freshness or effortless individuality of each client's look. The Zapp project began with an investigation

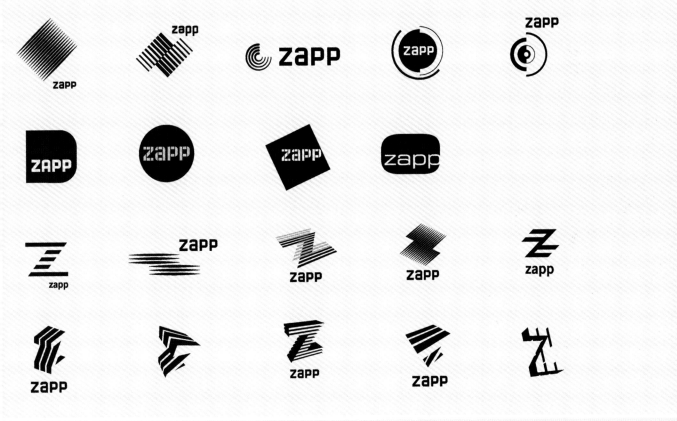

The Hesse Design team's exploration of the Zapp identity was methodical and well considered. The search employs a strategy based on the name, expressed typographically, and abstract form elements that interact in simple, but sophisticated and decisive ways. By exploring variation—and combinations of ideas seen in the variations—the designers are guided through a progressive process that yields highly resolved, purposeful marks.

of logotype concepts. The Hesse team, according to Klaus, sketches mostly digitally. While the designers confer and mutually audit each other, with Klaus providing direction as he himself participates, they tend to resolve each study to a high level that is considered final, even if they decide not to present it to the client. Each version is, in effect, ready to go—an occurrence of certain visual variables, complete in itself and not in need of refinement. ▌For this reason, Hesse and his team command a liberal timeframe for exploration.

The initial study for Zapp's logo took place over nine months, at which time Hesse presented three of the concepts to the client. ▌The rigor of the exploration was fortunate, because Hesse and his team would have to be confident in light of an unexpected twist. "Details we did not know beforehand compelled us to reveal the development process," Hesse says with trademark bemused detachment. "The result was that Zapp chose one of the alternative logos."

This set examines the relationship between letter strokes, counterspaces, and reversed, negative linear elements. Some of the studies also investigate splitting and mirroring of forms around an axis, and many test the shapes of the corners, both angular and curved. During the review of the full process, the client selected the final mark from within this sequence of studies.

A grid defines the thicknesses of strokes and the radii of various corners in different forms.

The logo the client selected demonstrates the skill and understanding of form Hesse brings to the table. The letterforms are constructed on a grid of very small units; the outer corners of those strokes, which would historically have been curved overall, are rendered with a circular radius. ▌The counterspaces, however, remain angular in shape to create a repetition of positive and negative form that offers a machined presentation. The one structural anomaly in the set—the Z—is forced to comply by cutting into its wayward diagonal stroke with a rectilinear counterform.

Robert Zapp
Werkstofftechnik GmbH
Zapp-Platz 1
40880 Ratingen
Tel +49 2102 710 0
Fax +49 2102 710 300
www.zapp.com

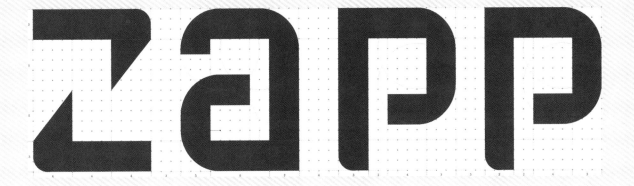

The contrast of curve and angle is an important aspect of the visual language of the letterforms. The alternation of these two states is evident in the contrast of the inner counters and the outer contours, as well as in their confrontation at close quarters.

Removing a rectilinear shape from the initial Z brings it into rhythmic and logical congruence with the other letters—which all naturally have interior or counters. This prevents the Z from visually disconnecting from the others because of its intrinsic structural difference.

The trade show booth exploits the linear language through materials, introducing a pattern of glossy and matte finishes into the environment.

To hear Hesse tell it, there were few, if any, revisions—to anything. Stationery, brochures, annual reports, website, and so on were organized, laid out, illustrated with clear, colorful photography showing products and people, and without much fuss. "The refinement," he says, "has been more related to the content." ▌Each stage of design and production is governed by the same methodical approach to solving a problem and making the result beautifully crafted, like a piece of furniture. "There are aspects to visual design, as in a chair, that are givens. The chair has to support weight against the pull of gravity. It must be comfortable to sit in. These things will never change. So some things, the maker of a chair will always do the same. But whether it is light or dark, cool metal or aged walnut—this is where there's a little room for fun," Klaus and Christine say.

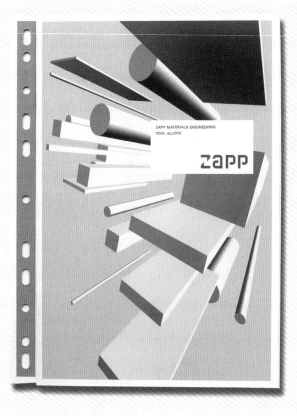

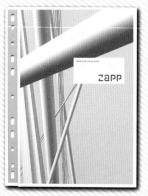

Applications follow strict grid structures and combine neutral sans-serif typography with a restrained color palette based on a light gray and three differentiators. Illustrations and photography are sourced or designed on a case-by-case basis, following guidelines established in an informal manual.

Both three-dimensionally rendered illustrations and photographs complement the luminous and linear qualities of the logotype.

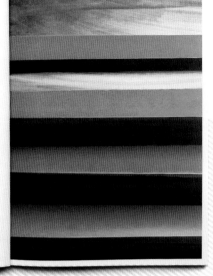

dem Kunden, der so seine individuelle Lösung finden konnte. Hervorzuheben sind hier die oberflächenveredelten Verfahren wie das Pulverbeschichten von Federschienenmaterial, die sich soförtert in der Automobilindustrie durchsetzen könnten, sowie andere technisch anspruchsvolle Anwendungen in Hauptmärkten wie der Handy-Industrie oder Nischenfeldern wie der Öl- und Gasindustrie.

Alles in allem: Die Zapp-Gruppe hat mit dem Wandel auf den Märkten auch im Geschäftsjahr 2005 Schritt gehalten, ist ständig in Bewegung und hervorragend aufgestellt für künftige Aufgaben. Zudem positioniert sich das Unternehmen immer stärker auf den wichtigen Weltmärkten als kompetenter Partner, der die Fähigkeit hat, Entwicklungen an den Märkten im Interesse der Kunden zu antizipieren. Wir setzen weiterhin mit Entschlossenheit auf die große Tradition der Zapp-Gruppe, die seit jeher Kunden, Qualität, Präzision und Flexibilität in den Vordergrund aller Aktivitäten stellt.

Im Geschäftsjahr 2006 werden wir auf diesem Weg weiter vorankommen. Ob die Vorboten eines Konjunkturfrühlings in Deutschland Bestand haben werden, ist unsicher. Gewiss ist, dass wir trotz weiter schwierigen Umfelds sicher, dass die Wachstums- und Erfolgsstory der Zapp-Gruppe – auch mit Blick auf künftig einzuleitende Strategie- und Investitionsschritte – unvermindert vorangetrieben wird. Das versprechen wir Ihnen.

Herzlichst
Ihre

Dr. Heiner Schunk   Carl Pfeffer

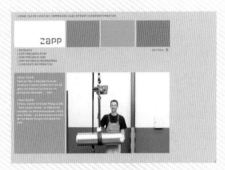

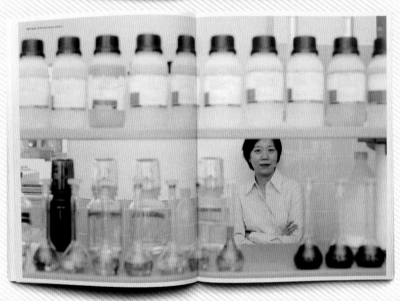

Images of workers bring a human element to meticulously staged and cropped photographs.

27

Red Canoe is a small, two-person studio that produces sophisticated design for sophisticated people—especially for people who like to read, as book cover design has lately been an important part of their practice. Having recently designed Laura Jensen Walker's first novel, *Reconstructing Natalie*, they were commissioned to develop the cover for the author's follow-up, *Miss Invisible*. "She writes in a witty style about serious real-world topics that people don't want to discuss," says studio partner Caroline Kavanagh. "Since the book design's purpose is to be an appropriate container for the content, that combination of factors calls for a special design approach." The first thing Kavanagh and partner Deb Koch do when beginning any project is research. For book cover designs, such as this one, that means reading the manuscript.

We're Talking about What's Not There

Some very rough pencil sketches made it into a refined form, including this discarded concept that the designers considered too literal once they saw it—meaning it would not make its way before the client as part of the presentation. Another, depicting an empty set of slippers on a scale, was more in line with the duality of the ideas they culled from reading the manuscript. The placement of the title in red on the scale's dial appears to indicate the protagonist has reached the weight at which she becomes invisible.

Usually, the publisher also sends over "tip sheets," or marketing outlines, that describe the demographic makeup of the target readership, the author's reach, other titles the readership may have liked, and so on. "If there's no manuscript, we read sample chapters, book proposals—anything we can beg, borrow, or steal from the client," explains Koch. ▌From reading, the designers make lists of key words and phrases that they can evaluate and discuss in terms of finding connections between ideas. For *Miss Invisible*, the strong title hinted at the story within—dichotomies in the relationships people have with food and the unfortunate societal consequences. "The character in the novel is fat, but she loves to bake; she's a nurturer," says Kavanagh. "Food is nurturing, but too much food is associated with being fat—and fat people are invisible in our society. Thin people often look away from fat people. Which is another double play—being fat, one would be hard to not see. So, the combination of these ideas is the entire concept for the cover." ▌Sketching, for this pair, is rare when undertaking the design of a cover. When it is used, it's as a quick means of communication

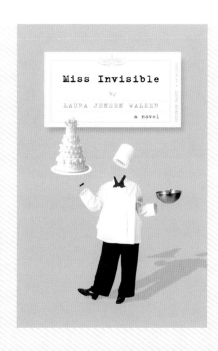

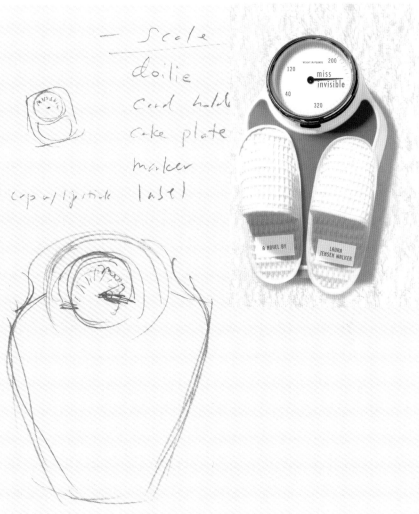

> Three ideas is often the rule. It means we have to be sure we can live with any one of them—but it's nearly impossible to not have a favorite runner in the group.

Deb Koch, Partner

Another humorous, albeit literal, interpretation focuses on the baking proclivities of the protagonist. A typewritten treatment for the title evokes the visual metaphor of a recipe card.

between the partners. "Even then, it's more likely we'd "talk" through Photoshop roughs," chimes in Koch. "The general starting point, however, is a new Photoshop file." ▋As Kavanagh works, the layers build up as she tests different combinations of backgrounds, images, and type treatments. "Let's just say that working files have, at times, had more layers than the application will allow," she says. Files are often saved anew to save the older material when a particular direction starts to go awry. "It sometimes happens that initial ideas, perhaps hastily rejected, turn out to have a gem of brilliance in them." ▋A little over two weeks later, Red Canoe presented three concepts for the *Miss Invisible* cover, pretty much a standard number for them. "Time and industry practice permitting, we'd prefer to show just one and go from there," Koch notes. ▋The presentations are delivered through e-mail as .PDF files, as the Red Canoe studio is, surprisingly, a sort of wilderness outpost in the middle of Tennessee. Bulleted write-ups are included in the presentation to stand in for the designers, who take time to carefully craft and edit their writing. "Our experience suggests

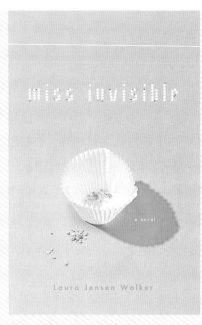

The approved concept made use of an existing photograph by the designers' colleague and longtime collaborator, Peter McArthur, that seemed to capture all the conceptual elements of the storyline—the dichotomous relationships between food, obesity, nurturing, visibility, and invisibility (consider that the cupcake itself has been "disappeared").

The major refinements to the layout were focused on the type and the background color. The legibility of the sprinkle-formed letters concerned the client. The designers first simplified the title treatment, starting out fresh from a dot-matrix font. They added in colored elements to create the sense that the sprinkles had fallen from the type. In a series of steps, they also darkened the background blue to help support the white letters. Eventually, the dots forming the letters were enlarged and an intermediate dropshadow removed.

In the title typography, the progression from most complex to most simple is also a progression from most literal to most abstract.

The strong symmetry of the layout is disturbed by the placement of the drop shadow and the crumbs, a decision that helps activate the large plain of blue space.

that some people are word people," muses Kavanagh. "They don't take in visual information on a visceral level, and it's crucial that they be able to read about the thinking. Other people see and do not read. We just have to present our thinking." ❚ The selected concept (an empty cupcake wrapper showing evidence of someone who is no longer there to be seen) was chosen because its thinking seemed so clear—nothing missing, nothing extra. "We make an assessment before client presentations .... If we don't have a "why" for something, then it is likely not needed," says Kavanagh.

A straightforward photograph and a clever title treatment allow the concept to speak loudly, yet still leave a bit of mystery. "Book covers, in our opinion, shouldn't try to tell the whole story; the element of curiosity is important."

> Our idea dictated the need for an image of a specific and real item, so photography was the clear choice. Also, the desired simplicity of the visual suggested a straight shot. Budgets only rarely allow for commissioned photography or illustration. Photographer Peter McArthur, who we have called upon for previous projects, has a stylistic approach that is direct, clean, and wonderfully colorful.

Caroline Kavanagh, Partner

The final cover shows some sprinkles that were added for effect, and the supporting typeface—Futura, a geometric sans serif—that corresponds formally with the line/dot language of the title and the large dot created by the cupcake paper.

28

City of Wodonga Visual Identity
GollingsPidgeon | St. Kilda, Australia

Wodonga is experiencing a boom. It's a small city in South Australia, in the province of Victoria. Its population of approximately 35,000 grew regularly at a rate of 1.8 percent between 2000 and 2005, making it one of Victoria's fastest growing provincial cities. Until recently, Wodonga has sat in the shadow of its larger sister city, Albury, across the River Murray. Following its sudden growth, the local government decided it ought to capitalize on the potential for tourism, as well as business and cultural development, and so enlisted design firm GollingsPidgeon to invigorate its identity… by creating one. A custom designed typeface, completely ownable by the community, offers a friendly signature for the growing community and brings history and present together in a colorful and engaging visual language.

Creating Visual Community

Pidgeon's notebooks show the writing and sketches that formed the bulk of his process in developing the city's new identity. Variations on letterform construction show how the same letter can be formed in different ways, allowing the designer to customize the structure to achieve a desired feeling.

I always refer to our library of reference books on design, history, photography, art, architecture, and fashion. I also have a wall with posters, postcards, typographic experiments, and my four-year-old daughter's paintings and drawings.

David Pidgeon, Principal

"It was one of those awkward briefs where the target audience is everyone," says David Pidgeon, the firm's creative director. "So our approach needed the flexibility to communicate at different levels." Pidgeon concentrated his effort on a typographic mark for the city's name that evoked the idea of linkage, of drawing a community together. ▌Focusing the identity in a type form, rather than in a symbol or icon, would mean it could exist in almost any environment and retain its presence. It would also likely avoid any sensitive political or cultural issues that could be raised because

of a particular image choice. "We try to present one concept only; however, we often present the thinking process that led there, which may include alternate solutions from along the way. In our initial proposal, we supported the typographic idea with references to a traditional coat of arms, and also cattle brands, as Wodonga has one of the biggest cattle sale yards in the region. The thinking was very preliminary; the client hated it, and considered taking the job away from us." ▌Despite this painful experience, Pidgeon felt that the typographic concept only need slight refining, but it was clear that

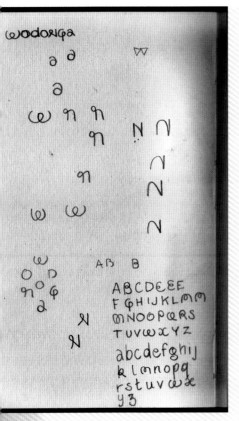

The first iterations of the Wodonga wordmark were formed primarily of existing letters, with the custom form alteration occurring in the W and G.

Sketches show various configurations for the letters, both in a line and triangular format. This latter development was a response to the idea of creating a crest, or coat of arms, for the city—a concept that was roundly dismissed by the city's board.

their aesthetic needed a major directional change. "The typographic resolution of this identity came from an experimental typeface that I had designed called Hex. It's based on the geometry of a hexagon and has no horizontal structural elements. I was able to use what I had learned from this process to create the character forms for Wodonga." Pidgeon made a second presentation of the new typographic mark alone; the city enthusiastically approved it the second time. ▌Pidgeon made minor adjustments to the forms, and built out the rest of the alphabet. And then, while developing the stationery, developed a visual language of symbols to represent the different aspects and activities of the city. The inspiration for these was the simplicity of the cattle branding concept discarded by the city during the first presentation. ▌This time around, however, a line language that related directly to the Wodonga wordmark was used to create figures into a modern language depicting various activities in the city. The figures can be used in isolation or conjunction with one another. "As we developed this idea, the client requested more and more symbols to represent the community and it is proposed that they continue to develop them over time." The resulting language is easily applied by various city agencies, helps customize their particular projects, and ensures consistency across the board.

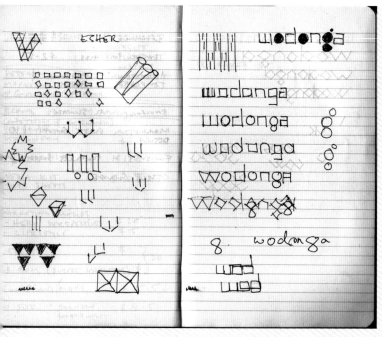

CITY OF WODONGA ◆ VIC

More elaborate construction configurations resulted as Pidgeon returned to the idea of showing linkage among the forms. His sketches led him to revisit a typeface he had created for an unrelated project, Hex, which was constructed using a hexagonal grid. Applying the Hex logic to a simpler structure, Pidgeon was able to construct a continuously linked wordmark. The interconnection of the strokes, like a script typeface, created a rhythmic flow among the characters and a strongly unified mark—a visual singularity. The progression from base form to letterform structure is shown here in a series of steps.

Pidgeon increased the weight of the strokes and rounded the terminals to create a more fluid contour; these adjustments not only strengthened the unity of the form, but softened its angularity, making it feel friendlier.

abcdefghijklmnop
qrstuvwxyz ! @ # $
% ^ & * ( ) – = + { } [ ] : ;
> < " ' , . ? / 1234567890

The visual form for this project was about creating a memorable mark that reinforces the concept of linkage within a community. The fact that the mark can also spell out the word *Wodonga* was of secondary concern. It was an issue that took the client some time to get their heads around; they wanted to seek more clarity in the typography while I fought to keep the strength of form.

David Pidgeon, Principal

The stationery evolved quickly, pairing the wordmark with a neutral sans serif in black ink on one side of each application, and printing a dramatic composition of the iconic figures on the reverse in the process inks—cyan, magenta, yellow, and black.

The client approved the new mark, and Pidgeon went about developing applications. One of the first steps was to develop the stationery; Pidgeon turned his attention to building out the rest of the alphabet, based on the characters in the city name. As he was doing so, he noticed a similarity between

some of the letters' iconic forms and the cattle brands with which he had experimented earlier. He was drawn to create a secondary system of icons depicting city activities, using the same visual language as the alphabet.

DESIGN EVOLUTION

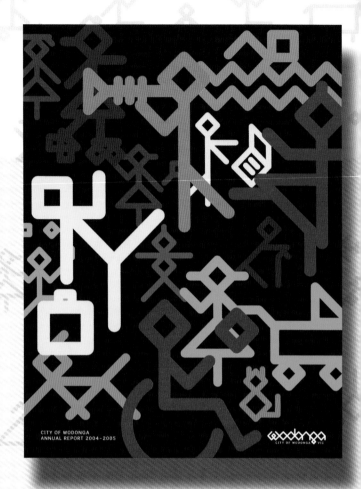

CITY OF WODONGA
ANNUAL REPORT 2004–2005

The components of the identity lend themselves to multiple uses and are flexible enough to be taken apart, repurposed, and turned into new forms as varied as illustrations of people to whimsical decorations on the side of a garbage truck.

The essential grid structure can be used in three-dimensional applications, such as the tree-root cover and public art, and to create other forms, such as the shield shape on the pylon signage.

The annual report cover presents the process primaries (magenta, cyan, yellow) in combination with additive secondary colors (orange, violet, and green). The simplicity of the color scheme is lively and fun, supporting the sense of friendliness in the mark and icons.

> I tend to keep refining rather than keeping too many variations.

David Pidgeon, Principal

SPORTS
& LEISURE
CENTRE

CITY OF WODONGA

The identity itself does not rely on color, but in application its forms can easily be translated into color, as seen in the flag banners (single and multiple color) and signage applications.

DESIGN EVOLUTION

29

The Calumet Open Space Reserve is a wetland preserve on the far south side of Chicago and, oddly, one of the city's principal manufacturing areas. As a way of addressing this bizarre paradox, the city has begun several green policy initiatives and envisioned an environmental education center, to be built in the area. The city's Department of Environment (DOE) organized a competition encouraging firms to submit proposals for the new center's design. Studio Blue, based in Chicago, was tapped to develop the poster that would act as a call for entries. A delicate tracery presents the meandering tangle of a bird's nest in the vocabulary of architectural blueprints and, in doing so, evokes discussions of sustainability and the blurring of natural and built environments.

This Building Is for the Birds

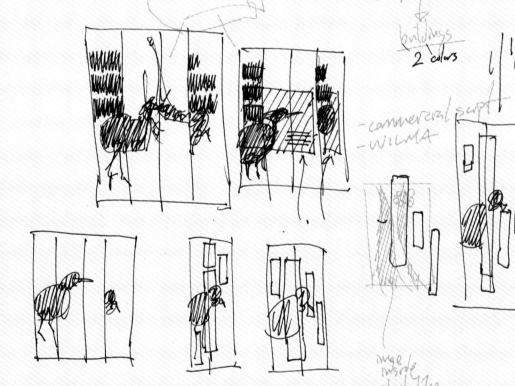

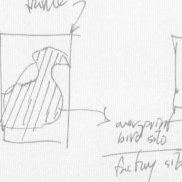

A cross section of early sketches shows an immediate fascination with bird forms, plants, and geometric elements in combination. Working with recognizable subjects allows a great deal of leeway for altering them to communicate ideas while keeping the message accessible.

Some sketches exploited the physicality of the folded poster itself as a way of splitting and reconfiguring the industrial and natural elements.

Moving from hand to digital sketching allowed for more specific juxtaposition of image components, as seen in this series of preliminary illustrations. Using illustration highlights the artificiality of the image combinations, some of which are both funny and disturbing; in particular, the bird wearing the welding mask and the factory spewing plants.

The studio begins projects collectively. Each member of the team is assigned a task—gathering visual reference or researching the client's needs in greater depth—and then the group meets for an "informal ideation." Cheryl Towler-Weese, one of the studio partners, describes this process as "like the game show *Win, Lose, or Draw*, with several people generating quick sketches on the fly. Sometimes these are just a word; sometimes it's representational. What we end up with," she continues, "is a wall covered with ideas. It might not look like anything, but it captures the desired tone of a project." ▊ For the competition poster, Towler-Weese and designers Tammy Baird and Garrett Niksch desired something unusual after that day's session. "I grew up not far from where the environmental center was to be built, so I was familiar with the landscape," says Towler-Weese. "In this part of the Midwest, nature and industry coexist in sometimes surprising ways." Evoking this idea in the poster seemed appropriate, given the future center's proposed site. ▊ The first sketches to go digital investigated birds as protagonists; this choice of animal came from local knowledge, as had

> With something like a poster or book cover, we like to present a range of solutions—something safe, something a bit riskier, and something in between. This is especially smart when dealing with city government, as with this project.
>
> Cheryl Towler-Weese, Partner

DESIGN EVOLUTION

the general direction—various birds nest along the Calumet River. Nicksch and Weese experimented with surreal juxtapositions of bird and industry, alternately unsettling and humorous—in one sketch, they paired the bird with an ominous factory image; a lighthearted approach showed the bird wearing a welder's helmet. ▎A related direction showed the bird's nest as a kind of architectural plan. Preliminary type treatments were added for the sake of the presentation, where overall concept and visual quality would be the pressing issues. Towler-Weese and Niksch prepared three versions.

When Studio Blue presents concepts to clients, they introduce their audience to the research and ideation processes that have taken place. "This better sets the stage for what they are about to see," she says.

> Because this competition would appeal to younger, more progressive architects, we wanted the poster to have a bit of a sly edge to it—something you might not catch on the first viewing.

Tammy Baird, Designer

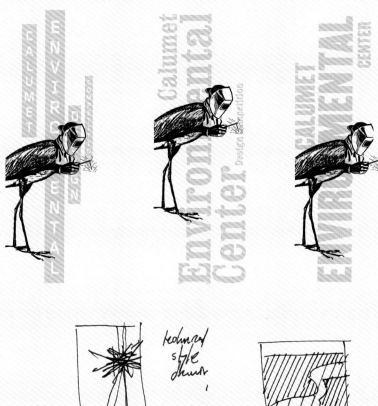

During this stage, the designers investigated using typography in combination with the images. The vertical arrangement of the text in these studies acts as counterpoint to the bird's diagonal thrust and alludes to smokestacks in a less literal way than previous illustrations.

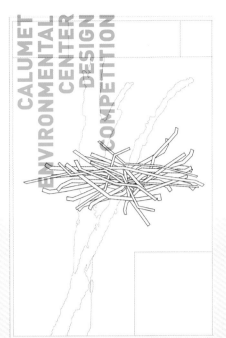

CALUMET ENVIRONMENTAL CENTER DESIGN COMPETITION

The client immediately like the nest concept, but had very specific input. The bird depicted in the tree was the wrong species for the area, the nest was much simpler and didn't evoke the tangle of an actual heron's nest. Also, the client felt like the skyline needed to more closely match the buildings near the actual site. ▌ Niksch and Baird addressed these requests and evolved the concept more thoroughly throughout a four subsequent revisions. Because the silhouettes of the heron and industrial skyline needed to evoke the specific environment along the river, photographs were taken at the site and these

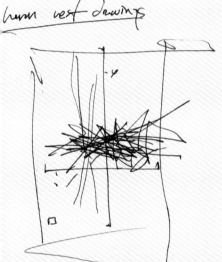

heron nest drawing

CALUMET
ENVIRONMENTAL
CENTER
DESIGN
COMPETITION

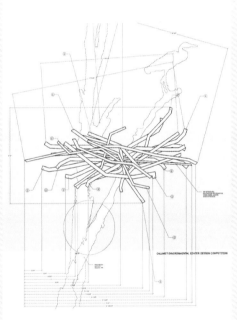

The idea of a nest, a bird's form of architecture, recurred in numerous sketches as the designers addressed image combinations. In these studies, the designer rapidly explores size, position, and relative value or density. A notation near one sketch suggests the strong idea of rendering the nest as a blueprint or architectural drawing.

The vertical type configuration makes its way into one of the first computer-generated nest drawings, scanned from a photograph and rendered with a CAD plotter. The strength of the solid type nearly overpowers the illustration.

Added diagrammatic elements highlighting the CAD rendering's spatial measurements bring complexity to the layout and clarify the concept of "bird architecture." Square-based breaking of space houses the tree/nest form in a sturdy structure, reinforcing its architectural quality. In a later iteration, a gentle gradation of cool blue helps to soften

the poster's linearity and introduces the perception of deeper space. Including the bird silhouette further clarifies the subject matter.

DESIGN EVOLUTION

were then traced using ScanFont—a program typically used to digitize handwriting when developing typefaces. This produced extremely accurate vector outlines for the elements that would establish the environment in which the nature center would be built. To add an architectural layer of meaning we dimensioned the nest (the heron's "house") using CAD software. "The result is a sort of absurdist blueprint," Niksch elaborates. "The dimensions you see in the poster are actually to scale."

> We like the multiplicity of narratives. It has more to say than what it simply says.

Cheryl Towler-Weese, Partner

The designers continued to develop the poster by introducing a built horizon, referring to the industrial heritage of the future center's site. Specificity was crucial in the depiction of the natural environment; Studio Blue's client at the DOE was very concerned that they depict the industrial buildings properly so the poster would accurately reflect the building site. This resulted in redrawing each element several times, based on different photographic sources, and numerous conference calls to discuss such minutia as the scale of the grain silos and proper number of factory windows.

Changing the overall color scheme from blue to green adds warmth and a more immediate association with the idea of environment.

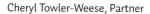

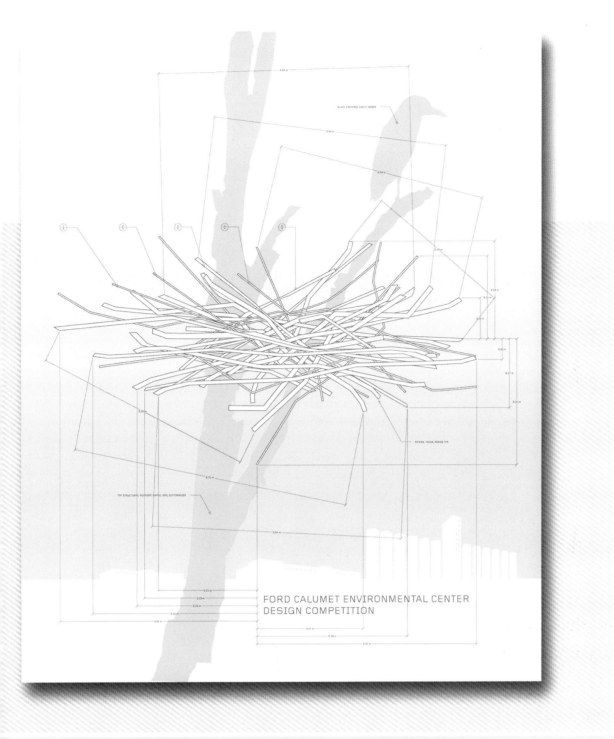

FORD CALUMET ENVIRONMENTAL CENTER
DESIGN COMPETITION

The gradation of the background field augments the spatial depth introduced by color; the flat color fill of the tree and bird silhouettes creates a perceived middle ground; maintaining the outline treatment of the nest thrusts it further into the foreground.

Reserving the red color for the diagrammatic lines helps separate them from the nest drawing so both elements are distinct. The choice of an intense red is complementary to the muted green used for tree, bird, and background.

The complexity of the drawn elements belies a strong yet subtle breaking of space through the format by a series of delicately canted diagonals; for example, the slight tilt of the tree's primary vertical is offset by its branch upward to the right and the slowly rising horizon of industrial buildings.

Although initially obscured by the cloud of lines, the asymmetrical spatial breaks yield strong negative shapes at decisively different intervals. Setting the type in all uppercase and using a light-weight, angular, sans serif font visually connects the type's linear quality to that of the illustration.

DESIGN EVOLUTION

30

Bottle Redesign: Shango Rum Liqueur
Wallace Church, Inc. | New York, USA

Premium luxury spirits are a dime a dozen. Consider, for instance, all the brands of high-end vodka currently available. Fighting for attention on a strictly visual level used to work, but within the crowded field of spirits cloaking themselves in subculture and lifestyle, the visual had better have backup. Shango is a brand of spiced rum liqueur whose brand traded on a cultural mystique to build loyalty among its target demographic, but wasn't telling its story. To do so effectively, the brand needed to be addressed from a new vantage point—one that Wallace Church, Inc., a New York strategic branding and packaging firm, discovered when they began their research.

Deep, Dark, and Delicious

The original bottle branding was overly complicated; the linear texture, all in white on the red surface, prevented consumers form easily distinguishing the forms and reading. In addition, the choice of illustrative elements failed to capture the symbolic depth of the mythology the brand intended to evoke.

The client wished to retain the red bottle, so the designers at Wallace Church produced the majority of their studies in this color scheme. The combination of red and white was one visual aspect that was accurate—these are the colors symbolic of Shango.

Shango is a godlike figure in Santéria, a Yoruba spiritual system carried to Cuba when slaves were brought to the island from Africa. The religion was forced underground because of its conflict with Catholicism, but it remains a powerful spiritual and cultural force in the Caribbean. "Shango is known and revered by many people," explains Stan Wallace, the firm's principal. ▌ The convergence of these and other variables (that rum is produced in Cuba, for one) drives the primary messaging of the brand—its naming after a god—and its positioning toward young, urban, African- and Latino-

American consumers. The brand was striving for a connection to cultural roots among members of these groups, as well as for romantic notions of power, myth, and elemental sexuality. ▌ The existing bottle design, despite its unusual red color, offered a mish-mash of pseudo-African iconography. Not only was the crowded detail busy and confusing, but it may have been considered insulting—a Tiki-style motif of leaves, spears, helmet, and faux-"tribal" typography. What was lacking—aside from good taste—was authenticity and emotion.

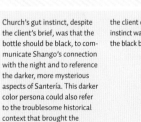

New concepts ranged from close-in studies of symbolic images related directly to Shango and Santería—the double-bladed axe and the ram—to more general Yoruba images, such as the mask; and onto symbolic concepts beyond specifically Caribbean mythology, including the endless serpent, blood and smoke, contemporary imagery

such as graffiti, digital textures, and illustrative figures. These latter concepts, although presented to the client, were considered not relevant enough to the mythology of Shango, despite being valuable in considering other avenues.

Church's gut instinct, despite the client's brief, was that the bottle should be black, to communicate Shango's connection with the night and to reference the darker, more mysterious aspects of Santería. This darker color persona could also refer to the troublesome historical context that brought the Yoruba religion to Cuba—the slave trade. Against expectation,

the client decided Church's instinct was right, and approved the black bottle design.

Designers at Wallace Church, armed with stories about Shango culled from a variety of sources and images provided by the client, began sketching new concepts. The project was going to happen on a relatively fast burn—six months from start to launch—so the investigation became digital very quickly. The client's brief requested the designers retain the bottle's original red color, because Shango is usually identified with red and white. ▌Most of the exploration attempted to bring credible references to the Yoruba legends, invoking iconography associated with Shango: his double-headed axe, a ram's head, mask forms, and so on. Stan Wallace, the firm's principal, made a presentation of fifteen concepts with his team. ▌One of the concepts shown deviated from the brief. "Although Shango is represented by red and white, we felt strongly that black would convey mysticism and the darker side of the story more effectively," says Wallace. "We presented a design to show how it would work, and the client went with the black bottle." ▌The black bottle featured a striking red face, almost masklike but blurred and ghostly. It seemed to be peering out from within the depths of the bottle, as though some entity had been captured inside. An elegant serif logotype and minimal descriptive text, surmounted by a delicate axe icon, complete a mysterious, austere, but somehow passionately narrative bottle. Shango's makers were pleased enough that very little refinement took place. ▌The typographic details were resolved quickly, and the face image—photographed in-house for budgetary reasons and manipulated digitally—underwent density and sharpness changes to test its reproduction quality on the bottle.

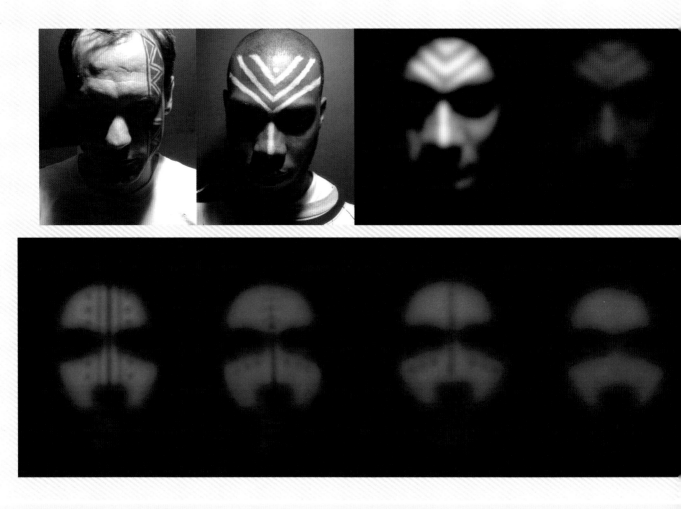

There was little change to the bottle design after the client approved the concept. An abstract icon was replaced with Shango's symbol, the double-bladed axe, and the point size of the type at the bottom made slightly larger. The all-uppercase setting was spaced more loosely to ensure better legibility; red dots were included to suggest burning coals.

The most attention was paid to the ghostly red face image that is the centerpiece of the design. Test photographs were taken of different models, both Caucasian and African American, with and without painted facial decoration. The high-contrast lighting provided the most sculptural quality, causing the face to resemble a mask. The image was manipulated using software.

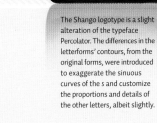

SHANGO

RUM LIQUEUR
* * *
RUM LIQUEUR
MADE WITH WHITE
RUM FROM TRINIDAD
BLENDED WITH
NATURAL FLAVOURS,
DAMIANA AND
GUARANA
* * *
35% ALC/VOL
(70 PROOF) 750mL

DESIGN EVOLUTION

The Shango logotype is a slight alteration of the typeface Percolator. The differences in the letterforms' contours, from the original forms, were introduced to exaggerate the sinuous curves of the s and customize the proportions and details of the other letters, albeit slightly.

31

Pigeons International Performance Promotional Poster
Thomas Csano | Montréal, Canada

As part of a celebration of their twentieth anniversary, Pigeons International, a Montréal theatrical dance company, organized a multimedia performance of three pieces they had performed previously, a trilogy of works by Paula de Vasconcelos investigating the state of planet Earth. Graphic designer Thomas Csano had created the poster for the first part, *Babylone*, nearly three years ago, when the Pigeons troupe had first performed it. Now, Csano would design a new poster to promote the three-part performance.

The History of the World in Three Acts

The poster Csano designed for *Babylone* made explicit reference to the Middle East through the use of tile patterns and the four-square star grid.

Csano's first sketches for *Trilogie* imagined a literal trilogy of geometric spaces, made up of mini posters based on the original design of the *Babylone* poster. While this idea establishes the tripartite nature of the performance very clearly, it doesn't quite capture the magnitude of the event, imparted by a larger title that encompasses all three.

Csano toyed with showing a Hand of Fatima as a central iconic image, but the client considered this idea too abstract and requested Csano use photographs from the performances of the individual works.

Each of the three performances in *La Trilogie de la Terre*, or *Trilogy of the Earth*, is a work devoted to exploring one temporal stage of the world's history: past, present, and future. The works address issues of evolution, nature, human triumph, and human tragedy. ▌Csano's original poster for *Babylone*, the performance focused on the past, had employed exotic typography, textures, and a grid motif inspired by Moroccan tile work. "I created a centered and balanced grid, and used a pattern effect inspired by graphic elements found in ancient civilizations," he recalls. In revisiting this visual concept at the request of his client at Pigeons, he was wary of treading over old ground, but understood that he had created something that resonated before. "It's not ideal," he mused, "but I'll have to make it work." In this case, he wouldn't have to establish the overall conceptual direction as he had the first time, but would instead have to reinvigorate it to make it relevant. ▌For the original *Babylone* poster, it had been a matter of discussing and brainstorming with his client to work out an idea that both though would be viable. According to Csano, this is a typical working method, even

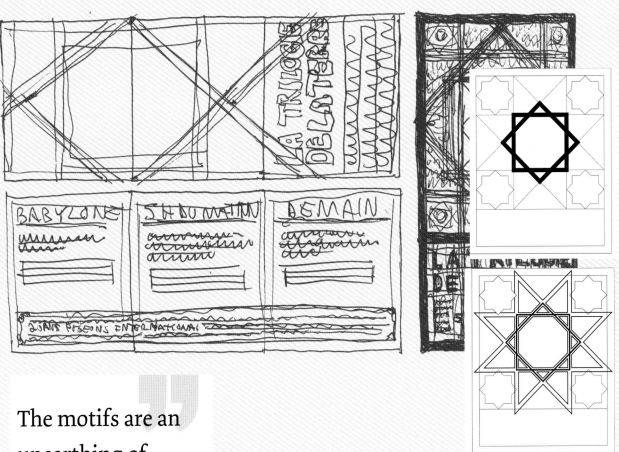

The images requested for inclusion by the client are first set in the four corners of the grid formation. The images are overlayed with sun symbols to help integrate their tonal qualities into the overall patterning around them.

The motifs are an unearthing of ancient cultures.

Thomas Csano, Principal

Project Case Studies **31** *Dance-Theater Performance Poster*

for corporate clients. ▌After his discussions, Csano works by hand first but then transfers to digital sketching very quickly. "I do a lot of visualizing an almost finished product in my head first; when I begin to actually work, the sketching is usually close to the final product," he says. "I make all the changes I need as I work. This specific design was resolved by altering and re-altering the same file." Csano continues the collaborative approach by showing clients the changes he makes, but usually no more than three times. ▌In the new poster,

the geometric grid remained a primary element, with a centrally located photograph. The linear elements of the grid were strengthened and the titling enlarged and moved downward to occupy the bottom third of the format. Less decorative type was selected, but one with a weathered texture to suggest age. The poster relies on a variety of symbolic gestures for communication, such as the aged quality, patterns, mandala forms, geometry, and the unspoken narrative in the photograph.

Variations test the relationships and relative saturation of the colors. A near-primary set of hues is used, but in each variation, it is slightly skewed. For example, in the first exploration, the red is colder, making it more analogous with the blue, which leans toward violet. In the next set, the red becomes hotter as it shifts toward orange, which creates a complementary relationship to the less-saturated blue. The relatively muted yellow remains constant throughout.

Along with color, the designer considers variations in the placement of the central grid and title, testing the arrangement of each to determine which creates the strongest set of relationships within the format. Elongating the format creates a more harmonious, mathematical relationship between the format and the central grid, based on the proportions of the golden section. The elongated format allows for the central grid configuration, including the photograph, to shift upward, while the title drops below; justified, the title creates a strong horizontal break between upper and lower portions.

> The picture is like a window in the present; this image shows a tension between man and woman, a duality between young and old. There seems to be a communication between the two that could be a discussion about the future.

Thomas Csano, Principal

The final color scheme skews all of the color into an analogous relationship of brownish reds and golds, with the blue component removed altogether. The corner images are replaced by one central image.

Within the photograph, a mysterious narrative is suggested by the two figures, who seem to embody opposites: male/female, young/old, forward/backward.

32

Sundance Film Festival 2007 Identity
AdamsMorioka, Inc. | Beverly Hills, California, USA

The explosion of the independent film movement in the U.S. is largely due to the vision of Robert Redford, actor, director, and founder of the Sundance Institute, an organization dedicated to supporting cinema outside the Hollywood studio system. The annual Sundance Film Festival, held in Park City, Utah, provides exposure for nascent filmmakers and a forum for innovation. For several years, the studio responsible for capturing the spirit of this trendsetting event has been AdamsMorioka, located in Beverly Hills, California. Studio principal Sean Adams and his team approach this annual project with passion, cognizant of the festival's preeminent position cultural arbiter and their role in maintaining a sense of aesthetic rigor. "Most independent film festivals fall into the trap of being "groovy." That's fine where applicable," Adams says. "But Sundance should never try too hard." After months of intensive work, the 2007 festival identity flared into being, delivering a seemingly effortless, powerful, elemental image.

Ignition Accomplished

Sense of Possibility   Sundance Studies AdamsMorioka

Each concept board records the name of the concept—this one was named "Sense of Possibility"—and shows how the concept would be expanded across a number of hypothetical collateral pieces. The "Sense of Possibility" concept used the iconic film frame catalyzed by different elements.

A concept about expectation proposed depicting a film-screen curtain hiding and revealing environments seen during the festival.

"We begin with my really terrible hand sketches. They're practically impossible to understand," says Adams. "Concurrently, we work digitally with the information from the previous year, to explore formats and typeface issues." ▮ The initial exploration phase is challenging for AdamsMorioka. Working directly with institute directors Robert Redford and Jan Fleming, as well as an internal group at Sundance, they find it difficult to decipher and prioritize the vast number of ideas that are generated. Adams notes that, in discussing the 2007 festival, Redford had a consistent vision

to communicate the idea of community and the rigors of making an independent film, which provided some focus. ▮ The period of ideation, furthermore, is relatively long and tends to overlap the previous one. "Since we've designed the festival for five years, it's difficult to say when one year's explorations stopped, and the next began. If I had to put a hard schedule on the exploration phase for this one, I'd say it lasted about three months," says Adams. ▮ The needs of the project—not simply creating image, but helping to move 50,000 people around the site—as well as the media's impact

on the festival's exposure, number among the team's considerations as they explore ideas. Although created for direct experience at the festival by film industry insiders, supporters, and the like, the imagery must transmit the primary idea quickly and clearly for those seeing it in print and on television, where most people are likely to come into contact with it—in a news feature or a segment of *Entertainment Tonight*, for example. ▮ For this year's exploration, the AdamsMorioka team—which consisted of Volker Dürre as project art director and designers Monica Schlaug and Chris Taillon—delved

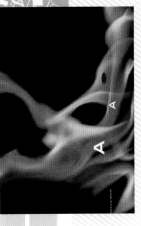

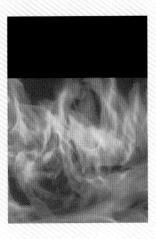

This concept proposed a playful collage of bird images, drawn and collaged, as an alternative to heavy conceptual themes. A winter-themed concept played with composing a variety of snowflakes made of film-industry figures and equipment.

Having a client with a creative sense, it often works best to share multiple ideas and then eliminate until you've come to an agreement on one. This prevents the inevitable "Did you try making it red?"

Sean Adams, Principal

This concept, called "Ignition," showed a flaring fire that explodes into flame across the collateral in differing configurations. The passion, intensity, and creative energy implied by this direction captured the ideas Redford and the Sundance marketing team felt were most important this year.

DESIGN EVOLUTION

into previous years' explorations to mine previously considered concepts, as well as evolved those in new directions and generated others from scratch. A dedicated Sundance hard drive organizes archived files for easy reference. In addition, the studio also maintains a library of shapes, color ideas, and visual artifacts that they can explore as they work. In the end, the team presented nearly seventy-five concepts, in several installments, to Redford and the Sundance team for consideration. "The truly terrible were left behind," Adams winks. But he explains the reasoning for such extensive presentation thus:

"Robert Redford's vision is the most important component. As an extraordinary filmmaker, he, along with Jan Fleming, has insight that always improves on an idea." ▌ Each concept is presented on a large board that includes notation about the ideas it's trying to convey and how it might be applied to known festival publications, such as the program guide. Some concepts are continually investigated as new ones are proposed, while others are discarded outright, but archived for future consideration. ▌ After the extensive discussion, the concept of fire as a primary image was determined to best

> We maintained the restraint to use fire only, without resorting to graphic or typographic tricks. We let the message be what it was.

Volker Dürre, Art Director

Following approval, the designers began to define the language of the ignition image and the behavior of the fire. These rough sketches envisioned a ball flaring from initial explosion, referencing the Sun, but not attempting a literal representation.

These images explore the circular field relative to the flare. The viewpoint and cropping were too suggestive of a solar eclipse's corona, rather than of an object sparking into ignition. The images without the solid object weren't clearly fire—looking a bit like fur—and the absence of a "kindling" object didn't establish the idea of ignition.

This image began to capture the sense of ignition, and the solid object was indistinct enough that its shape didn't suggest an identity for it.

represent the 2007 festival's message. An elemental idea, it suggested energy and the creative impulse to the team, as well as evoked notions of ritual and gathering, as around a campfire. "We focused on the energy of the fire, not the destructive aspect," explains Volker Dürre. "The object on fire is never shown. There is no burning film or other graphic element to confuse the message," he clarifies.

❚ Two weeks of design refinement followed, with little change in concept. The design team paired the flame idea with a custom typeface display use based on an extended slab serif,

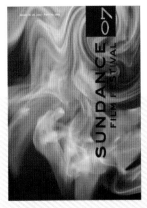

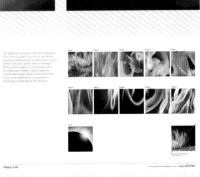
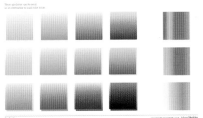
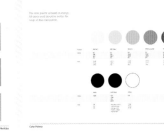

The ignition and flame images were eventually painted by an artist, who was able to capture the essential ignition, flare, and roiling flame activity the design team was after. It became clear that in order to avoid a negative interpretation—destruction—no burning object could be shown, with focus on the flames, not the source.

The design team developed coherent rules for cropping the fire, as well as guidelines for color, paper stocks, and typography, which were enumerated in a style guide.

Headlines were set in a customized slab serif based on Hellenic Wide, an old metal face originally released by the Bauer foundry. The alteration shown here was made to extend the letterforms and exaggerate their horizontal rhythm. A sans serif with slightly condensed proportions was chosen for setting complex volumes of information—film descriptions, timetables, credits, and so on. The condensed width offered a contrast to the headline display face, and it offered a variety of weights, plus italics, for detailed hierarchic needs within text. A third face, Boton, was selected as an in-between face—acting as a visual transition between the extended display and the condensed sans serif—because it is a slab serif of uniform stroke weight and condensed proportion. The designers developed a second weight to add flexibility in typographic color.

Hellenic Wide, because of its slightly Western feel and proportional similarity to the Sundance Film Festival logotype; a sans serif, Section, was chosen for informational text because of its versatility and assortment of weights; and a third typeface, Boton, was used as an in-between face, with an additional weight created to add flexibility. ▌The design refinement also included the development of a color palette, mostly warm hues, and formatting concepts, included grid structures, Festival logo placement, and image cropping. ▌"Quality and craftsmanship are integral to the message. Every element, from the arc of a specific flame, to the proportional relationship of the type to logo is refined," Adams continues. "The imagery is an illustration, painted by an extraordinary artist, Mike Lavallee at Killer Paint—the photography never had the crispness or resolution necessary for large scale pieces. Plus, it gave us control over the flames; not so easy with real fire," he elaborates. ▌In addition to organizing complex scheduling and event information to be clearly navigable, the various publications and collateral present information and imagery based on filmic traditions. Parts of

Near-fluorescent red, orange, and yellow paper stocks were used for single-ink collateral pieces, such as tickets and the stationery elements shown here (letterhead and envelope).

> Where would we be without a grid? I wouldn't cross the street without one.

the story are revealed as the viewer progresses through each piece, experiencing peaks and valleys, and a clear end point. Sometimes several crops of flame images coexist to signify the multiple viewpoints of individual film directors.

Sean Adams, Principal

The organic quality of the flame image permits endless variation in visualizing the concept; every occurrence of the flame is completely original and never repeats. Conceptually, this is a strong message that corresponds to the vision of Redford and the Sundance Festival with regard to independent filmmaking.

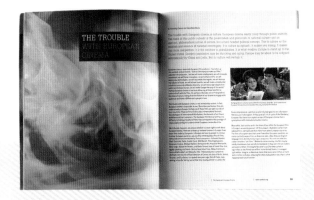

Page-spread sequences show the filmic sensibility the designers used to pace the content within publications, setting up slow crescendos countered by sudden, explosive fields of flame, as well as movement around the grids, articulated by shifts up and down among text and graphic elements.

All of the publications are set on a column grid whose proportions are defined in the style guide. This ensures rapid formatting and continuity of proportion and rhythm among the publications.

Crossing the Line

United Kingdom, 2006, 50 min., color, 35mm

Director/Screenwriter: Daniel Gordon
Executive Producers: John Battsek, Richard Klein, Paul Fi
Coproducer: Nicholas Bonner
Cinematographer: Nick Bennett
Editor: Peter Haddon
Sound: Steve Haywood
Narrator: Christian Slater

In 1962, Private James Dresnok, a 19-year-old American border guard in the notorious Korean DMZ, deserted the U.S. Army by crossing over into communist North Korea. As one of only four U.S. soldiers who defected to North Korea during the height of the Cold War, he was noticeably a stranger in a strange land. Although Dresnok was unsure about his future in the highly secretive communist country, the North Korean government found they could use his unusual circumstances in their propaganda campaign against the United States. Dresnok soon became a film star, playing the evil American again and again.

Crossing the Line expertly provides an in-depth portrait of the last American defector still residing in North Korea after 40 years. Director Daniel Gordon skillfully counterpoints Dresnok's own testimony against stark archival footage of the People's Republic and a haunting soundtrack. Further historical context is provided through interviews with his former commander and fellow soldiers, as well as a childhood friend who still awaits his return.

Crossing the Line is the unprecedented and complex story of a man who left the native country he felt unconnected to and found himself living in an alien nation he came to consider home.

—LISA VIOLA

Monday, January 22, 4:00 pm
Holiday Village Cinema IV, Park City
Tuesday, January 23, 9:15 am
Holiday Village Cinema III, Park City
Wednesday, January 24, 6:15 pm
Holiday Village Cinema III, Park City
Thursday, January 25, 7:30 pm
Broadway Centre Cinemas VI, SLC

114   World Cinema Competition: Documentary   2007 Sundance Film Festival

Enemies of Happiness
Voros lykkes fjender

Denmark, 2006, 58 min., color, Sony HD Cam
Dari/Pashtu with English subtitles

Directors: Eva Mulvad, Anja Al Erhayem
Cinematographer: Zillah Bowes
Editor: Adam Nielsen
Sound: Mikkel Groos
Music: Thomas Knak, Anders Remmer, Jesper Skårning
Graphics: Torsten Høeg Rasmussen

In September 2005, Afghanistan held its first parliamentary elections in 35 years. Among the candidates for 249 assembly seats was Malalai Joya, a courageous, controversial 27-year-old woman who had ignited outrage among hard-liners when she spoke out against corrupt warlords at the Grand Council of tribal elders in 2003. *Enemies of Happiness* is a revelatory portrait of this extraordinary freedom fighter and the way she won the hearts of voters, as well as a snapshot of life and politics in war-torn Afghanistan.

Amidst vivid, poetic images of Joya's dusty Farah Province, the film tracks the final weeks of her campaign, when death threats restrict her movements. But the parade of trusting constituents arriving on her doorstep leaves no doubt that Joya is a popular hero. Among her visitors is a 100-year-old man who treks two hours to offer loyalty and herbal medicine. King Solomon–style, Joya acts as folk mediator and advocate, adjudicating between a wife and her violent, drug-addicted husband and counseling a family forced to marry off their adolescent daughter to a much older man. Protected by armed guards, Joya heads to poor rural areas to address crowds of women, pledging to be their voice and "expose the enemies of peace, women, and democracy." In the presence of her fierce tenacity, we can imagine the future of an enlightened nation.

—CAROLINE LIBRESCO

Saturday, January 20, 2:30 pm
Holiday Village Cinema II, Park City
Sunday, January 21, 2:30 pm
Holiday Village Cinema II, Park City
Monday, January 22, 8:30 am
Holiday Village Cinema II, Park City
Tuesday, January 23, 9:00 pm
Broadway Centre Cinemas IV, SLC

Preceded by **Make a Wish**
Amanish

Director: Cherien Dabis
Palestinian Territories, 2006, 12 min., color, 35mm

A young Palestinian girl will do anything it takes to buy a birthday cake.

World Cinema Competition: Documentary   www.sundance.org   115

On pages where white space predominates, the flame motif is continued in a bright bar of color that helps orient the reader to the material as well as to the festival theme.

Almost all collateral pieces also include some type treatment in red, which connects the words to the central visual element of fire. The blocks of black are evocative of a darkened movie theater suddenly brought to life by the magic of independent film, as represented by the bursting flame.

33

Challenging an Assumption... or Five

Andrew Ashton is something of an iconoclast. Much of his work, with its complex amalgams of symbols, styles, and metaphors, threatens design establishment notions—stylistic dogma, popular visual trends, corporate pandering, reductivism—and defies many of the "rules" enumerated in this book. Fortunately, the maverick approach is supported, indisputably, by a rich understanding of those "rules" and the skill to break them productively. The managing committee for Melbourne, Australia's, annual design festival, then, likely approached Ashton with a combination of excitement and trepidation when they tapped him to develop the identity for the 2006 installment. Unified under the given theme glow, the Melbourne Design Festival's identity displays the weird intersection of ideas prevalent in Ashton's idiosyncratic process.

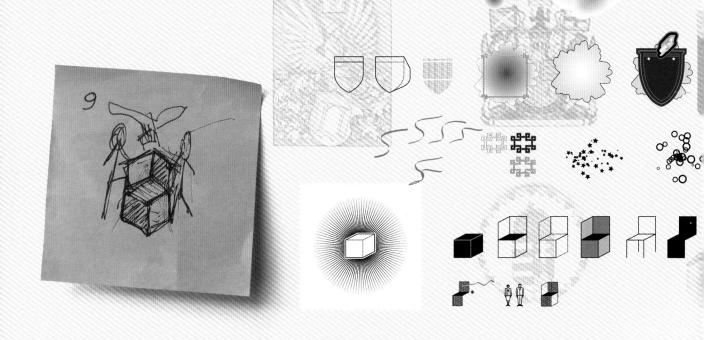

Ashton's process of discovery begins with a search for ways to envision not only the festival's theme, "glow," but also issues of relevance to contemporary design: power, historical significance, consumerism, politics, aesthetics, sexual equality, and so on.

Ashton envisioned a contemporary coat of arms derived, in part, from the conservative swing of Australian politics and the enforcement of national identity through such a heraldic device in government communications. Ashton's research in this vein unearthed a multitude of symbolic components with which to experiment: ribbons; shield forms, escutcheons, and chevrons; animals of power, such as the ram, deer, and lion; vines and plants of mystical potency; weaponry; and so on. Of interest is that conceptually, the coat of arms invokes ancient strategies of identification or branding.

The sketch for the coat of arms concept is shown here on a sticky note that survived a brainstorming session. It shows the basic arrangement of shield and flanked figures associated with heraldic emblems.

"I apply Newtown's Third Law to my process on a regular basis," Ashton says cryptically. "For every action there is an equal, if not greater, reaction. I like to understand a project's audience, to assess what influences their actions, and develop potential ideas around these findings." ▌ The Melbourne Design Festival's goal, in addition to celebrating the current state of design practice, is to involve the public and highlight design as part of their daily experience. Ashton is acutely aware of style trends and their insinuation into public consciousness and, characteristically, questions the source, value, and effect of such givens on visual—hence, public—culture. "The latest graphics software has brought to the fore the ability to render complex tonal images," says Ashton dubiously. "Subsequently, a rash of 3D-modeled corporate brand marks has appeared all over the world. To resist this trend," he states, "the studio approached the festival graphic based on optical art techniques—to develop a complex image without the aid of fine gradated tones." ▌ Purposely working under such predetermined and defiant conceits is a strategy Ashton imposes to fight cliché and push against boundaries. Assuming an expectation, in this case, for a design festival to be identified by an exciting image was also grounded in his perception that, given a broad selection of design industry events, prospective attendees would be selective, based on their judgment of its value from the image alone. "The less cliché the event's image, the less likely the event will address the cliché issues that marketers think designers want to address," Ashton says. ▌ Ashton presents concepts in two stages (see Case Study 25)—first, one in which broad ideas are explored together, and then a

> The vast majority of this audience is savvy to contemporary design. We wanted to challenge the viewer by presenting an image unlike any other currently being generated in the field.

Andrew Ashton, Principal

Potential image components, such as the Mason's calipers, undergo a series of studies in which Ashton tests variations to see what's possible, as well as what will work best in particular situations.

A refined digital sketch of the heraldic concept, supported by Ashton's research, communicates the idea well enough to the client that it is approved for further development.

DESIGN EVOLUTION

refined conceptual presentation, following the results of the initial discussion. "As the projects progress, we reference key stages," says Ashton. "These stages help confirm the final choice. Sometimes we will push an idea to its end even when we know that at a previous stage the idea was communicating at its best. Sometime a complete new idea can transpire from exhausting another." ▌Ashton's references in the initial stage of exploration, with the "glow" theme in mind, came about in consideration of Australian recent political conservatism and government enforcement

of the Australian coat of arms as an official national symbol. Ashton liked the idea of a heraldic symbol—a historic form of branding, and one that is familiar to many people—as a container for the more complex ideas he was gathering to evoke the theme itself. ▌"The function of the festival is to bring design to the public's attention," Ashton explains. "A design-inspired coat of arms seemed a good vehicle." Because design practice involves numerous fields of study and practice, education, social issues, and science, as well as communication and aesthetics, Ashton devel-

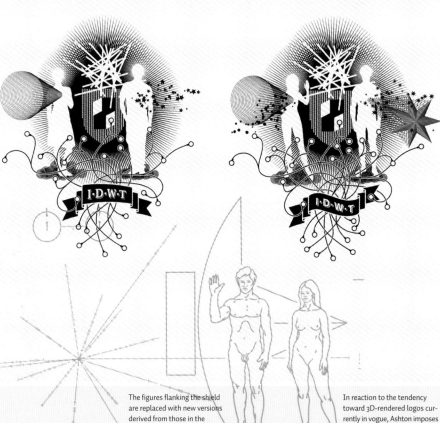

The figures flanking the shield are replaced with new versions derived from those in the pictographic, intergalactic greeting designed by Carl Sagan for the *Voyager I* craft launched in the late 1970s. In Ashton's version, however, the female waves in salutation, not the male.

In reaction to the tendency toward 3D-rendered logos currently in vogue, Ashton imposes a limitation on the coat of arms he will develop: it will consist of only high-contrast, optically reproducible forms— no continuous tone or gradients. An evolution of the coat of arms in this direction shows the primary symbolic components, reduced to a purely

black-and-white form: a radial, linear glow; linear structures; a spatter of stars; a shield form; a vine motif sprouting white globes; two figures; and a banner ribbon with insignia. This configuration is clearly sourced in the Australian coat of arms, seen adjacent.

An extruded star form is added to the right side of the configuration to offset the left-leaning stress created by the extrusion of concentric circles, and the vine motif is enlarged.

oped icon and symbol components that he combined within the coat of arms format, much as medieval heraldic imagery does. The coat of arms is laced with symbolism, from fractal theory to sexual equality. A fractal star, radiating lines, and a vine sprouting light globes mutually reinforce the festival theme.

❚ The refinement stage, following conceptual approval by the client, continued for a week, with the formal details being worked out. A bookish, but quirky serif face, Dolly, was selected for festival typography, and the color palette limited to a range of two colors,

another thumbing of the nose to expectations of extravagant production.

The festival logotype is set all lowercase and undergoes a similar spherical warping as the coat of arms.

In a last adjustment, the entire coat of arms was subjected to a filter-based distortion to create a bizarrely spherical warping.

34

ARQ (Murcia Archeological Museum)
Identity Program LSD | Madrid, Spain

One of the most common obstacles in creating visual communications for museums is the tendency to get weighted down by the history, rather than bringing the history into the present to resonate with contemporary audiences. Conservative, overly academic identities often do the opposite of what is needed: to make history come alive for people and invite their exploration. In contrast, the graphic program for this museum both respects the ancient tradition of this Spanish city's artisans and delivers a lively experience for the modern museumgoer, thanks to the deft intervention of Gabriel Martínez and Paz Martín of Madrid design studio LSD.

A Modern Journey among the Ruins

Painted and inscribed images from the museum's extensive collection of ancient Iberian pottery were contextually present for the designers as they began their exploration into a logotype. The idea of broken pottery—and the metaphor of fragmentation it suggested, of pieces put back together by archeology—informed initial studies. The designers examined the notion of breaking the acronym's letters apart.

As far as archeological history goes, the museum's collection offered a rich source of material for the designers. Murcia is an ancient city on Spain's Costa Blanca, and the museum holds a collection of Iberian artifacts from 1900 B.C.E., through the later Ottoman occupation, and forward into the present. Pottery, using the area's distinctive red-orange clay, is abundant in the collection, and it was to this material that the designers were immediately drawn. ▍Their initial investigations, into typographic marks, focused on the initials MAM—Museo Arqueológico de Murcia—in various configura-

tions that were reminiscent of fragments. Referring to images of pots, tablets, and other artifacts, the designers broke the letters apart to create a sense of archaeology's piecing together different times. This concept would later prove important as development progressed beyond the mark. ▍Their first proposal, however, had to do with the museum's name itself. "It was too institutional," says Martínez. In considering ways to attract the public's attention and make an enjoyable experience out of it, they realized the name could work against them. "We proposed a less formal

The designers proposed changing the museum's acronym from the literal MAM, which seemed too stodgy and institutional, to ARQ, which had a more contemporary sound and communicated the nature of the museum more directly. Martínez and Martín

demonstrated similar concepts for the logo in their presentation; the museum agreed and approved the concept.

The letters ARQ offer more varied form as part of their structure—the angled A, the curved Q, and the R, which mixes the two as a kind of transition. This progression from angle to curve lends the grouping a strong internal logic and greater complexity than does the MAM configuration.

name–ARQ–which could easily become a fun, familiar term." In a bold and unexpected move, the museum's board agreed, and the designers returned to the ideas they had been investigating, now using the three new letters. Toward the end of a three-month period, LSD presented their recommended identity mark—the rhythmically fragmented letters ARQ set in a contemporary serif face—and again met with museum approval. ▌Now, LSD turned their attention to the signage and collateral elements, including the stationery system. The pottery from the collection resurfaced as a

source of inspiration. Many of these artifacts were painted with intricate scenes from ancient daily life—animals, people hunting, ritual symbols and decorative geometric motifs. These elements seemed to lend themselves to the stationery, but Martínez was wary of the direction, hoping to avoid a dry, dusty-looking program. "We wanted to change the traditional feeling toward archeological collections and add notions such as discovery, enjoyment and learning," he recalls. He and Martín began to look into photographic images as well, in the hopes of finding some more modern textures.

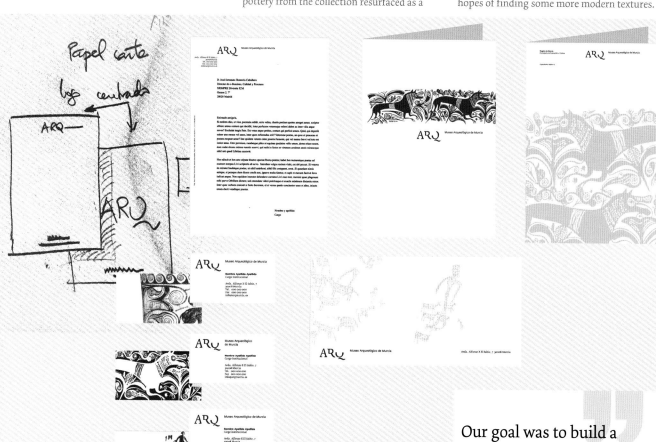

A palette of analogous clay reds and browns was sampled directly from the pottery. The closely related colors are similar in value but differ in temperature, from warmer to cooler (shifting from yellow into red).

The stationery development shows how the designers, certain that the pottery drawings needed to be a part of these documents, explored options for their use in tandem with typographic arrangements for the supporting text. In the final versions of the business card, the city's crest accompa-

nies such information, while the ARQ logo is kept separate on the reverse with the pottery drawings. The letterhead organizes the city's crest near the ARQ mark, and the pottery drawing is arranged in a horizontal band across the bottom. Note the relationships in alignment among type ele-

ments in both applications, as well as how elements proportion the spaces they break.

Our goal was to build a learning trip from the past. Through the interpretation of objects and bits of information, museumgoers will discover how people here lived.

Gabriel Martínez, Partner

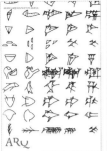

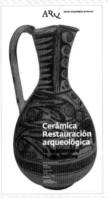

Initial studies for posters focused on typographic concepts, supported by the clay-colored images culled from the pottery. Decisive composition of the textural drawings plays with rhythmic type configurations.

The type family Fedra was adopted, using both its serif and sans-serif forms, to unify past and present, as well as to increase the visual unity of materials while providing opportunity for textural variation. The details of the letterforms evoke older styles of type drawing. The tittle of the lowercase *i* is a rotated diamond that lends a chiseled quality to that letter; open joints between bowls and stems, as in the lowercase *b*, evoke archaic forms.

The designers became conscious of all the applications beginning to feel too similar—even stuffy—and so discarded the typographic direction to explore photography. This study focuses on objects and relatively neutral coloration; the photographs are documentary and feel similar to the pottery drawings in their tonality and unaffected presentation.

Despite simple, yet dynamic, composition of imagery and corresponding typographic color, the designers determined this, too, was too programmatic and institutional.

The fragmentation of the logo suggested the same might be desirable for images. ▌The designers found that a simple splitting of a format in half, top to bottom, integrated well with the horizontal axis in the logo. Each area could contain a different image, or elements could travel across the divide to establish more direct connections. Experimenting with this idea in the stationery immediately proved too much, but it seemed to work well for more promotional elements.

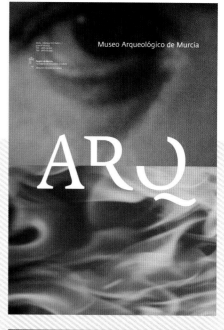

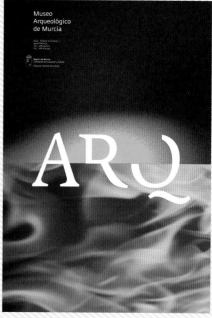

In the next poster study, the designers broke the format in half, situating the ARQ logotype across the break. Top and bottom could become independent of each other, creating an opportunity to make the connections between past and present that the designers felt important. A variety of image combinations was explored to see how relationships could be created, both conceptually and visually. The juxtaposition of different images top and bottom could profoundly affect the communication.

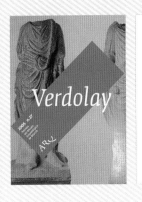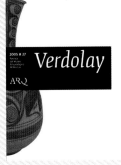

After numerous iterations of posters, signage, and a newsletter/magazine, the designers established two approaches to image use. "We chose illustration to relate directly to the collections and photography to build more abstract concepts for promotional purposes," says Martínez. The designers brought revisions of work in progress to their clients three times. This is a usual number of revision rounds for projects LSD has been involved. "Three is the limit!" Martínez says emphatically. ▌Supporting the program throughout was a dual serif/sans serif type family—Fedra, by Peter Bilak—that

Martínez and Martín took the museum newsletter through a similar process as the posters and stationery. The progression steps through photographic and, subsequently, strictly typographic presentation, supported by the ceramic images. The pottery is itself altered through added color to separate it slightly from the context of the institutional materials.

Simultaneously, the designers were developing signage and other materials. In response to the direction the posters had taken, their signage studies turned from illustration to incorporate photography. After evaluating this idea, they decided to keep the pottery drawings, and their associated color palette, for the signage as well, establishing these aspects of the visual language for the institution itself, in contrast to the photographic imagery being created for advertising and marketing communication.

allowed for tremendous flexibility in function and tone. The designers were also attracted to the set because it expressed a similar notion as their concepts for the imagery: "The two families perfectly join the concepts of tradition and present," Martínez says. A rich family of earth tones, including the color of the pottery's local clay, plus black and a rich blue, rounded out the concept.

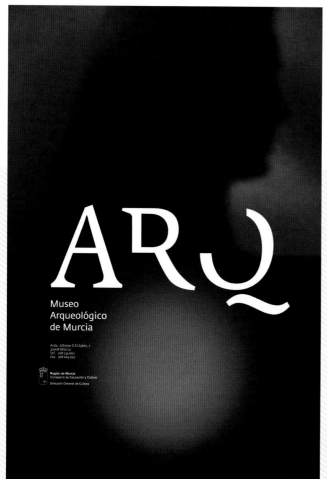

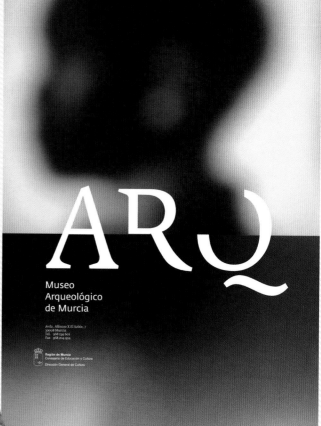

The final posters pushed the imagery into a more surreal area, leaving interpretation to the viewer. This idea encompasses the designers' goal of engaging the public and exciting them through the archaeological subject matter.

The promotional posters incorporate contrasting colors that both bridge and emphasize the horizontal split in the composition and the letters of the wordmark. The colors are softened and the images blurred, creating an intriguing tableau as well as an interesting contrast that makes the stark white and strong lines of the type stand out.

Salón de actos
Biblioteca
Taller de restauración
Tienda

Salas
Prehistoria a Edad de Bronce
Sala Usos múltiples
Administración
Sala Exposiciones temporales

2

Salón de actos
Biblioteca
Taller de restauración
Academias

1

salas
Ibérico a Paleocristiano
sala
Exposiciones temporales

0

Salas
Prehistoria a Edad de Bronce
Sala
Usos múltiples
Administración

-1

Almacenes

↑ Salas
Prehistoria a Edad de Bronce

← Sala
Usos múltiples
Administración

→ Tienda
Aseos

0

↑ salas
Ibérico a Paleocristiano

→ sala
Exposiciones temporales
Aseos

1

Región de Murcia
Consejería de Educación y Cultura

Dirección General de Cultura

Nombre Apellido Apellido
Cargo institucional

Avda. Alfonso X El Sabio, 7
30008 Murcia
Tel.   968 234 602
Fax   968 204 994
info@arqmurcia.es

ARQ Museo Arqueológico de Murcia

The system of images and
color palette used for
materials directly related
to the collections them-
selves proves to be very
versatile, whether used in
single color applications
such as stationery, in
monochromatic variations
such as signage, or in
multicolor collateral such
as brochures and T-shirts.

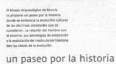

El Museo Arqueológico de Murcia
te propone un paseo por la historia
donde se evidencia la evolución cultural
de las distintas sociedades que se
sucedieron. La relación del hombre con
el entorno, sus estrategias de adaptación
y la explotación del medio donde habitaba
dan las claves de la evolución.

un paseo por la historia

ARQ Museo Arqueológico de Murcia

Guía español

35

**Swansea Waterfront Museum
Public Art Project**

Why Not Associates with Gordon Young |
London, United Kingdom

Form, function, landscape, and history come together
in this public art and design project realized for a museum
devoted to the industrial history of Swansea, a coastal
Welsh city. Once a powerful seaport, the city's heritage
spans shipbuilding, porcelain manufacturing, mining,
and the development of the world's first railway service.
This rich narrative is embodied in the museum's extensive
collection of industrial artifacts, housed in an austere
building designed by Wilkinson Eyre Architects that
evokes the early twentieth century's machine age.
Creating an environmental work to communicate the
museum's mission and engage the public fell to London's
Why Not Associates and frequent collaborator, artist
Gordon Young.

Machine Age Monoliths... And a Place to Sit

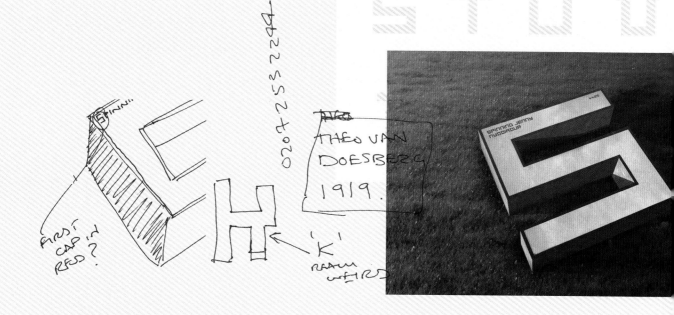

Early sketches focused on square-form sans-serif letters that reflect the area's industrial heritage, as well as the museum architecture. The first proposal conceived of a full alphabet of letters; each letter was to bear the name of an artifact from the museum's collection, set into the surface in Welsh and English, along with its museum catalogue number. The indi- vidual letterforms containing this text element are shown flat and in a computer-gener- ated rendering of the letters on site. The heavy outline indi- cates a concrete rim housing a terrazzo surface that holds steel text in place. The red ini- tial creates contrast and echoes details in the museum building.

The two-year process began with Why Not's partner and lead designer for the project, Andrew Altmann, sketching with Gordon Young on paper. Despite Why Not's characteristically digital work, their aesthetic remains rooted in craft, evidenced by their recent, similar public art commissions involving stone, glass, and brass typographic explorations. ▌ Early on, Altmann and Young focused on a typographic concept. First, it would discourage linking the museum with a specific image. Second, the designers could incorporate the Welsh language, an aspect

they felt important as a way of honoring local culture. Last, the monumental forms, cast in concrete and steel, could be used by visitors as benches. ▌ Taking cues from the architecture and its references to the Dutch De Stijl movement, Altmann chose a typeface with geometric structure to reflect the subject matter of the museum's collection. Schematic plans and computer-aided images of the proposed alphabet installed on the grounds represented this one concept, presented after two weeks of development. "We always try to present just one concept we believe in," says Altmann.

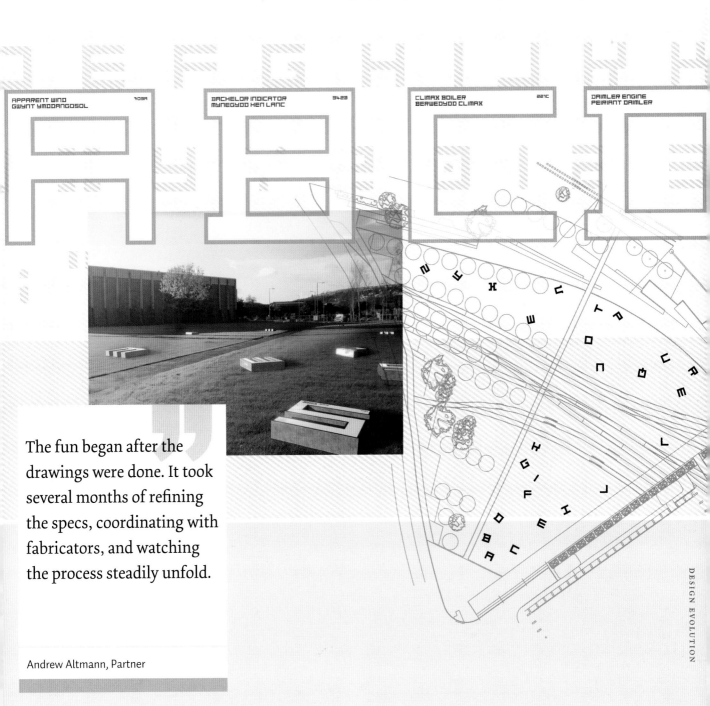

APPARENT WIND
GWYNT YMDDANGOSOL   709A

BACHELOR INDICATOR
MYNEGYDD HEN LANC   342B

CLIMAX BOILER
BERWEDYDD CLIMAX   221C

DAIMLER ENGINE
PEIRIANT DAIMLER

The fun began after the drawings were done. It took several months of refining the specs, coordinating with fabricators, and watching the process steadily unfold.

Andrew Altmann, Partner

The committee reviewing the design proposal approved the concept right away, but the building's architect had some objections—the letters appeared scattered haphazardly over the landscape, and he didn't like the typeface. "We thought it made sense, and there was also a cost consideration," remembers Altmann. "No curves! Much cheaper to make." ▌After further review, the designers opted for a typeface designed in the 1930s by A. M. Cassandre called Bifur. "Again, the font related to industry—Cassandre and all his transport posters. Plus," Altmann clarifies, "the design of the letters allowed us to create a more enclosed type of seating." It was also determined that a single phrase, instead of the scattered characters, would create a single line of elements whose geometry would complement the building and the site. ▌The committee, together with Altmann and Young, settled on the phrase Pobl+Machines—"people" in Welsh, linked with the industrial past. Once the phrase was approved, a two-year process of planning, drawing, production, and installation began.

The revised typeface, Bifur, has a similar industrial feeling to that originally selected—geometric structure and dramatic counterspaces all convey strength and precision. The presence of curvilinear elements, however, brings a counterpoint to the angularity of the other strokes, creating a richer experience of form. The shading in the letters, further-more, suggested a kind of two-level structure that lent itself to creating seating with backs and enclosed areas. Three-dimensional computer-aided renderings of the new phrase helped refine the seating levels and scale relationships to the site before fabrication.

Comparing the computer drawing at left and the pre-production maquette above reveals an adjustment in the punctuation. The ampersand that is truly part of the Bifur typeface's character set [at right] proved overly complicated relative to the other forms, as well as potentially confusing—is it an *N*? a *C*? The designers opted instead for a plus sign, whose simpler stroke configuration fits more clearly with that of the other characters, and is much more easily recognized as a character.

Following the client's final approval of the maquette, the individual base letters were fabricated in steel at full size. The sheer scale of the project becomes evident when a person stands in the midst of two of the base letters. The smaller texts were cut from metal plates and set into the surfaces of the base forms, countersunk within poured concrete. The contrast of rough and reflective surfaces at large and small scales creates a rich, tactile experience.

Finishing, transporting, and installing the finished letter benches required a small army and heavy machinery. With the letters set into the ground and a good polishing, the realized project was introduced to the Swansea public with great fanfare.

> Working with Gordon Young means we get the benefit of combining two disciplines. Together, we're able to reach a point that neither of us could have achieved on our own.

Andrew Altmann, Partner

The final, full-size letters were constructed by artist Russell Coleman. Their frames are stainless steel, filled with poured concrete set flush to the surface with the detail letter-forms. The supporting typography is set in a lightweight sans-serif face, Edward Johnston's font designed in 1916 for the London Underground. The mass of the letters is offset by the luminous, reflective quality of their stainless steel coats. The flecked concrete surface texture adds subtle detailing to the otherwise sleek surfaces. ▌The project was very well received by the client group at the Waterfront Museum and is a popular visiting spot for locals and visitors alike, who often come to spend time sitting in the park on the monumental benches.

The letters *cum sculpture cum* benches are further integrated into the larger landscape by their placement bisecting a walkway. The cool grays of the paving stones also beautifully complement the blues and grays of the letterforms themselves.

The monolithic seating enjoys regular patronage from museum visitors as well as from longtime locals.

36

Promotional Theater Poster:
Sennentuntschi
Mixer | Lucerne, Switzerland

One of the joys of designing is that it allows the designer to investigate areas they might otherwise never have encountered. Sometimes, these encounters are more interesting than others. Such was the case for Erich Brechbühl of Mixer, who found out just how interesting the task of designing could be when he undertook the design of a poster for a new play, premiering at the Theater Aeternam in Lucerne, Switzerland. "My research always begins anew with every project," Brechbühl says, preferring not to keep an image library as some designers do. For this poster, the research was a bit outside his usual realm of experience.

Yodel-ay Hee Hooooo... OOooohhh Yeah, Baby!

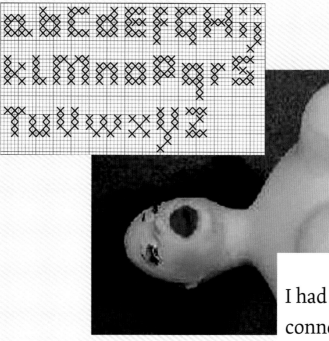

Brechbühl's extensive search for image reference introduced him to people he would otherwise never have met.

> I had the idea to connect modern elements with traditional crafts.

Erich Brechbühl, Principal

The play for which he was designing a poster revolved around two mountaineers who, feeling a little lonely, decide to craft their own version of a blow-up sex doll. Brechbühl decided immediately to somehow feature an image of the characters' creation on the poster. "I think it's very direct," he says. "I wanted to show, in a very simple way, what the play is about," he says, eyebrow raised. ▌Not sure, however, how to achieve the idea in a tasteful way—most likely, in some illustrative form—he set about collecting images of blow-up dolls, mostly downloaded from the Internet ... but since these were very

small, he found himself having to buy a few. ▌The most important issue was establishing proportions for the figure, as well as being able to determine how to represent details accurately. "There is a big difference between a woman's shape and ... this," he clarifies. In drawn form, being able to present the image as that of a doll, and not of a live person, would depend on capturing the doll's particular gesture, the shape of its shoulders, its characteristic expression. ▌Brechbühl, who had read the play, started sketching with pencil, making thumbnails to see what he could do with the image.

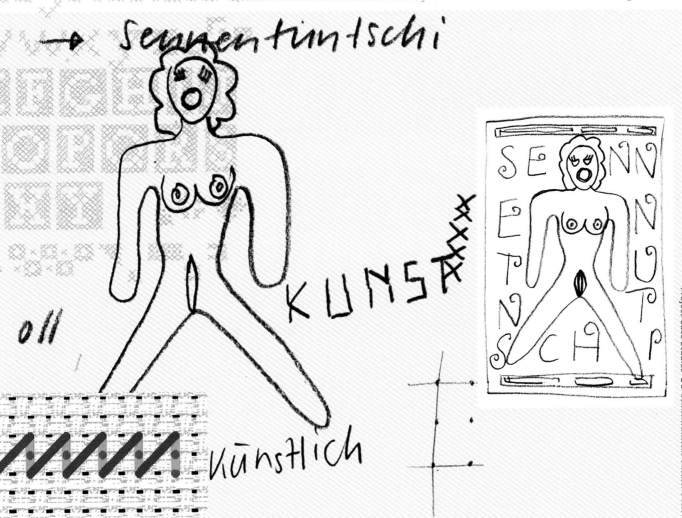

The designer gathered examples of hand-embroidered lettering from samples he found on the Internet in an effort to maintain the design's connection to craft and the handmade creation at the center of the play.

The differences between photography and illustration in terms of subject mediation are made explicit here. While some viewers may feel uncomfortable looking at photographs of the blow-up doll—which are completely credible because they appear "real"—

an illustrated version removes the real, physical quality and the potential for it to be perceived as "obscene."

The human figure, because it's such an iconic form, can be shown in a very distorted way and still be perceived as, simply, a human. The drawing of the doll required a certain specificity of gesture and proportion—the outward thrust of the arms, the strange protrusion of the shoulders, the

indistinct transition from the neck into the head, and so on— to transform the image recognizably for the viewer.

"I had the idea to connect modern elements with traditional crafts," he says. He looked for some rustic handicraft that could translate quickly for the audience; while blowing up a low-resolution image, the pixellation suggested cross-stitch embroidery—ironically, the kind that young women of an earlier time made as part of their wedding linens. ▎With this in mind, he roughed out a sketch depicting an embroidered image of the doll for his theater clients, and they approved. "For me it's normal to present one ideal concept. If the client isn't satisfied," he winces, "I'll work on another idea and present that one." ▎Brechbühl made vector drawings of the doll's contours. Then, at a very small size, he imposed a bitmap pattern so that the pixellation that occurred when he enlarged it would create the embroidery stitch pattern at the right scale. Once this was complete and the stitching texture transferred to the full-size vector drawing, he positioned the type elements.

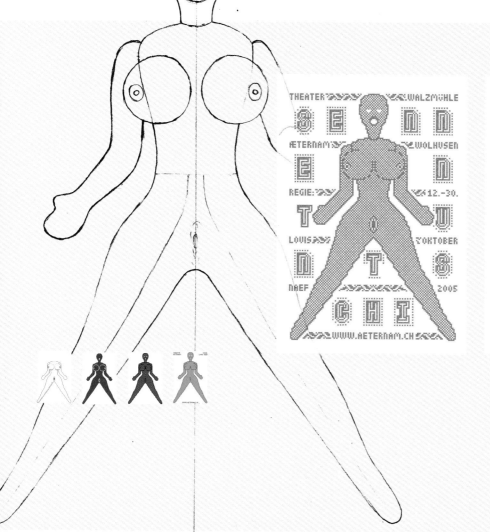

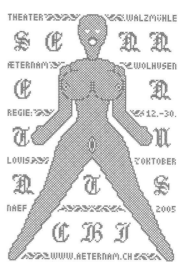

The tiny, original sequence of textured drawings that was transformed, through enlargement, into the model for the stitching pattern, is shown here.

Placing the figure centrally makes it confrontational and oddly welcoming. The designer offsets the static quality of the composition by introducing detailed surface activity and scale changes among the supporting typographic elements.

The bitmap typeface shares a structural characteristic with embroidery; context transforms the digital into the handcrafted.

These underwent a few changes, primarily because of evaluations Brechbühl made of the relative sizes and complexity of the typefaces—titling stitched in a similar way as the doll drawing, supported by a bitmap font (similar enough in texture to needlework) for the supporting information. The poster was reproduced as a silkscreen in one color ink on heavy stock.

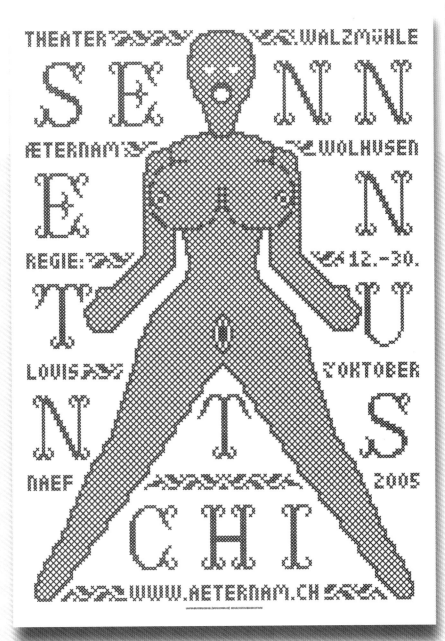

The choice of typeface for the titling in this pre-final version calls more attention to itself than the designer wanted, distracting from the doll image. This effect results from the weight of the typeface relative to the doll's lighter density, as well as the degree of positive and negative interplay within the individual letters.

In the final poster, the juxtaposition of the overblown female figure with the domestic qualities inherent in the needlework feeling of the type make a statement that is startling without being obscene, inspiring curiosity, engagement, and humor, while communicating clear messages about the content of the play itself.

37

Edison Innovation Foundation Website
Firstborn | New York and Los Angeles, USA

The brief suggested that the website desired by the client, a foundation dedicated to preserving the legacy of inventor Thomas Edison—the man responsible for the lightbulb, the vacuum tube, the phonograph, and motion pictures—should be as innovative as the man himself. No small feat, that task fell to multimedia developers Firstborn, who worked to create a striking interface for the experience that challenges conventional notions of navigation. "It was about creating a site that Edison would have been intrigued to interact with," says Firstborn executive producer Dan LaCivita. Freeform information structures that change page by page invite exploration and delight with unexpected discovery.

The Thrill
of Discovery

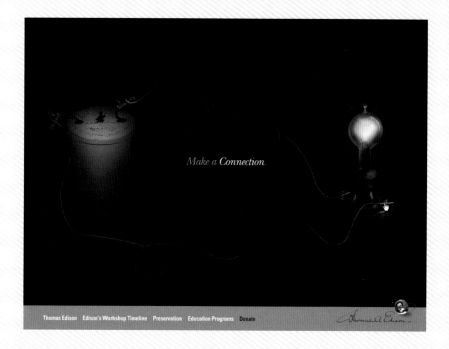

Make a Connection.

The first of three directions presented content in a conventional, horizontal-format browser page context, with A-level navigational links separated into a gray band at the bottom of the page. While the red Donate button remained constant to encourage visitors, color change in the nearby links indicated the link's state of activity and the location of the user.

A photographic depiction of Edison's first lightbulb connected literally with an aspirational headline to welcome users to the home page.

The Edison Innovation Foundation's primary goal in having the site developed was to support a massive capital campaign aimed at preserving Thomas Edison's Menlo Park laboratories, shops, library, and some 5,000 documents, which had fallen into neglect. One of the mandates the client presented Firstborn was that the site should avoid the stodgy quality of like sites produced by similar institutions. LaCivita and his team, led by art director Victor Brunetti and Flash developer Gicheol Lee, were happy to oblige. ▌ As part of the proposal and schedule, LaCivita and the client had already established the major content areas and of how many individual pages each would consist. Following a kickoff meeting to discuss the brief, Firstborn received initial assets from the client—marketing materials, Thomas Edison's trademark signature, image files, and text for the home page and one section to establish the navigation structure and visual style. ▌ While LaCivita prefers to focus on two strong concepts, in this case, Firstborn developed three and presented all of them. Each offered a distinctly different approach, focused on the timeline section of the site to help compare navigation. Two of the

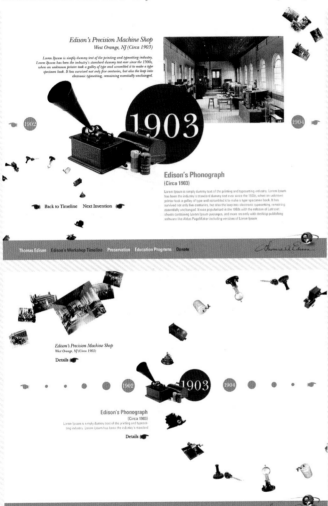

The timeline was presented as a linear configuration that scrolled across the screen as the user rotated a circular wheel made up of silhouettes of Edison's patents. The dots representing the years grew in size as they entered a central hot spot relative to a given patent's position and, if selected, expanded to a much larger size. An introductory image assumed a central position, while additional snapshots clustered to the upper right, and the silhouettes positioned lower left. Dingbat icons directed the user toward links, and images were captioned with short text.

directions presented content in a more conventional format, with A-level navigation links along the bottom. ▌In both versions, the timelines appeared as horizontal, linear structures with links to deeper content. One of these concepts showed smaller, scalable images interacting with graphic elements and type on a white background, while the other made use of full-screen imagery to place the user directly in the laboratory environment. ▌The third concept, however, came out of the process of exploring design patterns and programming scripts in the Flash software. "Every project is different," says Brunetti. "Sometimes you do a lot of sketching in pencil. Other times, you gather assets, create mood boards, and work with grid systems…" "…And other times," Gicheol Lee chimes in, "you may open up Flash to see what type of interesting layout can be created programmatically." Brunetti and Lee discovered a design pattern in Flash that could be used to create a navigational structure around a spiral that would change interactively—reordering itself as different content was accessed.

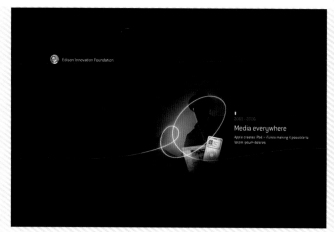

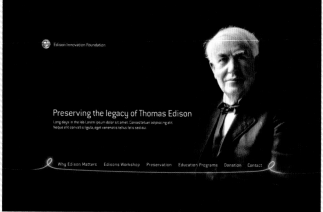

Where did the ideas for the site come from? Brainstorming. Lots of brainstorming.

Victor Brunetti, Art Director

A second concept also framed the site in a horizontal page format. In this direction, a launch animation followed the arc of an electric current or wire through a montage of historic technological events related to Edison's inventions.

Both the home page and the timeline subpage use full-bleed imagery. On the home page, a rich black-and-white portrait of Edison presented a horizontal navigation system, similar to that used in the first concept. The arcing current plays a role in highlighting the user's location within the site. On the timeline page, a film-strip of images scrolls across the screen, allowing users to access images relevant to the timeline, which is navigated below in a sliding-bar format.

It was this latter concept that the client approved as capturing Edison's spirit of discovery. The core, spiral navigation structure is made up not only of the A-level links, but also links to 100 of Edison's 1,300 patents, giving users access to the original patent papers. The A-level navigation links cause the spiral of text to rotate around a central icon—the Edison Foundation's logo—and present the accessed content in the most appropriate structure. ▮ The timeline, for example, forms into a chronological list presented as a vertical column that expands and contracts. In the Foundation's informational area, links scroll upward through a horizontal bar. All of the action occurs in a deep, colorful space that makes use of a full-screen browser; there are no frame- or window-formatted areas, so the navigation and content material appears to float unencumbered.

▮ After the concept was approved, the team spent three weeks refining imagery and

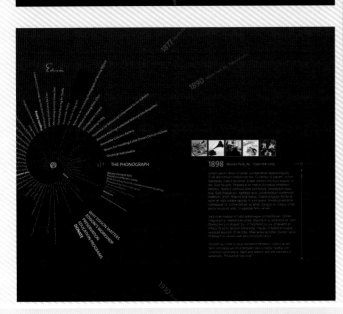

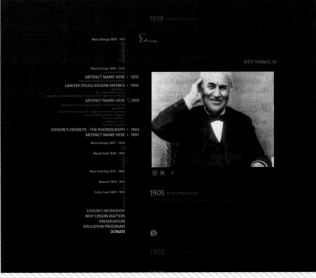

The third direction leapt into a different realm in all aspects. While the first two concepts made limited use of color, this one flooded the browser with a rich, slightly smoky greenish-blue hue. The navigation and the content, rather than constrained by a grid structure, bands, or other such devices, was displayed in a radiating spray of text from a central location, spiraling backward into deep space and creating a freeform shape. This text consisted of the names of roughly 100 of Edison's patents. Each page accessed by clicking the navigational links restructured the information. In the timeline, for example, a vertical column of information organizes the chronology and supporting images. The bold, luminous, and unconventional approach of this concept struck a chord with the client, representing to them the innovative spirit of the famous inventor.

content display structures, working with the client to edit and organize material, as well as select the most interesting patents for the spiral navigation. ▎From there, the team spent another five weeks programming the site and troubleshooting, presenting working prototypes twice for the client to review and make revisions. The team kept each iteration to compare differences in functionality, such as the transitions between pages. ▎"Sometimes, projects can have over a hundred versions as things progress," says LaCivita. The resulting site, launched merely three months after the

process began, helps reintroduce Thomas Edison's image to a contemporary audience in an energetic, inspirational context and allows them access to information about his profound technological contributions.

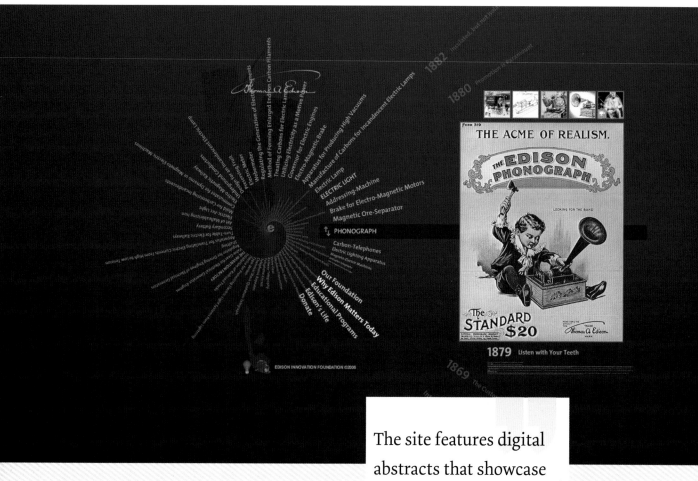

The central spiral on the site contains a list of every patent Edison ever held; as the titles are rolled over, pop up menus offer a downloadable PDF of the invention and a date of issue. Key navigational elements are in larger type to make them easier to find. The individual lines of the spiral morph and reassemble themselves into new shapes as one goes deeper into the site, but are always readily available, keeping the emphasis on the inventions that define the man.

The site features digital abstracts that showcase modern-day devices inspired by Edison's original creations.

Dan LaCivita, Executive Producer

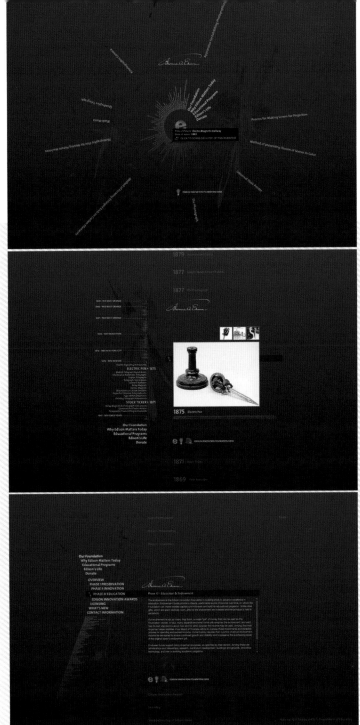

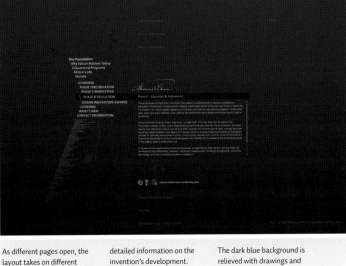

DESIGN EVOLUTION

As different pages open, the layout takes on different shapes. The opening sequence explodes outwards with innumerable ideas; interior pages maintain a constant connection to the inventions that are central to Edison's legacy. For example, click on a date and the spiral turns itself to highlight the appropriate invention and a pop up window gives detailed information on the invention's development.

The dark blue background is relieved with drawings and other information such as patent applications that show details of the products Edison invented. No matter where you are on the site, access to the main navigational elements as well as the list of patents is always available and easy to access.

38

Exhibition Catalog: *Branded and on Display*
Studio Blue | Chicago, USA

The design of exhibition catalogs typically follows certain conventions, maintaining a reserved presentation in page composition, typography, and graphic detailing in deference to the artwork. It sometimes happens, however, that an exhibition's conceptual underpinnings will suggest—even require—the accompanying catalog depart from such norms. Such is the case with this project—a catalog designed by Studio Blue of Chicago to accompany an exhibition at the Krannert Art Musuem, located on the campus of the University of Illinois at Urbana-Champaign. The exhibit, *Branded and on Display*, featured the work of artists whose work explores strategies of branding and the commoditized environment. Unconventional pacing, unexpected typography, and quirky color all help to extend the exhibition's ideas beyond its walls and into the catalog itself.

Mmmm... Culture. Where's My Checkbook?

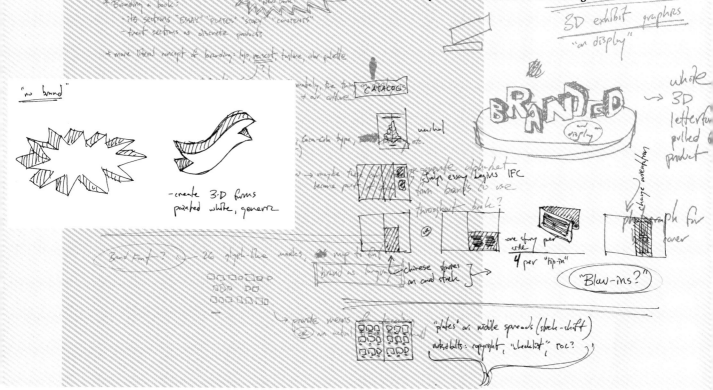

Unfortunately, schedule conflicts prevented the designers from meeting with the museum's curator before beginning the preliminary design exploration, having only a precis, sample images, and a few e-mails from which to work. Studio Blue partner, Cheryl Towler-Weese, and designer Garrett Niksch began the four-week process of exploring the design direction with hand sketching, working in the brainstorm sessions (see Case Study no. 29) that Towler-Weese describes as being like the old game show, "Win, Lose, or Draw."

▌Considering the exhibition, and bearing in mind that the audience—mostly students, given the museum's location—would be more receptive, the designers' approach avoided convention from the outset. "We looked at mail order catalogues," says Towler-Weese, "thinking that model would provide a nice twist on the typically conservative world of art books."

▌The designers compared various companies' strategies for presenting their products, and applied these same methods literally to the presentation of the artwork. The curator herself had proposed reproducing corporate brands throughout the book. "We could see that this

In their first approach, Studio Blue was working blind—having been unable to meet before beginning the process—and relying on a few e-mails from the client. However, they decided to reference mail-order catalogs as an appropriate form. The designers went right for the ultimate branded symbol, Andy Warhol's Brillo boxes, as a proposed cover image, selecting type styles and linear treatments to reflect the style of certain Northeast American clothing retailers.

The interior spreads reflected the same sensibility, presenting artwork in grid-based layouts typically found in such retail catalogs. The choice of light, neutral sans-serif, black bands, narrow gutters between images, and callout boxes all operate in an aesthetic favored by home furnishing and cooking retailers.

A second direction used logo-like shapes and colored text pages to suggest brands without actually showing any. The recognizable outer shapes of the brands played off the selection of type and color for the short stories. Artwork appeared isolated from text and in no particular order. The client wasn't satisfied with either direction, but this one seemed to have promise.

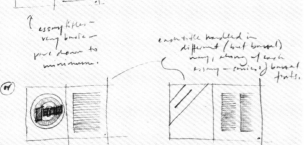

"
We generate many iterations and like to save each one. Saving ideas that might not, initially, hold any promise can help spark new ideas when unearthed later in the process.

Cheryl Towler-Weese, Partner

essays:

[typographic pin pullions; well logo words in text

put in title stuff here — numbers, etc. to keep left hand page minimal

essay titles — very bold — pared down to minimum

each title handled in different (but based) way, showing of each essay — series of based fonts

still quite titilation

Towler-Weese and Niksch began to rework the concept, focusing on the differences between the content—short stories, essays, and artwork— as well as the notion of evoking the brands in the short stories. Their efforts now revolved around the styles of the texts, initially using color and size as a way of differentiating between different components. Descriptive elements took on personality, related to their identity; essay text was treated in black and white. The designers narrowed their typeface selection down to Dolly, a serif face that feels bookish at smaller sizes, in its regular weight, but much more unusual at larger sizes in bold. Exaggerated details in the bold weight, along with exceptionally bulbous curves, gave it a plastic quality in this context. In this study, brand names are called out in bold.

would present an enormous rights issue," says Towler-Weese who, together with Niksch, spent time thinking about how they could evoke each brand without reproducing the logos. ▌In addition to the artwork, the book also would present nine short stories, each featuring a product brand as a central character. Treating the type for these individually—with color and typeface specific to the brand character—in contrast to the running text, became a way of suggesting brands without actually showing them. ▌Upon seeing the first, proposed concepts, the curator was able to

clarify her thinking with regard to the exhibition's artwork. The client wasn't comfortable with the studio's initial design concepts, which didn't accurately reflect the conceit of the exhibition. Knowing this, however, helped the designers better understand the form and structure the book needed. ▌"A good deal of alteration was needed to get the design to a place where the client felt satisfied," Towler-Weese says. She and Niksch stripped the artwork presentation down to allow, generally, one image per page, deliberately centered in a generic way. The running text, related to the

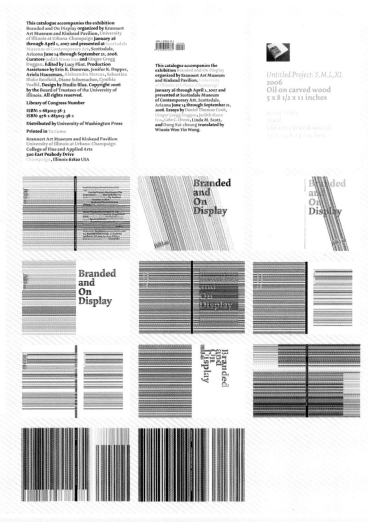

Tests of callouts set in Dolly revealed the interesting possibility of using the bold setting, in color, within running text to further differentiate brand names. Alternate typefaces—here, a slab serif—were still in consideration for various text elements.

Differentiating the short stories from the other texts meant evolving the earlier idea of evoking the brands they described by setting each story in its own typeface and color scheme. This choice introduced a kind of stylistic randomness that complemented the irregular sequencing of material.

The academic tone of the essay pages is enhanced by the use of the typeface Dolly, set in black, in regular weight, at a more conventional text size. Callouts showing individual works as support are also set centered on the page. As the relative dept of the paragraphs changes, the left-to-right alignment relationship is thrown into question, taking on a bland, arbitrary quality.

The client approved the direction and work began on the cover. The designers investigated a great many concepts, beginning with those that responded to the unconventional pacing by using a text-spread layout.

Of greater interest were ideas that related to the book's bar code, which had become an important element in one of the cover designs, and was also the subject of a work in the exhibit. Distorting this element created an abstract graphic element that could be

used in various dynamic ways. The client pushed the designers to explore this idea in as many iterations as possible.

DESIGN EVOLUTION

exhibition itself, became bookish, exaggerating the contrast between this content and the brand stories, which took on even more exaggerated color. ▌An earlier structural, idea, however, proved useful: art reproductions, essays, and brand stories would be interspersed with each other, seemingly at random, rather than be grouped, as they conventionally would. The unexpected, scattershot pacing suited the nature of the art and gave the book a slightly irreverent quality. ▌The designers also began to investigate the cover at this stage, its process itself a three-week exploration. "The client was

very involved and asked us to keep pushing our ideas further," says Niksch. "We ended up with many design iterations that we kept and compared." ▌Following approval of the cover, Towler-Weese and Niksch spent the remaining two months of development time executing layouts based on the approved design direction, which included two rounds of editorial revisions, and preparing the files for production.

The story that features Nokia is set on a cool gray-blue background in a bitmap typeface, emulating the look of SMS messaging text on a cell phone screen. Each of the short stories is as different, visually, as can be. This one commodifies Che Guevara as a brand, commenting wryly on the convergence of branding and politics.

Brand names are called out in the enormous text with colors drawn from their visual identities. The treatment simulates the visual effect of brands inserting themselves into public consciousness on the street.

The printed cover design shows the bar code expanded to fill the surface and translated into color.

Our particular favorite is the face used for the Hello Kitty short story—we would never get away with using type like that in any other art catalog.

Garrett Niksch, Designer

Artworks are shown individually, drably centered on the pages. Beginning with a color plate and then presenting text, out of expected order and in defiance of exhibition catalog conventions creates an unsettling effect. The unusual pacing disorients the reader; the designers also purposely removed page numbers at key points to augment this feeling.

39

Apparel Embroidery Patterns for Bonfire Snowboarding Company
Research Studios | London, United Kingdom

A Topography of Scale and Color

The sporting industry has been at the forefront of innovation in apparel for several decades. Not only have manufacturers influenced the shapes and styles of couture creations, but their products have steadily made their way off the tracks, slopes, and luge runs and onto the streets. Street wear, conversely, has had a chance to return the favor, as the rebel "extreme" sports popular with alternative youth culture—skating, mogul-jumping, motocross, and snowboarding—have organically adopted elements of everyday style. Bonfire Snowboarding Company is a manufacturer of gear for that particular sport whose subculture participants demand constant innovation in product. Research Studios, located in London, delivered a unique fabric pattern, with input from the client as a starting point. Bonfire was interested in using a camouflage pattern in its new lines of snowboarding apparel and accessories, and this was the jumping-off point of their brief to Jeff Knowles, designer at Research Studios.

> We developed a huge number of directions for the patterns; there were probably ten to fifteen options that we actually showed the client.

Jeff Knowles, Designer

After researching camouflage patterns to learn how they're made, Knowles created a base pattern as a guide and began to explore ways of reinventing it. From early on, he established an approach using smaller, pixel-like elements to make the camouflage part of contemporary culture, possibly commenting on the nature of cyber culture as a kind of camouflage.

"They wanted us to create a camouflage pattern that avoided the stereotypical army print," he says enthusiastically. The interesting formal aspect of this challenge was that camouflage prints—or "camo," for short—are designed to appear completely random, like the patterns of light and dark in wilderness settings, but are, in fact, repeated patterns. "I researched existing camo patterns to learn how they are created, and what it is that makes them different from a normal repeat pattern," Knowles says. ▌After building his own pattern base from which to work, Knowles began to investigate ways of treating the camo with a new approach. Working digitally from the beginning, and naturally drawn to things "high-tech," Knowles' starting point for exploration was pixel-based detailing—making up a larger pattern out of a smaller one. ▌For this project, what could be a standard process of formally presenting concepts and undergoing revisions in staged rounds didn't apply. Knowles experimented for several weeks with patterns made from various graphical elements, exploring alternative languages of greater and lesser complexity, density, and base pixel shape. "Every time a

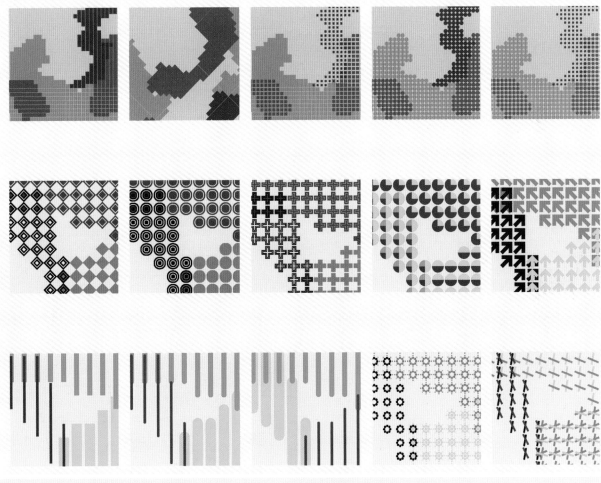

The pixel elements range from squares to lines to small pie-charts. By creating a simple system of variation—changing aspects of different pixels based on a specific visual logic—Knowles could create textural changes in the pattern simply by changing which kinds of pixel, of which density or complexity, appeared together.

By altering color, as well as form language, Knowles discovered he could perform these changes within the pattern independently of the overall camouflage shapes the pixel groupings defined. This variable added a tremendous complexity to the designs and a secondary, "transparent" layer to the camouflage.

change was made, other than a small adjustment, a new instance of the design was created," Knowles explains, "so I kept all the variations to compare." When he had generated a body of variations he thought would appeal to the client, he sent them via e-mail as a PDF file, and through discussion, selected one primary direction for refinement. ❙ Bonfire picked a pattern based on a system of concentric circles, some with thinner strokes, some thicker. The varying densities of circle components were distributed around the camo pattern in an alternate pattern. Compounding the complexity

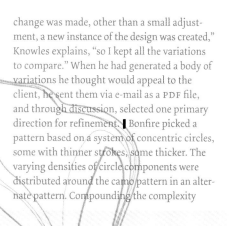

> From a distance, it looks like a solid camo, but as one gets closer you can view the detail in the design.

Jeff Knowles, Designer

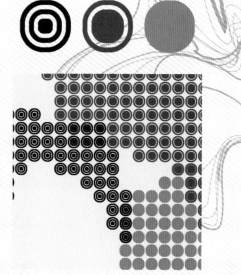

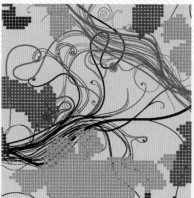

Knowles and the client chose this pattern, based on concentric circles of varying weights. The client, however, requested that a secondary, linear pattern be integrated within the base pattern.

Knowles turned to his colleague, Reece, who explored topographic mapping as a basis for his study of line languages. The progression here resulted in the final linear elements Knowles introduced into his base pattern.

The client imposed a palette based on the colorways they had already developed for the upcoming season's collection.

was color, which could also be distributed independent of any one kind of circle component. ❚ The client had only one request, other than minor, generalized refinement: they wanted a secondary, more fluid pattern introduced. For that, Knowles turned to colleague Ben Reece, who explored swirling lines while Knowles continued to refine the base pattern. Reece's studies took topography—the contour mapping of landscapes—as an inspiration, as well as splash forms that reminded him of snow. The swirling lines were incorporated as a separate vector layer into the base pattern, and then a

period of continued refinement ensued. "I would say 70 percent of the time (roughly ten days) was spent developing the initial ideas, the final 30 percent was refinement and color changes." Color, as it turned out, had been predetermined by the client as part of an overall colorway system for the season's collection, so Knowles simply had to apply the palette options in preparing the files for printing. ❚ The client spent two weeks in Japan at the printing factory. The pattern was so complex, the printing house had to develop new ways of printing to accurately reproduce it on fabric. The result

was a level of detail the printers hadn't seen before. ❚ Knowles was happy with the results of the process, although there were some skeptics on the client side. "Although they really liked the design, some people within the company were not to convinced it would be popular in the snowboarding market," Knowles says. "The jacket turned out to be one of their best-selling items."

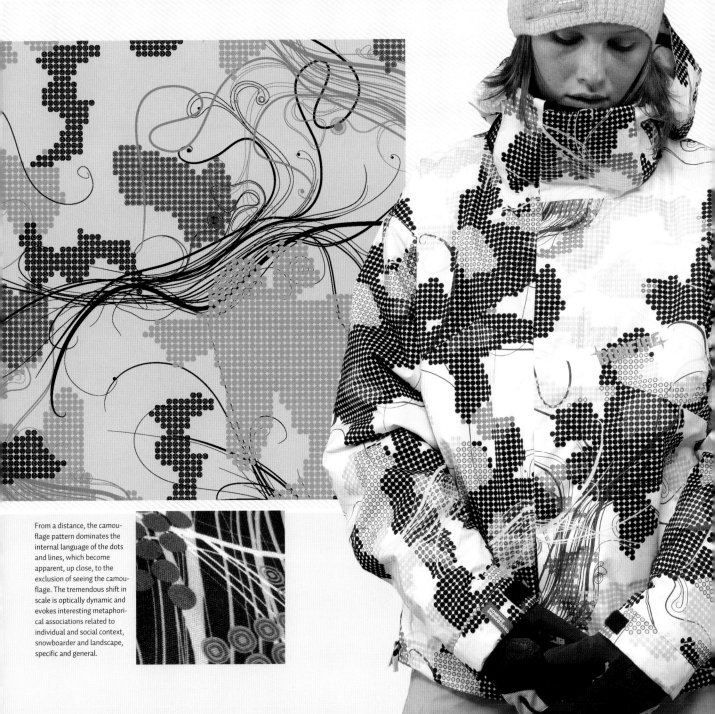

From a distance, the camouflage pattern dominates the internal language of the dots and lines, which become apparent, up close, to the exclusion of seeing the camouflage. The tremendous shift in scale is optically dynamic and evokes interesting metaphorical associations related to individual and social context, snowboarder and landscape, specific and general.

40

Renée Rhyner & Company Website
Red Canoe | Deer Lodge, Tennessee, USA

In the quest for profound communication and transcendent visual experience, designers sometimes forget that common sense often is the best source of profundity. There's a tremendous joy to experience in clear thinking and exquisite craftsmanship. This latter term is one that, oddly, can be applied to this website project for commercial artist representative Renée Rhyner & Company of Dallas, Texas. The site showcases the work of the artists Rhyner represents—in essence, it's a portfolio site. From intuitive organization to efficient click-through, and from typographic restraint to poetic pacing, the site's well-honed simplicity delivers a harmonic, well-considered experience.

Finding What I'm Looking For

Visual form, or "look and feel," evolves for the designers directly from solving problems, especially for websites. All of the layout choices in this site, which were made very quickly, were responses to the user's needs in interacting with the content.

With Web development, Red Canoe's method is less an exploration of options than the built result of answering questions. Studio partner Deb Koch says, "The bottom line in every case has to go be: "What is this site supposed to do for the client? Who is the audience?" ❙ The impulse to create convenience, and the advanced functionality that supports it, came from being part of the client's demographic. Koch and partner Caroline Kavanagh are constantly searching for images for projects such as book cover designs. "We know what we like and what we do not about sites—what we want when in a rush, what we enjoy when not in a rush." ❙ The designers take poorly designed sites they have encountered into serious consideration as they work. The solution they develop will very often come about from addressing a problem they've encountered somewhere else—to make the opposite of what they *don't* want. ❙ All of the decision making in Red Canoe's approach to Web development stems from functionality, not metaphor. It was answering those two first questions—want in a rush and enjoy at leisure—that led them to structure the Rhyner site's navigation as directly

An evolutionary phase in the design of the navigation shows how sensible the designers' approach was to the site's visual form. They briefly examined a set of graphic icons in the circular button elements to distinguish each of the artists; but, as these had no intrinsic meaning and were themselves images that could potentially compete for attention with the main content, they were discarded in favor of showing the artists' initials. This idea, which actually provides information, also worked as a way of integrating more type within the site.

The photographic content was the most important focus, so it was given a dominant position relative to other material; the proximity and size of the circular buttons immediately to the left of the image area immediately brings that navigation to the fore of one's attention. Appropriately, these buttons access the portfolios of the artists Rhyner represents, so the connection between image and image search is immediate and intuitive.

Separating A-levels of secondary importance—both physically and in terms of size and contrast treatment—reinforces their degree of importance.

as possible. A central image, tagged with the word "images," is supported to the left by a series of buttons listing artists represented by the client firm. The proximity of these buttons to the large image suggests the functionality after: go "here" to find images. The buttons lead to each photographer's respective area, with four options for navigating their work. All other content is small and located near the top—easily accessible, but clearly not the focus. These less important items are areas one might explore if time permits. ▌ The site's appearance developed quickly, again reflecting the answers

An opening image, paired with the word "IMAGES," makes this connection explicit and answers the question a user might ask: "What am I after?"

A neutral sans serif proved legible on screen and a logical choice for keeping quiet relative to the photographic content. Univers, as an option, especially in the condensed width, offered a number of weights for distinguishing hierarchy.

Clicking on an artist's link brings the user to that artist's area; a large image appears in the content area, and more in-depth navigation appears at top, set larger and all upper-case in a brighter value than the links at left.

The choice of a neutral background color was intended to avoid competing with the featured images. When the site was first being developed, the warmth of the brown enhanced the contrast and tonal quality of what were black-and-white images only, as none of Rhyner's artists

shot in color. Sometime after launch, when color images became part of the portfolio, the neutral background still served its purpose.

to a series of questions. The site features photographs? No images. The photographs reflect a wide variety of styles? Typography and color should be neutral so as not to conflict with them. The one stylistic device the studio employed was to tag the photographers with their initials, which became an important part of the typography in introduction screens and in the Personalities section, which both use large letterforms as a contrast to images. ▌It's only after working out the functionality, and the resulting appearance, that Deb and Caroline present the concept to their client—and that concept alone. This strategy, similarly, results from the partners' notion that they're solving a problem, and that the look and feel are a natural outgrowth, rather than a skin that could be applied to any understructure. ▌"Sometimes, we may show a "static rough," to which modifications are made, says Koch, "but still for one concept. From this point forward in the project—as in all the Web projects Red Canoe undertakes—such modifications were minor, and aimed solely at improving the experience. That process was roughly six months. ▌Within the relatively austere constraints Koch and Kavanagh imposed on themselves, there remained opportunity to create a rich and stately experience for users and, as is often said, the magic is in the details.

> I thought of this site and its original floorplan, as musical, so to speak. It has pacing and gently unfolds to reach the gems—the images.

Deb Koch, Partner

Changes in the library show the development of greater functionality and increased attention to the details of click-through and transition between states. Compare these two sequences of pages: The earlier iteration appears to the left and the revision to the right. The slight adjustment in how the cursor activates the link and the resulting change in the box behind shows an improved intuitive quality to the interaction. These changes are possible to see in a working model only, so the development is evolutionary and on the fly rather than iterative and comparable through an archive.

The lightbox display grid helps snap selected images into position as they are dragged into the grid's area of influence.

A sense of rhythmic pacing pervades the site as splash pages, which appear static on clicking into a new content area, surprisingly scroll to reveal additional imagery and selected quotations. In the News section, introductory lines of text scroll into view, followed by selected images, where appropriate. ▮ In the Personalities section, a more detailed version of the primary navigation situates itself in highlighted images, with each button bringing forth a short quotation, set in a bookish serif that brings texture and contrast to the overall sans serif typography throughout. ▮ The site undergoes constant updating—not simply the addition of new photographers or changing out the existing ones' portfolio samples—but adding new core functionality. Among these were a library, which archived images not shown on the site and allowed users to search them with a keyword. This function has now been expanded into a full-blown content management system that functions in both the front and back ends. ▮ The client and her represented artists will be able to upload, edit, and track images and data; site users will have access to a more conceptual keyword search, a lightbox feature,

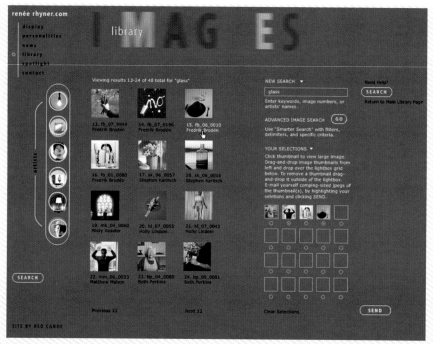

and thumbnail browsing, both by subject and by artist. ▌ The same attention to detail is given to each aspect of these functions, from the minimal number of clicks to access information, to pixel dimensions of a thumbnail image, to how that thumbnail appears or disappears from view as it is selected, added, discarded, or compared to others. ▌ Such ongoing enhancement is also apparent in the "site guest optional" sections, with a Display section—a scrolling slide show—and Spotlight—which showcases the work of an existing artist, or introduces a new one.

The leisurely Personalities section introduces animation; a slow transition from blank screen to image is countered by a shifting screen of vertical lines. This is followed by the appearance of small circular buttons that configure themselves within the image. On mouse-over, each calls up a quote from the photographer, set in Mrs. Eaves, a contemporary version of the transitional Baskerville serif.

The slowly paced animation is evident in the transitions between pages, especially in the Display section, where an introductory image scrolls from view to be replaced by another image.

Contributors

2FRESH
La Défense 9, Tour Ariane, E: 33
92088 Paris, France
Maslak, Beybi Giz Plaza, K: 26
34396 Istanbul, Turkey
www.2fresh.com
110 | 111 | 112 | 113 | 114 | 115

AdamsMorioka
8484 Wilshire Blvd., Suite 600
Beverly Hills, CA 90211 USA
www.adamsmorioka.com
170 | 171 | 172 | 173 | 174 | 175
218 | 219 | 220 | 221 | 222 | 223
224 | 225

Ah-Reum Han
School of Visual Arts
990 Sixth Ave., Suite 17J
New York, NY 10018 USA
onebeauty310@gmail.com
039

Armando Milani Design
Via Vivaio, 21
20122 Milan, Italy
087 | 088 | 089

Bruketa & Zinic
Zavrinica 17
Zagreb, Croatia 10000
www.bruketa-zinic.com
066 | 067 | 068 | 069 | 070 | 071
072 | 073

Thomas Csano
3655 St-Laurent Blvd.
Montreal, Quebec, Canada
H2X 2V6
www.thomascsano.com
214 | 215 | 216 | 217

Compass360
11 Davies Ave., Suite 200
Toronto, Ontario, Canada
M4M 2A9
www.compass360.com
160 | 161 | 162 | 163

doch design
Baaderstrasse 16
D-80469 Munich, Germany
www.dochdesign.de
028 | 102 | 103 | 104 | 105

Firstborn
630 9th Avenue
New York, NY 10036 USA
www.firstbornmultimedia.com
176 | 177 | 178 | 179 | 180 | 181
248 | 249 | 250 | 251 | 252 | 253

GollingsPidgeon
147 Chapel St.
St. Kilda, Victoria, Australia 3182
www.gollingspidgeon.com
038 | 148 | 149 | 150 | 151 | 198
199 | 200 | 201 | 202 | 203

Hesse Design
Duesseldorfer Strasse 16
Erkath, 40699 Germany
www.hesse-design.com
017 | 030 | 032 | 038 | 041 | 188
189 | 190 | 191 | 192 | 193

Hyosook Kang
School of Visual Arts
228 East 25th St., Apt. 10
New York, NY 10010 USA
yellowapple79@hotmail.com
025

Ideas on Purpose
307 Seventh Ave., Suite 701
New York, NY 10001 USA
www.ideasonpurpose.com
021 | 134 | 135 | 136 | 137 | 138 | 139

Kuhlmann Leavitt, Inc.
7810 Forsyth Blvd., 2W
St. Louis, MO 63105 USA
www.kuhlmannleavitt.com
060 | 061 | 062 | 063 | 064 | 065

Kym Abrams Design
213 West Institut Pl., Suite 608
Chicago, IL 60610 USA
www.kad.com
116 | 117 | 118 | 119 | 120 | 121

Laywan Kwan
610 W. 152nd St. #24
New York, NY 10031 USA
laywan@gmail.com
010

LSD
San Andrés 36, 2º p6
28004 Madrid, Spain
www.lsdspace.com
230 | 231 | 232 | 233 | 234 | 235
236 | 237

Mixer
Löwenplatz 5
6004 Lucerne, Switzerland
www.mixer.ch
106 | 107 | 108 | 109 | 244 | 245
246 | 247

Orangetango
88 Queen St.
H3C 09H Montreal, Quebec, Canada
www.orangetango.com
056 | 057 | 058 | 059

Un mundo feliz/a happy
world production
Madrid, Spain
www.unmundofeliz.org
122 | 123 | 124 | 125 | 126 | 127

paone design associates
240 South Twentieth St.
Philadelphia, PA 19103 USA
www.paonedesign.com
029 | 094 | 095 | 096 | 097 | 098
099 | 100 | 101

Parallax Design
447 Pulteney St.
Adelaide SA, Australia 5000
www.parallaxdesign.com.au
019 | 034 | 090 | 091 | 092 | 093
164 | 165 | 166 | 167 | 168 | 169

Planet Propaganda
605 Williamson St.
Madison, WI 53703 USA
www.planetpropaganda.com
152 | 153 | 154 | 155 | 156 | 157
158 | 159

Red Canoe
347 Clear Creek Trail
Deer Lodge, TN 37726 USA
www.redcanoe.com
194 | 195 | 196 | 197 | 264 | 265

Research Studios
94 Islington High Street
London N1 8EG United Kingdom
www.researchstudios.com
078 | 079 | 080 | 081 | 082 | 083 | 084
085 | 260 | 261 | 262 | 263

Sägenvier
Sägerstrasse 4
6850 Dornbirn, Austria
www.saegenvier.at
050 | 051 | 052 | 053 | 054 | 055

Leonardo Sonnoli
Via G. Rossini 16
Trieste 34231 Italy
leonardosonnoli@libero.it
025

STIM Visual Communication
238 South Third St., No. 4
Brooklyn, NY 11211 USA
tsamara_designer@hotmail.com
008 | 009 | 010 | 014 | 016 | 018 | 019
022 | 024 | 026 | 028 | 029 | 031 | 032
033 | 034 | 036 | 037 | 038 | 040

Strichpunkt
Schönleinstrasse 8A
70184 Stuttgart, Germany
www.strichpunkt-design.de
035 | 140 | 141 | 142 | 143 | 144 | 145
146 | 147

Studio Blue
800 W. Huron St., Suite 3N
Chicago, IL 60622 USA
www.studioblue.us
030 | 204 | 205 | 206 | 207 | 208 | 209
254 | 255 | 256 | 257 | 258 | 259

Studio Pip and Company
171 Greville St., Suite 5
Prahran, Victoria, Australia 3181
www.peoplethings.com
018 | 020 | 027 | 033 | 182 | 183 | 184
185 | 186 | 187 | 226 | 227 | 228 | 229

**Studio di progrttazione grafica
Sabina Oberholzer Renato Tagli**
Càd'Bariff
Cevio, Ticino, Switzerland, 6675
soberholzer@swissonline.ch
021 | 034

Surface
Peterstrasse 4
60313 Frankfurt am Main Germany
www.surface.de
023 | 031 | 034 | 074 | 075 | 076 | 077

Tactical Magic, LLC
1460 Madison Ave.
Memphis, TN 38104 USA
www.tacticalmagic.com
044 | 045 | 046 | 047 | 048 | 049

Tassinari / Vetta
Via G. Bruno 51
Rimini, Italy 47900
Leonardo@tassinarivetta.it
128 | 129 | 130 | 131 | 132 | 133

Vignelli Associates
130 East 67th St.
New York, NY 10021 USA
www.vignelli.com
006

Wallace Church
330 East 48th St.
New York, NY 10017 USA
www.wallacechurch.com
210 | 211 | 212 | 213

Why Not Associates
22c Shepherdess Walk
London N1 2AU, UK
www.whynotassociates.com
238 | 239 | 240 | 241 | 242 | 243

Acknowledgments

Just as the case studies presented within this book do, each book I write creates its own individual process. This one was no exception. And, as with all my previous books, a debt of gratitude is due a great many people. First on my list are the contributors, whose works made this volume possible: thank you for digging through your files for the often-tossed scraps of inspiration and overlooked middle steps of the projects you contributed. Hardworking designers–especially students–will benefit enormously from seeing the rough middle stages of the finished projects. And, of course, a huge and humble thank-you to the Rockport team (with a warm welcome to Emily Potts). In particular I'd like to thank David Martinell for being the trooper that he is. This book is dedicated to Beebee, my parents and friends, and to all my students past, present, and yet to be.

Timothy Samara is a graphic designer based in New York City, where he divides his time between teaching, writing, lecturing, and consulting through STIM Visual Communication. His seventeen-year career in branding and information design has exposed him to projects in print, packaging, environments, user interface design, and animation. He has been a senior art director at Ruder Finn Design, New York's largest public relations firm, and art director at Pettistudio, a small multidisciplinary design firm; before coming to New York, he was principal of Physiologic in upstate New York. In 1990, he graduated as a Trustee Scholar from the University of the Arts, Philadelphia. Mr. Samara is currently a faculty member at the School of Visual Arts, NYU, Purchase College, and Parsons School of Design, and has published five books to date, all from Rockport Publishers: *Making and Breaking the Grid,* (2003); *Typography Workbook* (2004); *Publication Design Workbook* (2005); *Type Style Finder* (2006); and, most recently, *Design Elements* (2007). Mr. Samara and his partner live in the Williamsburg neighborhood of Brooklyn, just over the river from Manhattan.